19 ABBOTT & JENKINS, BUILDERS & LUMBER DEALERS.
20 ANDOVER NATIONAL BANK.
21 ANDOVER SAVINGS BANK.
22 Wᴹ BARNETT, STOVES & RANGES, MFRS OF TIN & SHEET IRON WARE.
23 THOMAS HOWELL MFR & DEALER IN ALL KINDS OF FURNITURE.
24 E.PIKE DEALER IN OIL COOK & PARLOR STOVES & RANGES.
25 CHAS. S. PARKER. GENL. UNDERTAKER & DEALER IN
        CASKETS. COFFINS & ROBES.
26 ADAM FRAME. HORSE SHOEING & JOBBING
        WAGON & CARRIAGE WOOD WORK
27 JOHN W.FAULKNER HORSE SHOEING & JOBBING. WAGON & CARRIAGE WOOD WORK.
28 SMITH & MANNING. DRY GOODS & GROCERIES.
29 T.A.HOLT & CO. DRY GOODS & GROCERIES.
30 JOHN H. DEAN MERCHANT TAILOR, DEALER IN READY MADE
        CLOTHING & GENTS FURNISHING GOODS.
31 J.E.WHITNEY, WATCH MAKER & JEWELER.
32 VALPEY BRO'S. MEATS VEGETABLES & POULTRY,
33 JOHN H SOCHRENS, TONSORIAL ARTIST.
34 JOHN H. FLINT. PROVISIONS &C.

VER.

ETTS

TON.

ANDOVER

A CENTURY OF CHANGE
1896–1996

by
Eleanor Motley Richardson

in consultation with
The Publications Committee
Andover Historical Society:

James Batchelder, chair
Norma Gammon
Bernice Haggerty
Karen Herman
Nancy Jeton
Gratia Mahony
Charlotte Smith
Barbara Thibault
Ned Williams

Photographs edited by
Christine Gebhard

Published by
The Andover Historical Society

Sponsored by
The Eagle-Tribune
and the
Andover Townsman

THE DONNING COMPANY PUBLISHERS

THE ANDOVER TOWNSMAN

THE ANDOVER TOWNSMAN

ANDOVER TOWNSMAN

ANDOVER TOWNSMAN

The ANDOVER TOWNSMAN

ANDOVER TOWNSMAN

The Andover Townsman

Andover's weekly chronicle of all that makes this
community great, is pleased to sponsor
Andover, A Century of Change, 1896–1996.

The heritage *The Townsman* has chronicled since 1887 is a
heritage we share as Andoverites. The future it foretells
is a future we are pledged to help build.

The Andover Townsman
33 Chestnut Street   Andover, MA 01810

Publications Committee with author

Seated, clockwise from left are: Barbara Thibault, Norma Gammon, Bernice Haggerty, Christine Gebhard, Karen Herman, and author Eleanor Richardson. Standing are: Jim Batchelder, Ned Williams, and Gratia Mahony. Not pictured: Nancy Jeton and Charlotte Smith. Ray Sprague photo, 1994

The Donning Company, Virginia Beach, Virginia
    Steve Mull, General Manager
    Debra Y. Quesnel, Project Director
    Tracey Emmons-Schneider, Project Research Coordinator
    Elizabeth Bobbitt, Editor
    Tony Lillis, Marketing Director
    Dawn Kofroth, Production Manager

Additional copies may be ordered from:
Andover Historical Society, 97 Main St., Andover, MA 01810

Excerpt from *Becoming a Man: Half a Life Story*, copyright © 1992 by Paul Monette, reprinted by permission of Harcourt Brace & Company.

Photographs are from the Andover Historical Society Collection except those by Richard Graber, who generously donated five photographs for this publication. Photographs identified as *EMR photo* are by Eleanor Motley Richardson, late 1993 or 1994. Donald Look photographs date from 1943 to 1954 and Charles Henry Newman photos date from 1889 to the 1930s.

Library of Congress Cataloging in Publication Data:
Richardson, Eleanor Motley.
    Andover: a century of change, 1896-1996 / Eleanor Motley Richardson.
        p. cm.
    Includes bibliographical references (p.) and index.
    ISBN 0-89865-938-8
    1. Andover (Mass.: Town)—History. 2. Andover (Mass.: Town)—History—Pictorial works. I. Title.
    F74.A6R53 1995
    974.4'5—dc20

95-7906
CIP

Printed in the United States of America.

Contents

Foreword   7

Acknowledgments   9

Chapter One: **A Retrospective View**   11

Chapter Two: **Some Notable People of Andover— Ordinary, Extraordinary and Otherwise Interesting**   17

Chapter Three: **Preserving Andover's Character**   31

Chapter Four: **Associations and Organizations**   47

Chapter Five: **Entering the Modern Era**   61

Chapter Six: **Yesterday's Mills to Today's Industry**   79

Chapter Seven: **Faith Communities**   99

Chapter Eight: **Our Ethnic Heritage**   119

Chapter Nine: **The Face of "Main Street"**   133

Chapter Ten: **Andover's Pride in Education**   155

Chapter Eleven: **Plagues and Disasters**   177

Chapter Twelve: **The Evolution of Town Government**   189

Chapter Thirteen: **What We Did for Fun**   203

Chapter Fourteen: **Business and Family Profiles**   221

Appendix   249

   Andover Clergy since 1880

   School Administrators

   Selectmen and Town Managers

Endnotes   257

Bibliography   265

Index   267

**Amos Blanchard House, circa 1885, now home
of the Andover Historical Society, Andover's
Historical Museum and Research Center.**

Foreword

The Andover Historical Society has endeavored over the last four years to publish a book in connection with Andover's 350th Anniversary celebration. This book, *Andover: A Century of Change, 1896–1996*, is the culmination of that project. The society's mission, since its founding in 1911, is to maintain a museum and library where artifacts of local historical significance are collected, preserved, exhibited, and interpreted. Offering a wide range of educational programs and services for individuals and groups of all ages, the society encourages a greater appreciation for and understanding of local history and related preservation issues. This book reflects that philosophy through oral histories, historical fact, and period photographs. It paints a picture of our town's ethnic diversity, mores of the period, accomplishments, and frailties of the human experience of life. As a people, we all seek a sense of belonging, the connection that makes us a part of the fabric of the community, and yet allows us still to be individuals.

Andover: A Century of Change, 1896–1996 is an overview of our past one hundred years. The book's objective is to introduce the reader to the issues, projects, politics, and solutions that the community has faced and continues to face, as we move forward to the next century. To understand who we are, we must also understand where and how we have traveled to get to our destination. These stories are about the people and the organizations who became part of that fabric we know as Andover. We are grateful to the *Eagle-Tribune* and the *Andover Townsman* for their generous sponsorship, and to our local businesses and families whose profiles contributed to and supported the publication of this book.

Warmest regards,
James S. Batchelder
Chair, Publications Committee

The "Enchanted Bridge" once spanned the
Shawsheen River and joined Andover's North
and South Parishes.

Acknowledgments

The book has truly been a community effort, starting with members of the Andover Historical Society and especially its Publications Committee. The Historical Society staff, Barbara Thibault, director; Peg Hughes, assistant to the director; and Tom Edmonds, curator, have been constantly involved in the project as have many of the society's volunteers, notably Christine Gebhard, indefatigable photo editor, and Virginia Lopez Begg, who worked on community profiles.

Memorial Hall Library was most cooperative—James Sutton, director, and past directors Nancy Jacobson and Miriam Putnam, along with the reference desk personnel, in particular Leslie Baskin, Sydelle Cohen, and Nan Becker. The Board of Selectmen and town employees patiently fielded many requests, especially Town Manager Reginald ("Buzz") Stapczynski; Sandra Cassano, town manager's office; Town Clerk Randy Hanson and her staff; Rose Vandewallse, switchboard; Maywood Kenney, municipal maintenance; Public Works Director Robert McQuade; and Public Health Director Everett Penney.

We are also indebted to Phillips Academy—Ruth Quattlebaum, archivist; Donald McNemar, former headmaster; and Fred Stott, retired secretary. Richard Graber, James D. Doherty, Ruth Sharpe, and Adeline Wright patiently fielded questions. Ray Sprague prepared photos for publication. Rev. Peter Richardson, the author's husband, tolerated the mess and the stress, and kept her courage up. A major source for this book was oral history interviews with more than 150 Andover residents who gave time, memories, and photographs to bring this history alive. Their names appear in the text as they tell their stories. To them and all others who helped, my profound thanks. This is your book.

Eleanor Motley Richardson
December 31, 1994

Elm Square was named for the Centennial Elm. It was deemed a traffic hazard and regretfully removed in 1919. The elegant federal building behind it is the site of KAPS Menswear today.

Chapter One

A Retrospective View

In 1646 Rev. John Woodbridge and Edmond Faulkner purchased an area called Cochichawicke from the Sagamore Cutshamache for six English pounds and a coat. This confirmed a situation which had existed for some time: English settlers had lived in Andover at least since 1629. The town was incorporated May 6, 1646 (old calendar).

Early settlers became embroiled in wars with the Native Americans, threatened by loss of lands and freedom, from 1675 to 1698, and in the Witch Trials of 1692, in which fifty of them were accused, three hanged, and one died in prison. Andover Minutemen fought in the Battle of Bunker Hill on June 17, 1775, and throughout the Revolution. Andover sent 578 of its citizens off to serve in the Civil War. Their names are inscribed in Memorial Hall Library, built as a War Memorial in 1873.

The original town included what is now Andover, North Andover, part of Boxford, and South Lawrence. Boxford was set off in 1740 and Lawrence in 1847. In 1855 the town voted to divide into North Andover and Andover. Both were famous for private education. Phillips Academy was founded in 1778, Franklin Academy in 1799, Andover Theological Seminary in 1808, and Abbot Academy in 1829.

The town staged a five-day celebration of Andover's 250th Anniversary in 1896. Major observances followed in 1946, 1971, and 1976 (the nation's Bicentennial). As the 350th Anniversary approached, Andover Historical Society decided to publish a book spanning the most recent century and the Board of Selectmen appointed a town 350th Anniversary Committee to plan events for 1996.

What has been Andover's reaction to this century of change? One of the largest towns in the state, located on one of the state's major rivers, and boasting the county's highest hill, Andover has put approximately 25 percent of its 31.9 square miles in conservation. In mid-century, the intersection of two major highways brought an influx of population and made Andover desirable for industry. The town responded to the challenge with careful zoning and has attracted a high caliber of responsible corporations.

Originally a one-church town, Andover now is home to twenty-six religious congregations. An educational system once based on district schoolhouses now houses five thousand students in eight centralized schools. The acquisition of Andover Theological Seminary's campus by Phillips Academy in 1908 and the merger of Phillips and Abbot Academies in 1973 were landmarks in the growth

The house at 48 Central Street was known as "The Summer White House" for President Franklin Pierce, circa 1855.

West Parish was long considered the agricultural district of Andover. The George Flint farm seen here has been replaced by suburban homes on Bailey Road. Courtesy of Stephen Kearn

Horses and carriages find plenty of parking at the intersection of Main and Park Streets in this early 1890s view. Wakefield's brick meat market and the smaller wooden buildings at right were replaced by the Barnard Block in 1910.

A horse-drawn wagon delivers baked goods from Lawrence outside the Town House, while a high-wheeled bicycle's owner leaves it trustingly against a hitching post.

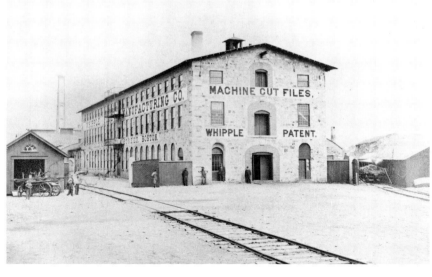

Near the Whipple File Company, Ballard Vale, is the "Hunneman Tub." The fire equipment is now in the Andover Historical Society Collection.

The John Smith house in Frye Village was later transformed into Shawsheen Manor, hotel for Shawsheen Village.

At the Frye Village mills, the bridge covers the Shawsheen River at what is today Haverhill Street in Shawsheen Village.

Abbot Village is the site of the earliest textile mill in Andover's South Parish.

and prestige of those institutions. While preserving its New England town meeting and selectmen, Andover voted in the Town Manager/Selectmen system in 1959. As lifelong resident Frederic Stott observed, "There is an integrity in Andover's town government, both elected and appointed. I cannot recall any malfeasance on the part of elected officials in the history of the town." The town's character still depends on each of its residents, whether their family has been here for 350 years or two weeks. It will be up to all of us to shape the Andover of the future.

Elizabeth Stuart Phelps wrote fifty-seven books and hundreds of stories, pamphlets, essays, and poems.

Chapter Two

Some Notable People of Andover—Ordinary, Extraordinary, and Otherwise Interesting

When residents are asked, "Who are the most famous people in Andover?" they have been known to answer, "George Bush, Jay Leno, and Morris Krinsky." Former President George Bush, Class of 1942, spent five years of his life at Phillips Academy. He has been notable for his loyalty and service to the institution, serving on the Board of Trustees from 1967 to 1980, and visiting again in 1989 after he became president. On that occasion, he told the students, "I loved those years. They did, indeed, teach the great and real business of living." Jay Leno, comedian and host of "The Tonight Show with Jay Leno," and a 1968 graduate of Andover High School also enjoys returning to Andover. He observes:

My wife Mavis finds it amazing that I keep in touch with my Andover friends. When I go back to Andover, my schools and even some of my teachers are still there. When my wife goes back to her old town in L.A., not only is her old school not there, the hill it was standing on is gone. They razed it to build a freeway. Los Angeles is like the witness protection act, every couple of years they wipe it all clean. New England values are so different. In Los Angeles, people work as teachers for a few years until they can do something else. My teachers in Andover were dedicated people.[1]

Morris Krinsky is second generation proprietor of the junkyard on Park Street, one block from the central business district. He was born in Andover in 1916, son of Hyman and Rebecca Krinsky. His father emigrated here from Russia before the czar was overthrown. An only child, Morris lost his mother when he was ten.

Krinsky graduated from Punchard High School in 1934. Later, he played on the Andover Town football team, and particularly remembers their big rival team, the Italian team from Lawrence. Krinsky says:

I sit and watch the people walk by. My generation can't afford to live here any more. Several old people used to come by and visit me every day. But they have stopped coming. Andover's kids can't afford to live here either. They just keep moving further up into New Hampshire and Maine. I've seen businesses come and go. Everyone thinks they're going to be a millionaire. There are too many eating places. I used to go to Town Meeting. There were always certain firebrands. They would argue for hours. Now at Town Meeting you just have time to blow your nose and it's over. There was a time in Town Meeting when one man called my junkyard a blight. Others said they wanted a colonial atmosphere, a row of

Much has changed in Andover over the past decades, but Krinsky's has been a constant presence since 1928. You can actually buy something useful from Morris, such as a six-paned window sash or a previously owned sink. A stroke suffered twelve years ago makes walking and speaking difficult for him, but it didn't touch his winning sense of humor. Posing for a photograph, he quips, "Be sure to get my Jay Leno profile." EMR photo

storefronts here. People ask me why I don't sell the place and move to Florida or a rest home. I say "baloney!"[2]

The high school that educated Leno and Krinsky has a fine record. In its Class of 1993, 91 percent of the graduates went on to further education, 83 percent to four-year colleges. The dropout rate is less than 1 percent. Some nationally known alumni include artist William Harnden Foster,'04; Brigadier General John E. Haggerty, '36; Dr. Roger Jenkins, '69, a pioneer in liver transplantation and hepatic-biliary surgery; and Michael Chiklis, '81, who stars on the television series "The Commish." Locally famous graduates are far too numerous to list.

Phillips Academy, simply called "Andover" beyond town borders, has produced many distinguished alumni in the twentieth century. Judge Gerhard Gesell, '28; U.S. Rep. Jim Shannon, '69; Massachusetts State Treasurer Joe Malone, '74; John F. Kennedy Jr.,'79; and Patrick Kennedy, '86, have all served in public life. Dr. Benjamin Spock,'21; the Rev. William Sloane Coffin, '42; composer Daniel Pinkham, '40; and Ring Lardner Jr., '32; are all nationally known. A great many have worked in theater: Humphrey Bogart, '20; actress Dana Delaney, '74; director Peter Sellars, '75; and Jack Lemmon, '43.

Abbot Academy, founded in 1829 to educate women, merged with Phillips Academy in 1973. Notable alumnae of this century include Marie Suzanne Loizeaux, '26, New Hampshire State representative for twelve years; Despina Plakias Messinesi, '29, travel editor for *Vogue Magazine*; composer Gwyneth Walker, '64; and Shirley Young, '51, vice president of General Motors and chairman of Grey Strategic Marketing.

We have our share of notable athletes. Jim Luscutoff, who played for the Boston Celtics, started a basketball camp in 1964 on Jenkins Road, where he and his wife, artist Lynn Luscutoff, still live. Daniel J. Sullivan played for the Baltimore Colts during Super Bowls III and V in 1969 and 1971, and skier Sharon Petzold was a 1992 Winter Olympics bronze medalist.

Like Morris Krinsky, a lot of old-timers and natives are nostalgic about the way Andover used to be when they were young—before the rapid population growth of the mid-century. Let the stories of its people in those years carry us back to 1896, the year our book begins.

In July that year, Andover lost one of its most famous citizens: Harriet Beecher Stowe (1811–1896). Although she lived here only from 1852 to 1864 while her husband, Calvin E. Stowe, was professor at Andover Theological Seminary, she penned six books here and the couple are buried in the Chapel Cemetery. Harriet's *Uncle Tom's Cabin*, completed in 1851, wielded national influence for the cause of Abolition. Six million copies were sold in twenty-two languages. When she met President Lincoln, he is reputed to have said, "So you're the little woman who wrote the book that made this great war!"[3] Mrs. Stowe's parties and lively sense of fun were something of a shock to the staid professors at the Theological Seminary.

Writer Elizabeth Stuart Phelps (1844–1911) was an alumna of Abbot Academy. Her most famous book, *The Gates Ajar* (1864), a diary of a young woman who had just lost her brother in the Civil War, was inspired by the war death of Phelps' first love. The book hit home for a generation of families and the book sold several million copies. Her tribute to Harriet Beecher Stowe tells us something about both women and nineteenth-century Andover:

Andover was a heavily masculine place. She (Mrs. Stowe) was used to eminent men, and to men who thought they were so, or meant to be or were thought to be

Bottom opposite page: An avid "dirt farmer" at her house on Elm Street, Bessie Goldsmith was a pillar of the Andover Garden Club. Upon her death in 1974, she left the 130-acre Goldsmith Reservation, near the North Reading border, as a conservation trust maintained under the stewardship of AVIS. Garden Club members in this Fiftieth Anniversary photo are, standing from left: Dot Hill, Arita Nichols, Bella Baker, unknown, Marilyn Swain, Maude Bramley, Alice Higgins, unknown, and Helen Wilkinson. Seated from left: Ruth Cleveland, a Federation guest, Dora Stewart, Bessie Goldsmith, unknown, and Geneva Killorin. Richard Graber photo, October 1967

by the ladies of their families and the pillars of their denomination. At the subject of eminent women the Hill had not arrived . . . And Mrs. Stowe's fame was clearly a fact so apart from the traditions and from the ideals that Andover was puzzled by it. The best of her good men were too feudal in their views of women, in those days, to understand a life like Mrs. Stowe's. It should be remembered that we have moved on, since then, so fast, and so far, that it is almost as hard now for us to understand the perplexity with which intelligent, even instructed men used to consider the phenomenon of a superior woman, as it was then for such men to understand such a woman at all.[4]

Of less international fame, but with more local impact, was journalist John N. Cole (1863–1922). Cole moved to Andover at age one. In 1887, at age twenty-three, he married Andover native Minnie White and started his own newspaper, the *Andover Townsman*. He purchased the *Lawrence Telegram* nine years later. For the past 106 years, the *Townsman* has faithfully recorded the pieces that make up the puzzle of Andover's history.

Local historians have also kept our roots alive. Outstanding is Sarah Loring Bailey (1834–1896), who wrote *Historical Sketches of Andover* in 1880. Claude M. Fuess (1885–1963), headmaster of Phillips Academy, wrote several histories, including *Andover: Symbol of New England—The Evolution of a Town*. His colleague, English professor Scott H. Paradise (1891–1959), published three histories, *Men of the Old School*, *History of Printing in Andover*, and the *Story of Essex County*.

Bessie Punchard Goldsmith (1882–1974), a *Townsman* columnist, policewoman,[6] and home economics teacher at the high school, was one memorable town character. Her father was principal of Punchard High School. A collection of her stories, "The Townswoman's Andover," is a small but informative

In 1903 John N. Cole was elected to the state legislature and in 1905 was chosen speaker of the House. In 1908 he retired from politics and returned to Andover where he became a respected voice at Town Meeting. But in 1916 the governor appointed him chair of the State Board of Waterways, and later state commissioner of Public Works. He died in 1922.[5]

booklet on the first half of this century. In the 1930s when women wore white gloves and hats to go downtown, Bessie would stride down the street in brown knickers, big boots, and a brown velvet tam o'shanter. She was also known to smoke a pipe. Yet she could dress up to pour tea at the November Club with the best of them.

Edward Roddy, Ph.D. (1921–1985), professor at Merrimack College, wrote *Mills, Mansions and Mergers: The Life of William M. Wood* and *Merrimack College: Genesis and Growth.* Juliet Haynes Mofford has written several award-winning local histories including the history of the North Parish Church, North Andover; *AVIS: A History in Conservation*; and *Greater Lawrence: A Bibliography*, which lists resources for Andover, Methuen, Lawrence, and North Andover. Robert Domingue wrote *Phillips Academy*, a history of the school's buildings. Shortly after the merger, Frederick S. Allis Jr. wrote a history of Phillips Academy and Susan McIntosh Lloyd wrote a history of Abbot Academy. Eleanor Campbell wrote *West of the Shawsheen*, a history of West Parish Church, in 1975.

Probably the best-loved children's author to live in our town is Monro Leaf, author of *Ferdinand the Bull* (1936). The Leafs lived in Andover from 1959 to 1965. Mystery writers also seem to thrive here. Susan Kelly has written seven murder mysteries. Her *Gemini Man* was named Best First Novel in 1985. Mary McGarry Morris, author of *Vanished* and *A Dangerous Woman*, wrote in secret for years, then published two very successful novels in a row, to the astonishment of her friends. Andrew Coburn, former crime reporter for the *Eagle-Tribune*, has written nine novels which have been translated into eight languages. Three were made into films in France.

Andover native Paul Monette won the National Book Award in 1992 for his *Becoming a Man: Half a Life Story*, relating his experiences growing up gay in Andover. Diagnosed with AIDS in 1991, Monette wrote six other novels plus *Borrowed Time: An AIDS Memoir*, and three poetry books. He died in early 1995.

While some wrote history, others recorded visual images. Photographer Charles Henry Newman was active from 1889 until the 1930s. Donald Look documented Andover from 1943 until 1954, followed by Richard Graber from 1962 to the present. Graber explains:

Moving to Andover from Indiana was like moving to a foreign country. Everything was different here. So I did a lot of observing. Whenever I saw we were about to lose something, like the old fire station behind the Town House, I would photograph it and code it GHS (that's the Graber Historical Society.) I'd assemble photo essays on town issues in the windows of my shop. One illustrated the town's clear-cutting all the trees on the future site of the High School. Next to it, I put a Bible verse: "They create a wasteland and call it peace." Dick Bowen, the Town Manager, was furious. "I could look up a Bible quote, too," he said. I didn't tell him I'd made up my Bible quote. And at that point we became good friends.[7]

Professional painters have included William Harnden Foster, William Abbot Cheever, Frances Dalton, Howard Coon, Marietta Amy, Jean De Rosa, and David Sullivan, among others. Many of the older homes in town display portraits by Dalton and Sullivan, or landscapes by Coon.

William Harnden Foster (1886–1941), left, was widely known as a painter and wildlife writer. He edited *National Sportsman* and *Hunting and Fishing* magazines, and invented skeet shooting. He illustrated covers for *Harper's*, the *Saturday Evening Post*, and the first L. L. Bean catalogue. Foster lived his adult life in Wilmington, Delaware, but retired to 71 Chestnut Street, Andover. Here, he canoes in Ballardvale with Charles Davies.

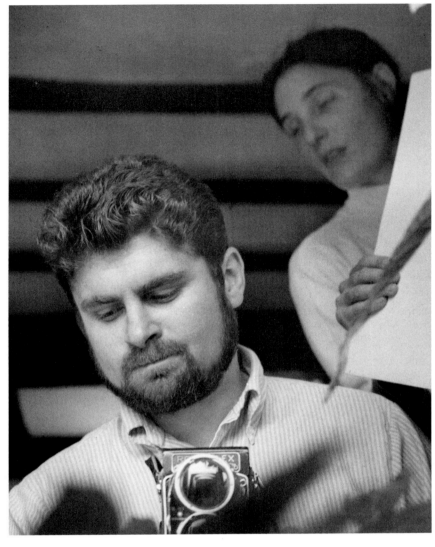

Photographer Richard Graber opened a shop in the Musgrove Building in 1962. He and his wife Rachel (background) were activists in the social issues of the 1960s, particularly education. Richard Graber photo, 1969

Other citizens left a legacy of natural wilderness areas in the face of inevitable growth. One of the first was Alice Buck, a graduate of Abbot Academy. It was she who led the movement to save Indian Ridge, the first privately purchased conservation land in Andover and one of the earliest in the Commonwealth.

Indian Ridge, behind Andover High School, is important to geologists as a glacial kame formed by a prehistoric glacial river. Native Americans often camped on the ridge, and many an artifact has been discovered there. It is covered by a stand of very old trees. In 1897 Alice Buck and others fought tirelessly to save Indian Ridge from being destroyed by town lumbering and gravel-mining operations.[8] They raised $3,500 of the $4,000 needed before the deadline came. At the last minute, the Abbot family who was selling the property knocked $500 off the price, since it was for "a public park."[9]

While some conserved land, others saw historic buildings in danger. Frederick E. Cheever (1888–1975) loved old houses and loved Andover's history. His home on Bancroft Road had been in the Bancroft and Cheever families since 1788. The barn housed Cheever's extensive antique collection, some of which he donated to the Historical Society, along with funds for an exhibit gallery there in memory of his mother, Alice Bancroft Cheever. A Punchard graduate, Cheever served as town postmaster and later took up real estate, developing Cheever Circle and Johnson Acres. In selling real estate, he reflected a bias of the times. Thayer Warshaw and his wife Bernice, one of the first Jewish families to move to Andover in 1948, remember Cheever saying to them as he drove by a particular neighborhood, "Of course your kind . . . I can't show you houses here. You are not allowed to live here."[10]

However, Fred Cheever helped turn the tide of destruction of historic sites in Andover. Bill Dalton, in his memoir, *Local Touch*, observed:

During the later '40s, '50s, and early '60s, the world wanted to move into the future as quickly as possible. The past had been horrible. World War I, the Great Depression, and World War II caused people to wish the past away. The old was gone and good riddance. Out-of-date buildings were not religious items to be preserved, they were just things that were in the way.[11]

Dalton recalls the town meeting in the mid-1960s when Fred Cheever stood up and "with a squeaky voice" told citizens of Andover he would personally contribute $500 toward saving and restoring the old Town House. The Town Hall upstairs had seen many years of significant community events. Dalton feels that without Cheever's one voice, the Town House would have been demolished.

William Madison Wood (1858–1926) left a new village in Andover as his legacy. Wood was born in Martha's Vineyard, one of ten children of Portuguese and English forbears. Sometime after age eleven, when selling apples on the street to support his widowed mother, brothers, and sisters, he caught the attention of a New Bedford cotton mill owner, who found him a start at the bottom in textiles. By 1885 Wood's accomplishments led to a meeting with a Lowell industrialist, Frederick Ayer, whose other enterprises were threatened by the

Addison Le Boutillier (1872–1951) was architect of houses at 10 (pictured), 14, and 18 Orchard Street, the 1917 Punchard High School (now the Town Offices), and Shawsheen School, 1924. He also designed bookplates; jewelry for Bigelow, Kennard, and Company; and pottery and catalogues for Boston's Grueby Pottery.

impending failure of a large but unprofitable Lawrence cotton mill. Ayer asked Wood to try to salvage the operation. Wood introduced cost pricing in each stage of processing, and succeeded in an impressively short time.[12]

In 1888 Ayer's daughter Ellen married William Wood, and three of their four children were born in Andover. The couple purchased the former North Main Street residence of millowner John Dove, naming it "Arden." Wood's grandson Cornelius A. Wood Jr. resides there today with his wife Rosalyn.

In 1905 the company built the Wood Mill in Lawrence, the largest worsted mill in the world. That same year, Wood took over as president. Following World War I, Wood brought the headquarters to Andover, renaming the old Frye Village (at North Main and Haverhill Streets) Shawsheen Village, and erecting a one-million-square-foot mill, an administration building, and an architecturally integrated village to house all levels of management.

Wood took a personal interest in his workers and their families. A story told by Cornelius Wood Jr. took place at the boys' camp run by American Woolen in Boxford:

One summer when Wood arrived to award prizes, the camp director told him, "We have two boys here who are equally good at athletics. You must decide which of them is to get first prize and which second." Wood took the boys aside and asked if they were willing to settle it with a baseball. Whoever threw the ball farthest would win. The boys agreed, the ball was thrown, and the prize awarded. Afterward, Wood took the runner-up aside and told him, "Anyone with the talent to be second can go the distance and become first." That Christmas the boy received a book from Wood, inscribed, "To the boy who I know will be first."

But even while Shawsheen was being built, Wood was suffering personal reverses. His youngest daughter, Irene, died of influenza in 1918 and in 1922 his oldest son, William, was killed in a tragic automobile accident on Route 28 in Reading. A marked decline in textile industry profits followed World War I. Worn down from years of hard work, Wood suffered a stroke, leading to severe depression about his inability to carry on as fully as before. On February 2, 1926, at age sixty-eight, he took his own life in Florida. His experiment in city planning may not have worked entirely, but he made a lasting mark on Andover.

While Wood had the means to physically change the landscape, ordinary citizens made their influence felt in a different way. They raised families, instilled values in their children, and built small businesses on Main Street. Margaret Hart Doherty, a native of Ireland, lost her husband in a railroad accident at the Andover station in 1887, but raised a family that became early leaders in the Catholic community and the town. William, the second oldest, married Josephine Powers in 1899, building her a house at 21 Harding Street, where they raised five children. Their oldest son, John, was the first baby to be baptized in the rebuilt St. Augustine's Church in 1900. Their daughter Margaret was the first child enrolled at St. Augustine's School when it opened in 1915 and their son Bill was the first child to receive a diploma from the school. Josephine Doherty and her friend Agnes Cunningham were two of the first Catholic Women to join the League of Women Voters. Bill was elected to the School Committee in 1931, serving thirty-nine years.

"In those days," says Bill's brother Jim, "You would never find a Catholic, a Black, or a Jew on any town committee except the Democratic Town Committee. Catholic girls would not be hired to work in the banks, the insurance companies, or at Phillips Academy."[13] All School Committee meetings were closed to the

President of American Woolen Company from 1905 to 1924, William Madison Wood was Andover's most famous citizen in his day. His was the largest woolen company in the world, employing forty thousand in sixty mills over eight states. Its headquarters in Shawsheen Village from 1923 to 1925 had a profound influence on the town. Courtesy of Cornelius A. Wood Jr.

public until Bill's election. Bill was a reporter for the *Lawrence Daily Eagle* and the *Evening Tribune* and once he was elected, a report of their doings went into the paper the day after each meeting. "There was hell to pay," says Jim. "They went right to Rogers, the publisher, in Lawrence to complain. He just laughed at them. Nobody bullied Alexander Rogers."[14] Jim was elected Town Moderator in 1978, a position he has held for the past sixteen years.

Like Josephine Doherty, Mary E. (Buntin) Dalton had to make it on her own. Her husband, Harry Clement Dalton, had gone to Wyoming to prepare a home for his family, while Mary stayed home in Amesbury with the four children. Before she could join him, he was killed in a train accident and Mary, aged thirty-two, was left to fend for herself.

In 1907 her attorney persuaded her to take over a store in Andover. She opened "The Metropolitan" bakery, soda fountain, candy shop, and employment agency. The second year, she found a house on the corner of Chestnut and Main Streets, where her children, Harry, Charles, William, and Frances, could easily run back and forth to the store. Mary Dalton's descendants became key leaders in the community. Four were presidents of the senior class or the student council at the high school and five were captains of varsity athletic teams. Her son Charles owned and operated Dalton's Drug Store on the corner of Main and Park Streets. Charles' son, Bill, served as selectman and town moderator, then went on to become Chairman and Commissioner of Labor Relations for the state. Mary Dalton's only daughter, Frances, inspired two generations of art students as a teacher at the high school.[15]

Beverly Darling also sought haven in Andover. Her husband, suffering from multiple sclerosis, was no longer able to work, so they moved here in 1948 to be closer to his family. Beverly had four children plus her aging mother living with them.[16]

"I always hated business and had no interest in it," says Beverly looking back. For someone who had no interest in business, she did rather well. Not only was she the first woman to own her own real estate business in Andover— Darling Associates Incorporated at 33 Chestnut Street— she was also the first person in Andover to get her Graduate Realtor Institute (GRI) certificate. Her interest in people made her tremendously successful. In 1973 she won national recognition for her office interiors from the National Association of Realtors and was listed in *Who's Who of American Women*. She was elected first vice president of the Greater Lawrence Board of Real Estate, chair of the Multiple Listing Service, and state director of the Real Estate Board.

Darling also chaired the committee for $13 million worth of school buildings and co-chaired the Collins Center Committee. She was president of the League of Women Voters and the Parents' League, chaired the board of the Andover Consumers' Cooperative and served as vestrywoman at Christ Church.

The "Supermoms" of today may well ask how Beverly Darling managed to juggle so much. The answer was Ruth Brian, her housekeeper. As a young girl, Ruthie was a ward of the state when Beverly first hired her to run the house and care for her children. After forty-three years, Ruthie is still ready with a jovial welcome at the door when visitors arrive at the Darling house on Alden Street.

Newly arrived immigrants, Scots-Irish in particular, could get emergency help through Mary Dalton at the "Metropolitan," 42 Main Street. The secret was a silent benefactor, Mary Wentworth French, onetime member of the School Committee. Her husband, Edward V. French, was president of Arkwright Insurance Company and board chairman of Factory Mutual Insurance Company.

Another successful business in the center was Ford's Coffee Shop. Following service in World War II, Tom Koravos worked the late shift at a lunch counter in a Lowell drugstore. His parents had emigrated from Northern Greece in the early 1900s. Tom used his free mornings to drive through surrounding towns looking for a small coffee shop that he could own himself. Fourteen Main Street had been purchased in 1942 by Harold E. Heseltine and Leslie Ford Powers. Soon afterward, Powers left town but his middle name stuck to the business. When Tom and Stella Koravos purchased the shop in 1954, they kept the name. That same year, they were able to buy a house on Elm Street from Harry Axelrod. Tom says:

I was thrilled at what I was doing. If you like what you're doing, you're going to do a good job. The whole family pitched in—I could always count on them. In the old days, we knew every man who came in the door, what he did for work, knew his wife and his kids by name. Now there are so many that I can't know them all. One day, I had to go out and run some errands. It was a Wednesday afternoon, when the Phillips students were allowed to come downtown. I left my wife in charge and told her not to take any checks. When I got back and she had left for the day, I opened the cash drawer and there was a check. I looked in the corner and it said, "John F. Kennedy Jr." I picked up the phone and called Stella. "Tom, now don't give me hell," she said. "The boys didn't have any money and I decided that a check was better than nothing at all." "Stella, did you know whose check that was?" I asked her. "No, all those kids look alike to me," she answered.[17]

Ford's came to be a gathering place for local and state politicians. There was a time when you would see longtime selectmen Sid White, Roy Hardy, or Phil Allen lunching at Ford's. In later years, you might have seen Jerry Cohen and Sue Tucker, or Paul Cronin ordering up spinach pie while they discussed issues at the State House.

Roy Hardy (1892–1955) served a long and distinguished term on the Board of Selectmen (1936–1954). Hardy was descended from an old Andover family and graduated from both Punchard and Phillips, and MIT. He owned bowling alleys in Lawrence and on Park Street, Andover, and served as president of the Andover Guild, the Community Chest, and the Red Cross, and as treasurer of South Church, among many other community activities.

Selectman Sidney P. White (1899–1983), whose term overlapped Hardy's by five years, is one of those recalled as "Mr. Andover." Also descended from

Now retired, Beverly Darling is a nationally recognized collector of miniature furniture, and continues her practice of sculpture and watercolor. Recently, she started writing poetry. Her gardens have been featured on the Massachusetts Federation of Garden tours. EMR photo

Tom and Stella Koravos owned Ford's Coffee Shop, 14 Main Street, from 1954 to 1994. They commissioned the Main Street mural from Dorothy Piercy in 1957. EMR photo

Andover's early settlers, White was a dairy farmer by profession. A plaque cast in his honor reads, "Sidney P. White, in recognition of forty years of devoted service to the citizens and town of Andover. Planning Board 1934–1951; Animal Inspector 1936–1944, 1957; Board of Public Works 1938–1956; Merrimack River Valley Sewage Board 1942–1956; Board of Selectmen and Welfare 1949–1961; Board of Assessors 1949–1959; Board of Selectmen 1966–1972." White held an eighteen-year record of perfect attendance at all boards of which he was a member.

While White and Hardy were in the limelight, others served quietly. Leo Daley (1900–1991) attended both Punchard and Phillips, graduating from Harvard in 1927. A gifted athlete, he was elected to the Andover Sports Hall of Fame in 1980. He was awarded an honorary doctorate of commercial science by Merrimack College at its sixteenth commencement. Daley served on the board of Memorial Hall Library, Spring Grove Cemetery, the town Finance Committee, and the Red Cross, was a lifetime member of the Andover Historical Society, and was active in St. Augustine's Church. Daley was a stockbroker, retiring at age eighty as senior vice president of Harris, Upham Company in Boston. From 1970 to 1990, he served on the Andover Retirement Board as a volunteer, investing all retirement funds for the town. When he stepped down at ninety, his replacement started at a salary of $40,000 a year.

Daley bridged the gap between Phillips Academy and the town below. Another notable ambassador between town and gown was Philip K. Allen, also called "Mr. Andover" by many. Allen was introduced to Andover by his father and uncles who had attended Phillips. His uncle, Bernard (Barney) Allen, was once a controversial member of the Academy faculty. Phil graduated from Phillips Academy in 1929 and went on to Yale and Harvard. In 1936 he returned to the Academy to teach. He remembers how removed Phillips was from the rest of the community and that there were incidents of "rough stuff" between the "townies" and Academy students.[18] He left to enter World War II as a private. He was released a lieutenant colonel.

Allen returned to Andover and served as state senator (1946–1948) and state chairman of the Republican Party. He then worked in Washington for Leverett

Prior to 1960, Sid White owned and operated Wild Rose Farm on Lowell Street, but in 1960, moved his herd to ancestral family land at 5 Argilla Road (the Abbot-Baker house) and set up a dairy bar known as Rose Glen on nearby Andover Street.

State Senator Philip K. Allen, his wife Elizabeth, and their children pose for a portrait, circa 1947.

Joshua L. Miner began the Colorado Outward Bound School in 1962, and with the support of headmaster John Kemper, Phillips Academy adopted elements of the program. Today there are five Outward Bound Schools and several Outward Bound centers in the country. Sixty thousand teachers have been through such courses, and public schools have begun to work elements of it into their curricula. Miner estimates the program now impacts one to two million people per year. EMR photo

Saltonstall as clerk of the Armed Services Committee, and for the Defense Department. Returning to Andover, he assumed the post of general manager for finance at WGBH-TV in 1957. He ran for selectman in 1958, serving until 1971. Allen believes he was the first from Phillips to run for selectman.

Allen served on the Boards of Trustees at Phillips (1966–1980) and Abbot (1948–1956; 1958–1973). Always a conciliator, he helped to bring about the merger between the two historic schools. Phil and his wife, Elizabeth Warner Allen, left Andover in 1992 for a retirement home, donating their large 1830 house at 1 Highland Street to the Academy.

Joshua L. Miner came to Phillips to teach science and physics in 1952. A former battery commander under General Patton, he had just completed two years' teaching at Gordonstoun School in Scotland under German educator Kurt Hahn. But Miner did not find America fertile soil for Hahn's ideals of selfless service and testing one's limits. He remembers the early 1950s as the peak of American national arrogance until Sputnik forced a severe self-examination. Then the climate improved for his dream of an Outward Bound program in this country. It "took off like a big bird"[19] in the early 1960s.

Thayer Warshaw is another nationally known educator. Born in 1915 in Lawrence, he attended Lawrence schools until eighth grade, then Phillips Academy. He graduated from Harvard in 1933, then worked twenty-two years in the family car dealership. He and his wife, Bernice, moved to Andover in 1948 seeking a good education for their children. Warshaw was a member of the first Sunday School class at Temple Emanuel in Lawrence, and was involved in the Temple's move to Andover in 1978. Bernice started Andover's first cooperative nursery school in 1958 at Free Church.

In 1957 Warshaw returned to Harvard for a master's in education. Upon graduating, he got a job in the Newton Public Schools, where he developed curricula to teach "What's in the Bible: People, Events, and Some Familiar Quotations," so students could understand literary allusions—a very tricky business just as prayer in the schools became a hot issue. When he wrote up his program for the *English Journal*, it was reprinted in the *Congressional Journal* and the *Christian Science Monitor*. From there, it was picked up by newspapers all over the country.

Warshaw helped form the Shawsheen Village Improvement Society soon after moving to town. In 1977 he became involved in the Ballardvale Improvement Society. He served on the Board of Taxpayers Association in the 1950s, the Public Welfare Committee, the Master Plan Committee, and was town representative to the Merrimack Valley Transit Authority. Warshaw was known for asking diplomatic questions at Town Meeting. "I asked, not because I didn't understand, but because I thought things better be explained," he says. At first, his questions were all but ignored by the moderator. Soon, however, he had people coming to him, asking him to ask their questions.[20]

Selectman J. Everett Collins served in World War I, then worked as auditor for Kemper Insurance Company. He married his high school sweetheart, Elizabeth Abbot, and they raised four sons. Choir director of Calvary Baptist Church in Lawrence for fifty years, he organized the Andover Male Choir in 1931. In 1934 they called in a "women's auxiliary" to do Handel's "Messiah." This became a tradition for the next fifty years with Collins conducting. After retiring from Kemper, Collins conducted choral groups at Andover High and West Middle School. When the performing arts center was dedicated in 1983, it was named The Collins Center.

For many years, the districting of the state legislature was such that we had few members representing Andover. Paul Cronin was one of the first to break through this barrier. Paul's family moved to Ballardvale when he was five. At twenty-three he was the youngest selectman ever elected in Andover or in Massachusetts, serving from 1963 to 1966. He helped defeat urban renewal in Andover in 1962. During his term, Andover built a high school and two elementary schools without increasing the tax rate. The projects were funded through a series of bond issues. Cronin served as state representative from 1967 to 1969.

In 1972 Cronin was elected to Congress, the first member from Andover in this century, serving the 5th Massachusetts District from 1973 to 1975. He was voted outstanding freshman member of Congress by his peers, but two years later was defeated over the Vietnam issue. "I thought there was a right way and a wrong way to get out of Vietnam and I knew we were making headway," says Cronin. "My house at the corner of Punchard and Bartlet Streets was picketed twenty-four hours a day; my kids had to be escorted to school, and my mother-in-law had a heart attack on the front steps. It was a crazy two years."[21] The primary in 1974 was held the weekend that President Ford pardoned Nixon for Watergate. Cronin was defeated by Paul Tsongas. Cronin was appointed to the Massachusetts Port Authority in 1991, and today works in international consulting.

Jerry Cohen grew up in Winthrop, moving to Andover in 1967. Changing careers from sales and marketing of food products, he enrolled at Suffolk Law School, where he met politicians and worked in the shadow of the State House. In 1973 he joined Andover's Democratic Town Committee and in 1974 ran for the state legislature, serving in the House of Representatives from 1975 to 1983. Cohen was involved in overhauling the state's construction contract law and the design selection process, and in Proposition 2 1/2 in 1980. Once the referendum passed, Cohen chaired the committee that wrote the statute. He taught at Merrimack College from 1974 to 1983, and presently serves as adjunct professor at Suffolk Law School while a practicing attorney.[22]

Susan Tucker came to Andover in the 1960s and soon was deeply involved in the League of Women Voters, elected president in 1974. She served on the Development and Industrial Commission. She remembers, "It was clear that the town was going to grow. The question was, How? Many volunteers put in an inordinate amount of time on the planning." When Cohen resigned in 1982, Tucker ran for the state legislature, the first woman from Andover to serve in the House of Representatives. She served four terms, with special emphasis on education improvement and domestic violence prevention, writing and passing major reform of domestic violence laws in Massachusetts.[23]

It would be impossible to write biographies of all the notable people in Andover during the past hundred years. As of 1994, the population is close to thirty thousand. We have outgrown our ability to recognize everyone by name. Although we would like to give every worthy leader in town government his or her due and would like to outline the development of every business, we can only bring to mind a few citizens who are representative of their time, their profession, and the themes of change in the lives of their fellow townspeople.

J. Everett Collins (1894–1986) served twenty years as selectman, one term on the School Committee, and fourteen years as state representative. He was a fine tenor and conductor and an exceptional athlete. He was the only one elected to both Athletic and Fine Arts Halls of Fame at Andover High School.

Alice Buck's Indian Ridge Association merged with AVIS in 1915, giving AVIS its first substantial piece of property.

Chapter Three

Preserving Andover's Character

Claus Dengler pulled his car to the side of Reservation Road under the Indian Ridge sign and set out along the path. He hiked north up the long glacial kame into the hardwoods, and looked down to his right through colorful leaves at the huge new Andover High School. It was 1968. When the path began to descend, he turned and struck out to the south, down around a huge leafy bowl in the woods. He walked through a deep pine forest with soft needles under his feet, then continued the circle through a small rise of oaks. Stopping to rest, he noticed a sizable boulder to his left off the trail with some kind of plaque attached to it. Pulling branches aside, he read, "In Memory of Miss Alice Buck, by whose loving interest and untiring effort the perpetual use of this woodland by the people of Andover was secured in 1897." Some of the bolts were missing and there were nicks from wanton bullets. Who was Alice Buck? he wondered.

Dengler was president of AVIS, the Andover Village Improvement Society. AVIS owned the land he walked on, and had for many years. The next time he met with the Board of Directors, he asked, "Who was Alice Buck?" Nobody knew.

Dengler figured that he had an excuse not to know the answer, but surely Al Retelle or Harold Rafton, hero of acquiring land for future generations, ought to know. He took the plaque over to the Vocational Technical School, where a sympathetic teacher put his class to work repairing it. Then he pursued the idea of writing a history of AVIS. "I bumped into a boulder and that gave me the necessary kick in the rear," he says. "I looked around for a writer and finally ended with local historian Juliet Haines Mofford." The result was Mofford's *AVIS—A History in Conservation.*

The story began in 1894 when forty people gathered in the new November Club on Locke Street to see whether there was any interest in founding a society to beautify the town. Other towns had begun to form such associations. Thirty people joined AVIS that evening. A week later, May 7, 1894, they adopted bylaws stating:

Its object shall be to improve and ornament the streets and public grounds of Andover, by planting and cultivating trees, cleaning and repairing sidewalks, and doing such other acts as shall tend to beautify and adorn said streets and grounds.[1]

William G. Goldsmith was the first president. Goldsmith had been principal of Punchard High School and was then town postmaster. Emma Lincoln, daughter of the Universalist minister, was elected secretary, and John N. Cole, publisher

An emigrant from Lübeck, Germany, in 1951, Claus Dengler joined AVIS out of a love for the outdoors and friendship for Al Retelle, AVIS president from 1960 to 1965. EMR photo

of the *Townsman*, treasurer pro tem. Shortly afterward, George A. Parker was elected permanent treasurer.[2] These officers were assisted by a fifteen-member executive committee. From the beginning, prominent citizens, both men and women, were on the board. However, AVIS was not originally a landholding organization. Its more pressing task was cleanup. It is hard to imagine the town in the days before trash collection, when it was not uncommon for homeowners

The Rev. Frederick Palmer of Christ Church sent a letter to the *Townsman* on April 23, 1894, before AVIS's first meeting, suggesting, "The ragged-looking bank of rock near the Railroad Station ought to be made into an ornament, instead of remaining, as at present, an eyesore."[3] This became one of the society's first projects.

to simply throw their trash out the back door, creating mountains of tin cans. "Village improvement was an event of the industrial age," says Dengler, "and so was trash." Dumping occurred wherever a corner of land looked unused.

Not only was unsightly land cleaned up, but bushes and trees were planted to enhance its beauty. AVIS cleared and planted triangles at North Main and Stevens (then Marland) Streets, Main Street at Hidden Road, and Summer Street at Upland Road. Mary Byers Smith donated "Roger's Dell" at the intersection of School Street and Lupine Road.[4]

In the 1890s AVIS members cleared paths in Carmel Woods, the first town-owned conservation land. Carmel Hill had been the woodlot for the town

In 1921 the town sold the Almshouse to William M. Wood. Newman photo

Almshouse, deeded to Andover by North Andover when the towns split in 1855. In 1869 the town chose "Mount Carmel" as a site for the town cemetery, but the plan was abandoned due to the "impropitious nature of the soil for burial purposes." (The name, Mount Carmel, was a Biblical reference dating back to Andover Seminary days.)

In 1919 there were only seven residents left at the Almshouse, so in 1921 the town sold the fields and buildings to William M. Wood.[5] The town built a new infirmary on Carmel Hill in 1922. In 1967 the town considered Carmel Hill for a new school, but sloping terrain discouraged them. At Harold Rafton's urging, Carmel Woods was deeded to the Conservation Commission at Town Meeting in 1969. The issue was not dead, however. In 1971 the Housing Authority again selected Carmel Woods, this time for elderly housing. But investigation revealed that land put into conservation can only change its use or agency by a two-thirds vote of the legislature, a majority vote of the Conservation Commission, and a two-thirds vote of Town Meeting. Carmel Woods was safe.

Ten years after AVIS was formed, the Andover Natural History Society held its first meeting, June 4, 1904, at the Town House, with its object "to investigate and to promote an interest in everything pertaining to the natural history of Andover, Massachusetts."[6] At the June 4 meeting, Florence Abbot and Clara Putnam spoke on birds, Miss Putnam making special mention of the flycatcher family. Mr. Goldsmith spoke on the flower of the horse chestnut, and other plants in flower were exhibited by members. A "field meeting" was held two weeks later at the garden of Mr. Tyer, where members observed a fine collection of native ferns and a bed of foxglove in full bloom. At the third meeting, committees were set up: "Carmel Park," "Flora," "Birds," and "Insects." At the December meeting, "the winter habit of skunk cabbage was discussed."[7]

In 1915 the Natural History Society set up a fifteen-hundred-acre State Reservation and Game Sanctuary, stretching from Indian Ridge to Pomp's Pond. There is no indication that the society ever owned the land, but members erected more than forty-two bird boxes in the area including Foster's Farm. The reservation was duly approved by the Massachusetts State Fish and Game Protective Association.

The Andover Natural History Society gradually dwindled away. The minutes of May 14, 1935, report that "Several members expressed a feeling that there were so many other activities in town that it would be futile to continue." It was voted to disband.

Not only organizations but individuals and families took initiative in preserving undeveloped land for future generations. Charles and Mabel Saunders Ward bought the Holt farmhouse, built circa 1709, as a summer home and gentleman's farm in 1917. The property included Holt Hill (Ward Hill), the highest in Essex County (420 feet), and a fine example of a northern quaking bog. It was Charles Ward's wish "to have a portion of the property, and all of it eventually, used in some suitable manner to benefit some deserving

State conservation efforts came to Andover in 1916, with the purchase of Harold Parker State Forest. The site was nineteenth-century farmland, grown up to woods, lumbered, and scarred by fires. The state bought up such "wasteland" (at $5 an acre) to develop forestlands. The year that the forest in Andover, North Andover, and Middleton was purchased, Harold Parker, chairman of the State Forest Commission, died suddenly, so the forest was named for him. From 1933 to 1941, Civilian Conservation Corps units built roads, trails, ponds, administrative and recreational structures, and planted red and white pine. Today, the forest totals 3,014 acres, 30 percent in Andover.

organization." Charles died in 1933, and in 1940 Mabel gave 107 acres to the Trustees of Reservations in his memory, naming it the Charles W. Ward Reservation. The Trustees of Reservations was and is strictly a private organization with no state aid.

During her lifetime, Mabel Ward bought abutting land and more was donated, until the reservation encompassed 276 acres. Her grandson, John Kimball, took over its stewardship upon her death in 1956 and, helped by his wife Margaret and other family members, has purchased additional land so it now totals 670 acres.

In tandem with the birth of land conservation groups came local historical societies. America had celebrated her Centennial in 1876, and older towns were becoming aware that they had some history to preserve. The Andover Historical Society held its first public meeting April 14, 1911, with its object:

John Kimball says, "Beauty takes a tremendous amount of work. Fields grow up to brush, orchards run to brambles, and stone walls are buried in trees without constant care. When I took over the Ward Reservation in 1956, you couldn't see anything but trees from the top of Holt Hill. I had to re-open the view. The solstice stones were put there by my grandmother in about 1940—I was there when they did it. She had been to visit Stonehenge in England and wanted one of her own. Four stones indicate the four directions, and others mark the rising and setting sun at the winter and summer solstices."[8] EMR photo

. . . to cultivate and encourage an interest in historical and antiquarian research; to collect and treasure significant Historical matter and antiquarian relics; and to found and maintain a museum where such collections shall be preserved and exhibited, thus making a valuable, interesting and educational feature in the life of Andover.[9]

The first officers were Dr. Charles E. Abbott, president; Sarah Wilson Carter, first vice president; Nathaniel E. Bartlett, second vice president; Agnes Park, secretary; George Abbott, treasurer; and John V. Holt, librarian. At the May 15 meeting in lower Town Hall, the Cornell Fund was announced: "left for a collection of Historical furniture—garments and implements to be put in Memorial Hall if thought best." By October 1911 the society possessed: "a picture of Andover taken in 1857; a map of the town still older; a veritable carpet bag; and some old dresses and bonnets and embroideries and some books and papers of value with offers of more things when we have a place to put them." In December 1913

In 1915 the Andover Historical Society found a temporary home in the Andrews house, a federal house at the southwest corner of Main and Chestnut Streets. At first the society rented one room, but soon overflowed into a second. In 1931 it was torn down to build a new United States Post Office.

George Francis Dow of the Essex Institute gave a talk on "Andover and Other Old English Towns."[10]

Caroline Underhill (1867–1956) acquired the 1819 Amos Blanchard house at 97 Main Street from her sister, Julia Underhill Robinson, in 1924. In 1926 the society voted unanimously to purchase the Robinson property, but only $800 of the $18,000 needed was pledged. In 1929 Miss Underhill agreed to sell the property for a yearly payment of $420 during her lifetime with the stipulation that she have life tenancy.

Miss Underhill, who studied under Melville Dewey, had been head librarian at the Utica (New York) Public Library. She became curator of the Andover Historical Society, serving more than twenty-five years. She diligently catalogued the society's possessions, joined in research projects with members and visitors, expanded the library, and invited school classes for tours. The society's newsletter observed in her later years, "Frail, burdened with failing eyesight, she nevertheless enjoyed sitting in her Boston rocker in the North Parlor, receiving visitors with whom she could discuss the various treasures in the house."[11]

A notable volunteer was Charlotte Helen Abbot (1844–1921), schoolteacher, dressmaker, and columnist for twenty-five years for the *Townsman*. She started genealogy as a hobby, but eventually became a professional genealogist. Her valuable collection of genealogical information on Andover families remains at the Andover Historical Society.

Margaret Dodge succeeded Miss Underhill as resident curator from 1957 to 1963. Barbara Sessions served as curator from 1963 to 1971. A new meeting room and the Cheever Room were added in 1965. Katherine M. Gordon was resident hostess/director from 1972 to 1975, and from 1975 to 1978, Carl and Priscilla Blomerth were resident custodians. Under the curatorship (1976–1978) of John P. Brucksch, construction started on the Susanne Smith Purdon Wing, and the survey of eight hundred historically relevant structures in Andover for the Andover Historical Commission was begun.

The early focus of the historical society was mainly on artifacts and lectures. Preservation of buildings, if it happened at all, was carried out by private owners. For example, William Wood saved some of the older buildings in Frye Village when he created the Shawsheen Village, moving them to Balmoral and Argyle Streets. Likewise, when Phillips Academy took over the former Andover

Harriet Beecher Stowe's house, once on Chapel Avenue, was rescued and recycled several times. When the Stowes came to Andover, Harriet requested the former carpentry shop be renovated as a residence. When they left, it became a student boardinghouse, and in 1888, an inn. In 1929 Phillips Academy decided to replace it with a modern inn, but, conscious of its history, moved it to 80 Bartlet Street.[12]

Brechin Hall, the Seminary library, was razed in 1929.

This house was moved from Main Street Terrace to 150 Main Street in 1955, making way for a new bank.

Theological Seminary campus in the early twentieth century, it saved several buildings on Seminary Row. Foxcroft Hall was rebuilt in 1912, Bartlet Hall was rebuilt after being damaged by fire in 1914, and Bartlet Chapel was moved, restored, and renamed Pearson Hall in 1922. Samaritan House, the 1824 infirmary, was moved from Chapel Avenue to 6 School Street in 1929.[13]

Thomas Cochran, Class of 1890, a J. P. Morgan partner, took the lead in renovating the Phillips campus between 1924 and 1931. But many landmarks were destroyed in the process: Little Sanhedran (1875) was razed after the construction of Paul Revere Hall and the old stone chapel (1876) was razed in 1931.[14] But to his credit, Cochran created the Moncrieff Cochran Sanctuary for birds and wildlife, eighty-six acres abutting the campus.

Down in the town, a new wave of changes began in the 1950s. As Andover's population grew, new schools were built and old ones dismantled. In 1962, an urban renewal project was proposed. "It was really urban destruction," says photographer Richard Graber. The plan, largely federally and state-funded, referred to the central business district as "blighted" and would have razed all the buildings on Main Street from Chestnut to the Musgrove building with the exception of the Andover Bank. A new Town Hall and Fire Department would have been built where High Street meets Elm. Ultimately, the Finance Committee recommended that the project would not justify the expense to the town. It was defeated at Town Meeting in 1963. Even today, historic buildings are being lost. The firehouse on Park Street, boasting a handsome tower with an unforgettable bell, met the wrecker's ball in 1970. Phillips Academy's Cheever House (1840s) at the intersection of Main and School Streets disappeared one summer morning in

1981 and the last Latin Commons (1834) was destroyed in 1988. The old schoolhouse in Ballardvale, used as a library and community building, was razed in 1981. The Turner farmland at 331 South Main Street was lost to development. Conservationists put it on the town warrant in 1978 and a young farmer was ready to lease it. But it was voted down and the imposing homes of Orchard Crossing fill its fields instead.

A portion of the Andover Industrial Park, owned by Digital Equipment Corporation and Hewlett-Packard, now occupies the site of the former Shattuck Farm. When development on the property escalated in 1980, Wendy Frontiero,

Andover's Historical Commission consultant, sent a distress signal to the Massachusetts Historical Commission. As a result, time was granted for an archaeological dig before four Native American sites were bulldozed. Soon everybody got into the act: the Historical Society, the Conservation Commission, Hewlett-Packard, and Digital. Two reports were published, "An Archaeological Survey and the Documentary History of the Shattuck Farm, Andover, Massachusetts," 1981, and "The Camp in the Bend in the River," by Barbara E. Luedtke, in 1985 through the University of Massachusetts at Boston, both supported by the Catherine G. Shattuck Memorial Trust and the Massachusetts Historical Commission.

Shattuck Farm (1718), on a beautiful site bordering the Merrimack River at 125 River Road, was another loss. A restaurant in the main house served baked beans cooked in an old brick oven every Saturday night, and an ice cream stand and country store offered further goodies. An operating farm for 250 years, it encompassed seven distinct Native American sites. The location had been in continuous use for 8,000 years. Jim Batchelder, former president of the Andover Historical Society, remembers, "The house was re-sited on High Plain Road. But it's not facing the right direction and it doesn't look the same." [15]

Architect Jane Griswold moved to Andover in 1971 and served on the Zoning Board from 1975 to 1993. "Every time someone wanted a zoning variance, we went to look at the building," she says, so she learned quickly about the town's historic buildings. As an architect, she designed twenty to thirty additions per year, which furthered her explorations.

In 1988 Architect Jane Griswold began writing a column for the *Eagle-Tribune*. She says, "The newspaper thought then that there might be six houses in the Merrimack Valley worth writing about. They had no concept of the wealth, quantity, and variety of our architectural record. I wanted to make it popular and acceptable to talk about old buildings." Pictured is the Moses Foster Estate, once at Elm and Whittier Streets.

Griswold feels attitudes toward old buildings are changing. The Ayer Mill Clock Tower in Lawrence has been restored, a visible inspiration, and the historical societies of Andover, North Andover, Methuen, and Lawrence have begun to work together. "Andover has always had a reasonably good sense of its history," she says, "But we are part of the valley. The town lines are arbitrary."[16]

Construction of Routes 93 and 495 was bound to bring business and population growth to the valley. The pinch for land was nothing new in Andover. As early as 1675, residents had complained land was scarce and their children could no longer live there:

. . . whereas many of ye petitioners are much straitened in their p'sonall accommodations and most of their children grown up and many others of ye petitioners wholly destitute of land for settlement and soe under a necessity to look out for inlargment and places of habitation . . . [17]

As Andover's farms became history, farm buildings were destroyed. Between 1976 and 1989 alone, historic barns were torn down at 9 Bancroft Road, 112 Main Street, 87 and 237 River Road, 38 Phillips Street, 362 Salem Street, 62–64 Argilla Road (burned), and 117 Elm Street. Pictured is the Burtt farm at 35–37 Elm Street, just east of Free Church.

The Conservation Commission was formed by Town Meeting in 1960 after an act of the legislature to promote and coordinate all conservation acts for air, water, land, and natural resources in the Commonwealth. It differed from AVIS in that it was a public agency while AVIS was private. It could raise money from many sources including bond issues, and could even take land by eminent domain.

In 1967 Town Manager Richard Bowen proposed to the Selectmen that a fund be created to acquire land for conservation. Bill Stewart asked him how much he had in mind. Bowen thought carefully. "I wanted a figure that would

gain people's attention but not cause them to faint," he recalls. "I said '$250,000.' There was a big sucking sound. A quarter of a million dollars was a lot of money in those days."

Peggy Keck, an AVIS trustee, remembers Town Meeting in 1967 as a high point of her life.

I was chair of a League of Women Voters committee to study conservation issues in Andover. The Committee concluded the only way to protect conservation land permanently was to buy it. At first the selectmen were opposed to buying open space. At least one of them owned large parcels of land and wanted to develop them. Also, many townspeople were opposed to taking the land off the tax rolls. Dick Bowen challenged the selectmen.

The League went into action, providing information and getting a good turnout for the Town Meeting. I gave talks and slide shows to anyone who would listen. Harold Rafton buttonholed people on the street. Harold and Bob Henderson, president of the Andover Bank and chairman of the Conservation Commission, gave eloquent speeches at Town Meeting. The proposal passed unanimously, a great victory.[18]

Virginia "Deena" Hammond served on the Planning Board from 1955 to 1965 and in 1966, Town Manager Maynard Austin appointed her to the Conservation Commission. She was hired by the town in 1977, serving ten years. During her tenure, a great deal of land was purchased with the help of state aid. The Conservation Commission would go to Town Meeting for money to buy a parcel and, when the state sent them back a 50 percent rebate, the Commission would persuade Town Meeting to vote it back into conservation, building up a land purchase fund. After a while this source dried up. Combined with parcels given by developers and town land deeded to conservation by Town Meeting, the Commission now controls 140 properties totaling 1600 acres.

When Deena Hammond was hired by the town, she prevailed upon Bob Pustell to chair the Conservation Commission. Margaret and Bob Pustell moved to Andover in 1975 to escape the auto exhaust of Melrose, where Bob had served on the Planning Board and as alderman for twenty years. He had seen the last open spaces filled in Melrose. He knew that good conservation meant good business and a good quality of life. Bob observes:

What makes a good city? Open spaces. The higher the population density, the worse the living quarters and the more it costs to live there. Proximity to open land makes it desirable and drives land values up, provided it is convenient to where jobs are. Thus the town collects more money per unit toward the cost of administering the town. The more open space, the more the town collects in taxes per unit. If you have a fair amount of open space, no matter how crowded our community becomes, it will still remain attractive.[19]

The Hammond Reservation was bequeathed to AVIS by Deena Hammond's father-in-law, Edward Hammond Sr., AVIS president from 1943 to 1946 and investment chair from 1950 to 1965. "He and Harold Rafton lived next door to each other and disagreed about many things," says Deena, "chiefly whether to build up AVIS's

The Taft family donated thirty-seven acres of the Gray-Taft farmland, 232 Salem Street, to AVIS during the 1970s, naming it the Amy Gordon Taft Reservation.

39

nest egg or to spend it on land. Harold said, 'You have to start using this money' and got them to change the charter so they could. 'Land value can only go up,' Harold would say. 'They're simply not making any more of it.'"

While the Conservation Commission was using state aid to protect the remaining open land, Harold Rafton (1890–1982) was instigating a renaissance within AVIS. Nat Smith, a mathematics teacher at Phillips and current AVIS president, describes Rafton and his work with great affection:

Harold was a sickly child with a problem in his leg. It became so bad that he had to take a year off from college, going on endless long walks to build up his strength. It was probably then that he developed his love for the outdoors. But he didn't really get involved in conservation until after his retirement in 1955.

Once Harold got his eye on a site, he would protect it against all comers. AVIS had no money and he had to build our holdings by putting together small parcels. He loved people and would become part of their lives. He would help an old lady with offspring living out of state to sell off lots along the street where land values were high, then to donate her back swamp land to AVIS. She got a tax break, her heirs got the money from the prime real estate, she lived on in the old house, and everyone was happy. The wetlands were just what AVIS wanted, for animal habitats, trails, and watersheds.

Harold would get up before the Town Meeting, align the facts, and present them with clarity and force. He was enjoyed by everybody. He was bright, dedicated, and trustworthy. When he wanted to get his way, it was difficult to stop him. Once he telephoned me on Christmas morning. I said, "Harold, it's Christmas, I have small children, I have to go." He just didn't get the idea, said he had to talk to me for about a half hour. Finally I had to hang up on him.[20]

Harold Rafton was a task-oriented idealist who found a niche with a passion. His wife, Helen, with her love of flowers and beauty, probably influenced his choice.

Harold Rafton almost single-handedly procured the land along the Merrimack River, much of it purchased in 1840 by the founders of Lawrence. Rafton tracked down the Essex Company in Boston and persuaded them to sell twenty-seven acres with 2.5 miles of frontage in 1960.[21] Bit by bit, he bought up other parcels abutting the river to create Deer Jump Reservation. Between 1969 and 1975, the town acquired frontage from Deer Jump Reservation almost to the Lawrence line, the only breaks being Phillips Academy boathouse land and St. Francis Seminary's one hundred acres. In 1968 the largest parcel of AVIS land, bordered by High Plain, Chandler, and River Roads and Routes 495 and 93, was named the Harold R. Rafton Reservation. Juliet Mofford wrote, "When the Raftons joined AVIS efforts in 1955, the Society owned only twenty-three acres located on Indian Ridge. At the time of Harold's death in 1982, AVIS held nearly 850 acres."[22] AVIS has enjoyed unprecedented growth. At its centennial in 1994, membership stood at eight hundred.

The Andover Historical Society underwent a revival of its own in the mid-1970s, when the Board of Directors developed a long-range plan. In 1978 it hired

Roger's Dell, at School Street and Lupine Road, became a pet project of Louise Van Everen. While AVIS has continued to acquire land, in recent years it has focused on stewardship. Since 1971 a network of volunteer wardens, usually residents abutting AVIS land, looks after each property. Says Nat Smith, "There are people who don't know about Andover's wildflowers, fields, and streams here in town. You don't have to drive 150 miles north to find them."

its first professional director/curator, Marsha Rooney, who consolidated the excellent work done by previous curators and volunteers. With the assistance of President Marilyn Burns, Rooney worked toward the society's accreditation by the American Association of Museums (AAM). All aspects of the organization had to meet AAM guidelines. The society received accreditation in 1986, one of only three small historical societies in the state to get it.

Karen Herman, president from 1986 to 1988, observed, "We wanted to reach out to a broader ethnic and cultural base than the collections of the society reflected at that time." The museum instituted an interpretive program, "Andover at Work in the 1820s," with all fifth graders in town participating. The society already had a strong commitment to education—programs for schoolchildren had begun as early as 1940—but the fifth grade living history program initiated in 1980 was part of a strategic plan.

To strengthen the educational effort, the Historical Society hired Barbara Thibault as curator of education in 1986. She continued under Director/Curators Clark Pearce and Charlotte Smith. Thibault used her background in historic building preservation to develop walking tours and initiated programs in nursing homes. She was named director in July 1993, and Tom Edmonds joined the staff as curator in December. A third professional, Peg Hughes, is assistant to the director.

Reflecting the renaissance of conservation and preservation, the Historical Commission was created in 1970. According to John Sullivan, former chair, the commission was founded "to persuade people to preserve the historic fabric of the community." The first chair was Philip Allen.

The relationship of the Historical Commission to the Historical Society is similar to that of the Conservation Commission to AVIS. Like the Conservation Commission, the Historical Commission gets its power from federal, state, and local legislation. It is appointed by town government, while the Historical Society is a private organization. The Historical Commission focuses primarily on buildings and the architectural history of Andover. These four organizations often work cooperatively.

The Historical Commission developed a preservation plan and executed a reconnaissance survey developed by the Massachusetts Historic Commission completed

Volunteers contribute hundreds of hours to the Historical Society. Celebrating the 1991 exterior restoration are, standing from left: Nancy Larsen, Gratia Mahony, Hanne Castle, Priscilla Alden, Laurie Winters, Carol Majahad , George Trickett, May Bell, Jack Herman, Barbara Swift, Norma Gammon, Karen Herman, Bernice Haggerty, Margaret Roberts, Ruth Sharpe, and Jim Batchelder. Middle row: Nat Stevens, guest, and James Theophanis. Seated are staff members Peg Hughes, assistant to the director; Barbara Thibault, curator of education (now director); and Charlotte Smith, director.

From the historic properties survey, seven National Register districts were established and more than forty structures listed on the National Register of Historic Places. Pictured is 12 Highvale Lane, Ballardvale.

in 1977. Loose-leaf notebooks at the Andover Historical Society and Memorial Hall Library list almost every building by street with photographs and background information. They are constantly updated by the Historical Society.

The Commission attempted to have Central Street designated a Local Historic District in 1976, creating design review over proposed changes, but this was voted down. "Andover people have tended to encourage preservation on their own," says Sullivan. "For example, the houses on Central Street are almost all in excellent shape and historically correct from a preservation standpoint."23 Commission members still believe that local historic districts under Chapter 40C are necessary to assure preservation of Andover's historic structures.

In 1981, under Town Manager Jared Clark, the 1917 Punchard High School

on Bartlet Street was adapted for reuse as Town Offices, the town's first preservation project. This opened the way to restoring the 1858 Town House. The Historical Commission joined forces with the Historical Society to lobby for restoration of the town's first municipal building, saved from destruction in the 1960s. Members of both organizations, with the wholehearted support of Town Manager Ken Mahony and Selectman Jerry Silverman, fought hard at Town Meeting in 1987 to get the necessary $2.6 million appropriated.

The Town House, with meeting room on the second floor, had been partitioned into offices during World War II. Old photographs were consulted and the Boston architectural firm of Ann Beha Associates engaged. Michael Orlando, an elderly Italian fresco painter from Melrose, was called out of retirement to restore the ceiling decorations. Chandeliers found in the attic were reproduced. Arches on the large windows upstairs were exposed, and the stage was liberated from a clutter of partitions by Mansco Construction Company of Woburn.

The Historical Commission won a victory when the Demolition Delay Ordinance passed in 1991. This enables the commission to delay demolition of buildings up to six months if they are on the National Register of Historic Places or in a National Register District. Had the ordinance been in place, Shawsheen Manor and Cheever House would not have disappeared overnight. Commission members also encourage downtown businesses to preserve historic structures, presenting annual awards jointly with the Historical Society to individuals who preserve significant properties.

Some newer conservation organizations in town are the Appalachian Mountain Club (AMC) and the Andover Trails Committee. The Andover Committee of the AMC was formed in 1975. Louise Van Everen wrote:

The Andover group was given birth on a trail in Pinkham Notch, July 1975. Dorothy and Jim Christopher and Louise Van Everen were climbing. Dorothy made a chance remark, "Do you know that in the Andover area alone, there are 160 AMC members? Maybe we could have an informal social hour and become acquainted with our fellow members." It was agreed . . . About eighty members came to the first meeting at Fred Stott's house on October 21, 1975.[25]

Members build bridges, clear trails, and lead weekly hikes on Andover

Andover has completed its part of the Bay Circuit from Harold Parker State Forest to the Tewksbury line. In places, private property owners have granted permission for connections between conservation lands. In November 1993, Andover Marriott opened access to the Merrimack River Trail. Pictured from left are: Kathy Hersh, trails coordinator for the Merrimack River Watershed Council; Charlie Clist, general manager at the Marriott; Dave Archibald, senior engineer; Liz Tentarelli, chair of Andover's Trails Committee; and Robert Pustell, Conservation Commission chair. David Powell, Spectrum Photography

conservation land year round. Twice a year they host a lecture and social event. For the past fifteen years, the AMC has co-sponsored walking tours with the Historical Society, led by Warren "Bud" Lewis.

The Andover Trails Committee was formed in 1962 by Alan French and Deena Hammond. After lapsing for a number of years, it was revived in 1990, when it joined the Bay Circuit Alliance. The Bay Circuit was envisioned in the 1890s but not established by legislation until 1956. It was to be a two-hundred-mile "arc of green spaces, roads, and trails stretching from Newbury in the north, west through Framingham, to Duxbury in the south. . . "[27] It was formally incorporated as the Bay Circuit Alliance in 1992, and Alan French was named chairperson. The Alliance is formed of grassroots organizations in fifty towns circling Boston. In October 1994 French was the first to hike the trail continuously—a distance of about 195 miles. For the past four years, the Trails Committee has participated in annual treks to publicize the Bay Circuit. Liz Tentarelli recalls one memorable occasion:

In 1992 we held Trek Three from Lowell National Historical Park to the Ward Reservation in Andover, a distance of 18 miles. About twenty-six people showed up on an extremely hot June day. Alan French arranged for a canoe shuttle around the Trull Brook Golf Course in Tewksbury, which didn't want hikers on their grounds lest they be killed by flying golf balls. We had people of various ages and abilities, including one wonderful retired lady from Georgetown who trekked the entire Bay Circuit that year. We had to get them in and out of canoes, dodge mosquitoes, and avoid poison ivy. We started from Lowell at 8:15 a.m. and pulled into the Ward Reservation at 4 p.m. Fading into legend, it became known as "The Andover Death March."[28]

The Historical Commission and Historical Society joined the fight to save Draper Hall (center) on the Abbot campus in 1988. A zoning change would allow the buildings to be used for multi-family dwelling units. John Sullivan says, "Certain developers were opposed to the change, because if the buildings could not be recycled, they would have to be sold, thus releasing a major piece of real estate. The Historical Commission was strongly for the zoning change and felt it would help preserve a significant part of Andover's heritage. It was a hard-fought battle but it was approved at Town Meeting after heated discussion."[26] The Academy renovated McKeen Hall (right) in 1991 for use as administrative offices, and the trustees are now committed to preserving Abbot Circle. Abbot Hall is at left.

In 1922 the Square and Compass Club, a social club for master Masons, was formed. The club bought John Flint's estate on the corner of Elm and High Streets. Some major town leaders were members: insurance magnate Burton Flagg and Selectmen Roy Hardy and Sidney White. Jim Doherty says, "Decisions on town government were made Saturday night at the Square and Compass Club, finalized at South Church the next morning, and executed at the Selectmen's meeting Monday night."[1] While Catholics were not excluded from the Masons, they knew they would be immediately excommunicated if they joined.

Chapter Four

Associations and Organizations

The oldest continuous association in Andover is St. Matthew's Lodge of Masons, a fraternal organization founded in 1822. Its parent organization had been founded in 1733 in Boston, for mutual aid to members and the wider community. In 1826 the Masons built a handsome brick building at 23 Main Street. But Masons' historian Bob Domingue tells that shortly after St. Matthew's Lodge was founded, the nation underwent a violent anti-Masonic movement which drove St. Matthew's Lodge underground.

The Grand Lodge was obliged to call in all charters, but Andover buried its charter in the cellar of Merrill Pettingill's blacksmith shop on Punchard Avenue and refused to give it back. By 1845 persecution was over and the Masons came out of hiding but they had lost their building. In 1831 they sold it to the Andover National Bank and the Masons continued to meet there in rented space until 1964, when their new building was constructed at 7 High Street.

The Ladies' Benevolent Society, founded in 1831 by wives of Academy and Seminary faculty, also combined service with socializing. The society, nicknamed "Benevie," runs a close second to the Masons in longevity. Early meetings opened with scripture readings and a song, then someone read while others sewed for the poor. They took a break in the middle of the meeting, stipulating "The refreshment shall be perfectly simple, consisting only of tea, bread and butter, and one kind of cake (gingerbread being considered as such) . . ." Harriet Beecher Stowe was an active member. During World War I, the Ladies' Benevolent Society, chaired by Mrs. Horace H. (Catherine) Tyer, produced tremendous amounts of goods for the soldiers overseas. Lacking adequate means of shipping their goods, they gradually affiliated with the Andover Red Cross, which was established as a separate organization. The new Andover Red Cross chapter boasted 3,150 members in 1917. In one three-month period, workers used 793 pounds of yarn to knit for the troops.

Red Cross Director Barbara Loomer and Mary Angus assist a mother and child in 1952. The Red Cross sponsored blood drives, home health care, and helped displaced families. Volunteers raised money, ran a school dental program, and transported patients. Visiting nurse Marie Campbell drove a car with a red cross on the side. She was succeeded by Mildred Lowe and Helen Woodbury. In 1950 the Visiting Nurse Association became independent, but continued sharing space at the Square and Compass Club. The Red Cross purchased 4 Punchard Avenue in 1957. In 1976, largely due to the reduction of United Fund allocations, the Red Cross and the Visiting Nurse Association were dissolved in Andover and joined with Lawrence.

Veterans' groups were organized after each war to help returning servicemen: the Grand Army of the Republic in 1865, with its sister group, the Women's Relief Corps; the Soldiers' Aid Society after the Spanish-American War in 1898; American Legion Post 8 in 1919; Veterans of Foreign Wars Post 2128 in 1931 and its Auxiliary in 1932; and AMVETS Post 43 in 1946. The Servicemen's Fund assisted the families of those away during and after World War II. Disabled American Veterans, founded in 1947, helped the physically and psychologically wounded. Newman photo

The Andover Guild, originally the Society for Organized Charity, focused on the needs of children and youth. It built a Guild House at 10 Brook Street in 1896 (now the Knights of Columbus Hall). The Stamp Saving Society, one of its first projects, taught children how to save their money, penny by penny. In two and a half years, children deposited $1,000. The guild organized evening classes at Punchard High School, cooking classes in Abbot Village, and started the first experimental kindergarten, which was taken over by the town, only to be dropped in 1911. It was not reinstated until 1946. The guild started a boys' club in 1895 and a girls' club in 1901. The Guild House was taken over by the YMCA in 1968.

The League of Women Voters appealed to a younger membership than the more traditional women's clubs. Many capable college-educated women were at home raising children. Current President and former Selectman Virginia Cole, who joined in 1952, observed, "I was tired of finding women to talk to who only were interested in diapers. I knew there had to be some intelligent young women out there who were interested in social and political issues."[3] By the late 1950s the League became a pivotal force in changing to the Town Manager system. The Andover Taxpayers' Association joined the league in its efforts. The Taxpayers' Association, "dedicated to efficient and economical town government," studied all proposed expenditures by the town and made recommendations to the Town Meeting from 1932 to 1965.

Neighborhood associations were another way to gather community support. The Ballardvale Improvement Society (1916) and Shawsheen Village Improvement Society (1921) were formed for village beautification. The West Andover Neighborhood Association met at North School. Friends of Shawsheen (1978) opposed the expansion of the Andover Companies into a residential area; Argilla Road Neighborhood Association (1987) opposed condominium development at

Women formed the Andover Equal Suffrage League in 1912. After they achieved the vote, it metamorphosed into the League of Women Voters in 1921, with a membership of 326. By Andover's first election in 1920, 1,557 women had registered to vote and all but 110 exercised that right. In fact, 91 percent of all registered voters cast their ballots in the 1920 election.[2]

Residents of Carter's Corner, at the intersection of South Main Street, Rocky Hill, and Boston Roads, formed an association to honor those serving in World War II. Pictured is Laura Earley Richards. The Indian Ridge Community Association had a similar purpose. Courtesy of Leo Bernard

49

the corner of Argilla Road and Andover Street; and Central Andover Residents' Association (1989) opposed a comprehensive permit for forty housing units on wetlands off Summer Street.

On a lighter note, musical organizations were always popular. The American Legion founded a band in 1932 and the Andover Community Orchestra was formed

The Andover Brass Band (pictured on Memorial Day 1937) enjoyed a long career from 1878 to 1941. It practiced weekly at the Musgrove building, performing on Sunday afternoons at the Park bandstand to enthusiastic audiences. A member recalls their repertoire as Victor Herbert, Gilbert and Sullivan, and old-time waltzes—"Bridal Rose" (Lavallee) and "Nights of Gladness."

The Punchard Girls' Band was founded by high school music teacher Miriam Sweeney McArdle in 1940. It was the only all-girl marching band in the state, winning many awards. It merged with the boys' band in 1972. Look photo, 1942

in 1939. Singers could join the Andover Choral Society, which appeared briefly in 1873, 1882, and in 1915. Today's Choral Society, an offshoot of the Andover Male Choir, began in 1934 and continues today under the direction of Allen Combs. Sweet Adelines women's barbershoppers started a chapter in 1974. The New England Classical Singers, founded in 1968, are an outgrowth of the North Reading Choral Society, as is the Treble Chorus of New England.

Many social and fraternal organizations put on theatrical performances for their members, using the Town Hall. A troupe known as the Barnstormers gave its first performance in 1911 and disbanded in 1926. The Adventurers made their theatrical debut in 1936. In 1972 the Andover Community Theater (later the Andover Theatre Company) was born. It chose "George Washington Slept Here" for its first performance, even though George Washington had only breakfasted in Andover.

The November Club, founded in 1889 by Miss Elizabeth Handy, staged a large number of dramatic productions. Its 1892 shingle-style Victorian building on Love Lane (now 6 Locke Street) is listed on the National Register of Historic Places, the first women's clubhouse in New England. Originally from South Church and Academy Hill, many members were high-powered intellects who designed a program of lectures, courses, and concerts. Speakers ranged from Julia Ward Howe in 1892 to Henry Cabot Lodge in 1934 to Joyce Brothers in 1959. Bessie Goldsmith, club historian, reported in her Seventy-fifth Anniversary memoir that one member, Mrs. George McKeen, had to "steal time away from her first baby to help her husband make original translations from the Greek." By mid-century, the November Club boasted five hundred members and was active in many philanthropic causes.

From before 1920 until well into the 1980s, dancing classes were given at the club. A diary published recently by the *Andover Townsman*, reflected Donald Mulvey's experiences at age twelve in 1944:

Nov. 29: Tonight I said I was alright so Mother let me go to dancing school. Stern and me had a blast. Curtains were going up mysteriously and every time one went up old lady Bailey said "Whoever put that up will have to leave." It was glorious . . . March 28: At dancing school today I was rolling marbles on the floor to Johnny Young. Mrs. Bailey took them all away. April 11: We threw marbles around but finally Miss Bailey told us to stop or we would have to leave. Most of us stopped.4

In 1985 remaining members sold the November clubhouse to the Unitarian Universalist Church. They contributed part of the proceeds to Memorial Hall Library, creating a November Club Room. The club stopped holding monthly meetings in 1989 and voted itself out of existence in 1994.

The Shawsheen Village Woman's Club gathers for its annual meeting in 1950. From left are Mrs. Albert Curtis, unknown, Rose O'Connor, Helen Caswell, Fran Miller, and Helen Bevans. The club was founded in 1921 "to learn, to teach, to serve and to enjoy," and brought women in the new village together, including "first lady" Ellen Wood. During the Depression, it provided shoes and milk for needy youngsters and supported a women's chorus. Today, it is the oldest surviving women's club in town. Subgroups include bowling, bridge, golf, creative arts, a veterans' committee, and a singles group which provides support and companionship of women for women, organizing meals out, trips to the movies, and help in time of need. Each year, the club raises scholarships for Andover youth.

The Andover Club was a social center for elite men, with three rooms in the Musgrove building. It was formed in 1895 "for the purpose of the literary, social and intellectual improvement of the members." Men would drop in casually for an evening cigar and a game of billiards, and in their heyday, would put on Saturday night events attracting more than five hundred people. They competed with clubs from neighboring towns in whist, pool, billiards, and bowling. In 1931 they turned over their rooms to the Andover Veterans of Foreign Wars.

The Tuesday Club, a women's club, had its beginnings in 1904 as the "Every Wednesday Club." The name was changed when Wednesday was found to be inconvenient. Its object was "the advancement of a wider culture among its members, the encouragement of literary efforts, and mutual helpfulness." Along with teas, musicales, and evening parties, the group studied one country per year: Italy the first year, England the second, and Massachusetts the third. The club adopted a child, Katherine Koch, aged nine, who had been left alone in the world, sending her to a Goodwill School in Maine, then to business college. Unfortunately, Katherine had always been frail, and died in her early twenties. The Tuesday Club ceased to function in 1968.

The Andona Society is a major contributor to camperships and college scholarships. Founded in 1952, the club name combines Andover with the Latin word *dona* ("give.") This women's club began by supporting the Andover Home for Aged People with visits and equipment. Rapidly expanding in membership and scope, the club by 1956 had initiated the fundraisers Clown Town and an annual ball. Later traditions were a Spring Fashion Gala in March and participation in the Sidewalk Bazaar in June. Today the club donates more than $30,000 a year to sports and recreation, education and citizenship, and health and welfare. It has supported everything from preschool testing for amblyopia (lazy eye) to a teen center.

While Andover was well-known for its schools and mills, it was largely a farming community in the nineteenth century. Farmers formed the Grange in 1895. Arthur Peatman wrote a charming memoir in 1988, observing:

The Grange was much needed in a rural area. It directed new interests for both the young and the old. It was a place to meet both old friends and new; a place of gathering where one could hear the latest gossip, what events were happening in the world, who had new babies, who was in ill health, and who needed a helping hand in these difficult times; also a place where young men began to realize that there were girls, [and] *likewise, the girls found young men . . . it created cohesion amongst these hardworking, struggling, poor, farm folk. They truly believed in the old adage, "Together we stand—divided we fall."*[5]

Meetings were characterized by singing, drill teams, visits to other Granges, and lots of good food. The Grange was famous for its oyster stew dinners prepared

The Grange Hall was built near the site of the West Parish Cemetery's stone arch in 1895. The white clapboard building was moved onto Shawsheen Road behind West Parish Church when the cemetery was improved in 1908. It was razed in 1972.

by Burke Thornton, and tickets were quickly sold out. Peatman continues:

Many farmers during this time were still working horses in the fields, woods, and on the land. Many of us however seemed to have some sort of motorized vehicle for the highways—all old models and many of junk yard vintage but with a song and a prayer, the local garage, and one's handy abilities, they somehow ran. As one looked out at those vehicles on a bitter cold meeting night, you would see a clear cold moon and all sorts of assorted, used horse blankets covering the radiators. Even then, they were tough hand-cranking to get them started.[5]

When the Grange membership began to wane in 1961, the Hall was opened as a teen center. When West Parish bought out the surviving Grange members in 1971, Peatman's son, Glenn, took down the building and rebuilt it as a garage on his property at 403 River Road.

Other fraternal organizations blossomed. The International Order of Odd Fellows opened a chapter in 1894 and its sister organization, the Rebekahs, in 1904; the Knights of Pythias started up in 1909, with the Pythian Sisters following in 1914; Eastern Star, sister organization to the Masons, was founded in 1922; the Lions Club in 1930; and Andover Lodge of Elks in 1961. Secrecy added to the thrill of these societies. Secret rituals, ceremonies, oaths, and handshakes characterized their traditions. Even the fraternities at Phillips Academy were known as "secret societies." Most fraternal organizations were engaged in philanthropic causes.

Clan Johnston was Scottish, founded in 1908 to provide life insurance for the millworkers of Abbot Village. Its record book tells of its early members and

Many cultural groups also banded together. The German Club in Ballardvale built a clubhouse in 1885 at 154 Andover Street. The club was known for its singing and the classes it organized in the 1890s. Jack Murnane and his family, descendants of the club's founder, Emil Hoffman, live in the building today. Hoffman was superintendent of the Craighead and Kintz factory.[6]

In 1923 six fraternal organizations purchased the Morrison Block on Park Street, renovating it and naming it the Andover Fraternal Building. A complex schedule provided time for each club and for other town organizations. The building was replaced by the business block at 40 Park Street in 1965.

mission.7 The first member listed was George Guthrie, April 3, 1908. Members were fairly young: the average age of the first twenty members was twenty-seven. Many listed their mothers as beneficiaries and most listed their birthplace as Scotland. Few settlements were paid on these young, healthy men. The first was William Coutts, a millworker, who lived at 33 Shawsheen Road. He joined November 20, 1908, at age thirty-seven, and died in June 1913 at age forty-two. His wife, Jessie Ann Coutts, was paid $500 upon his death.

While the clan's first responsibility was to look after its members, it also sought to preserve the culture of its homeland, while ardently supporting the ideals of its new country. It supported a Glee Club, Male Quartet, and a double quartet of trombone players. Its neighboring Clan MacPherson from Lawrence was famous for its bagpipe band, which started up in 1921 and continues today. Although the last entry in Clan Johnston's membership book is dated 1968, ten members continue to meet at the Andover Senior Center.

Other cultural groups followed: the Ancient Order of Hibernians, celebrating Irish culture, in 1912; American Hellenic Progressive Association, celebrating Greek culture, in 1924; the Sons of the American Revolution in 1940; Sons of Italy, founded by Prince Spaghetti magnate and Andover resident Joseph Pellegrino in 1956; and the Campbell Highlanders in 1975.

The Andover Chinese Cultural Exchange was founded in 1983 by seventy-nine Chinese Americans raising families in a new country. They hoped to foster ethnic awareness and pride in their children and to engage in cultural exchange with the community. Through a costume demonstration at the Peabody Museum of Salem in 1986, a Chinese New Year celebration at Andover Town Hall in 1990, and a fashion show at Merrimack College, they have introduced Andover to their three-thousand-year-old culture. Pictured wearing costumes of the different dynasties are, from left: Ting-Shing Hsu, Jennifer Wu, and Stephanie and Jeff Kuo. Courtesy of E. Mei Shen-Hsien

While many groups were primarily social, others focused on a specific interest: archaeology, art, natural history, gardening, bridge, cameras, herbs, birds, antique cars, and meditation. Andover Garden Club was an outgrowth of the November Club in 1927. Emphasis was on practical gardening, and members took field trips to farm and garden conferences as they do today. In 1935 the club entered the Boston Flower Show for the first time. Bessie Goldsmith was asked upon her return what she thought of the Boston show. She replied, "Too much mink and not enough manure." However, 1950s photos of the Andover Garden Club in the *Townsman* also show a remarkable amount of mink.

Bessie maintained extensive gardens around her house at 60 Elm Street. Claus Dengler recalls that one day Bessie invited his wife, Eartha, up to her house to see a special flower in her garden. Claus was not too interested in the flowers, but noticed that Bessie had a remarkable tomato patch. "How do you grow such wonderful tomatoes?" he asked her. "Well," she replied, "I catch squirrels and gas them in my oven. Then I bury one squirrel under each tomato plant." Dengler suspected his wife was going to be ill, so they thanked Bessie and left quickly.

During World War II, club members staged garden tours to raise money for foreign relief, maintained a garden at Fort Devens, and shuttled bouquets to Lowell General Hospital.

They gave victory garden and canning demonstrations. In latter years, the club has maintained Andover Historical Society's Stearns Garden and decorated its rooms for the holidays. It plants flower barrels on Main Street, tends Bicentennial Park on Central Street, and fills the urns by the Town House. Members visit nursing homes monthly offering "garden therapy." Today the club numbers 130, plus twenty-four Junior Garden Club members.

When the Spade and Trowel Garden Club organized in 1954, it limited membership to thirty. Notable for its public service, members take gifts to nursing home residents in winter and decorate Memorial Hall Library for the holidays. In warmer seasons, they maintain gardens at Chestnut Court and plant trees on Arbor Day. In May 1994 they staged an "Art in Bloom" project at Phillips Academy's Addison Gallery, placing bouquets in each gallery to pick up the colors and mood of the paintings.

The Newcomers' Club was founded in 1950 to welcome incoming residents and continues to thrive today. The Village Garden Club of Andover grew out of the Newcomers Club in 1968. It provides plants for parties at the Senior Center and has donated plantings at the library and the fire station. It joins other clubs in the Garden Club Federation in such projects as planting on Interstate Route 95 around the "Entering Massachusetts" sign.

Not content to just improve the visual quality of the community, Andover residents have long been committed to growing strong, intelligent children. The first Mothers' Club was started at John Dove School in 1900. A 1909 newspaper brief mentions that Mothers' Clubs from the John Dove School, Bradlee School in Ballardvale, and Indian Ridge School in Abbot Village, all met at Jackson School in Andover Center for a lecture on Women's Suffrage by Mrs. M. S. McCurdy, an anti-suffragist.[8]

In 1922 the Shawsheen Parent-Teacher Association was formed at the Richardson School, followed by the Ballardvale PTA in 1929 and Central Schools PTA in 1935. St. Augustine's Catholic School Guild was founded in 1948. PTAs held programs on citizenship, visual education, hygiene, and home nursing. They studied nutrition and redecorated school lunchrooms. They helped with flood relief in 1936 and founded three Brownie troops. A school-wide organization was formed in 1991, the Andover Fund for Education, raising money to "maintain excellence in our schools in the face of changing financial reality."

A Girl Scout Council was formed in Lawrence in 1919 and Andover troops worked out of that organization. In 1920 the City Missionary of Boston opened Camp Andover for city children, at the north end of Pomp's Pond, on Foster family land. In 1940 the Girl Scout Council of Greater Lawrence established Camp Maude Eaton, named after one of the council's founders. Merrimack River Girl Scout Council was headquartered at 89 North Main Street, Andover, from 1963 until its 1980 merger with the Spar and Spindle Council.

Mothers also associated to cope with common problems. The Parents' League helped teenagers to find summer jobs and ski lessons in the 1950s and 1960s. The Children's Theater

Andover Boy Scout Troop 1 came to the Baptist Church in 1912. Today Andover has six Boy Scout and six Cub Scout troops. In 1921 Camp Manning held its first session on the south end of Pomp's Pond. The Boy Scout camp pulled out in the early 1950s and, after about ten years of private ownership, it was purchased by the town as a recreation area in 1963.

Workshop, founded by the league in 1955, became an independent community project in 1957. Under Artistic Director Virginia Powel, schoolchildren fifth grade and above rehearsed in the carriage house of the James Smith residence, now the parking lot for Olde Andover Village. By 1960 more than one hundred boys and girls were involved.

LaLeche League helped mothers with breast-feeding starting in 1965. The Mother Connection organized a network in 1982 that today encompasses thirty-five communities with five hundred members. They promote workshops, field trips, and rap sessions, a baby-sitting cooperative, and a toy-lending library. Parent to Parent, focusing on parenting education, was founded in 1990.

Educational and social action forces came together with a bang in 1967 when A Better Chance (ABC) was instituted. The program had begun a year before in Hanover, New Hampshire, to help students who were educationally disadvantaged and academically talented. Margot Bixby was involved in its founding:

Margot and George Bixby, who came to Andover from the Midwest in 1959, served as a host family for three ABC students. Margot comments, "When you come into a town and you care about things, and you want to be sure the quality of life in a community is there, you have to be part of that motivating force. And the benefits of that are just incredible, because all of a sudden, you find your quality of life is so enhanced because you're connecting with people you would never, ever connect with if you didn't reach out. It was very important for the Town of Andover to have ABC here for their quality of life." EMR photo

It was funded at first by the Tucker Foundation, part of the Rockefeller Foundation. The first director of the ABC Public School Program was a former math teacher at Phillips, Tom Mikula. Academically talented students were recruited from all over the country and brought to Hanover to be tutored by Dartmouth students for ten weeks, then placed in schools who had agreed to educate them. While these students had been placed in private schools before, organizers felt this was not enough. Andover was the second public school system in the country after Hanover to sponsor a program. Bob Klie orchestrated it with very careful preparation, asking the town to waive tuition for these students. The Boston Globe *wrote a story along with area newspapers—it was a big thing. Our first director here was Bill Deacon, an Andover High School teacher, with his wife, Nancy.*[9]

ABC was a hot issue. Philip Allen, selectman at the time, remembers the heavily attended Town Meeting where the vote was taken. One selectman insisted on a secret ballot, sure it would be defeated. It passed 528 to 119. ABC has now operated more than twenty-five years. "We're very proud of them," says Allen. "Most have gone on to college."[10] A residence for ABC students at 134 Main Street was purchased in 1967.

While many organizations appeal to the mind, others appeal to the body. William Wood's championship golf course in Shawsheen Village was incorporated in 1925 as the Andover Country Club, today numbering 450 members. Ballardvale had its own club, the YMAC (Young Men's Athletic Club). Andover Sportsman's Club was founded in 1934 at Harold Parker State Forest to conserve wildlife. It hosts a popular fishing derby every spring. Indian Ridge Country Club was started in 1961 by Daniel E. Hogan, president of Standex Corporation. In 1977 it was purchased by the DeMoulas Corporation and today has about three hundred members.

An early bicycle club gathers behind the Town House.

The Young Men's Christian Association (YMCA) is no longer limited to youth, males, or Christians. Its facility at 165 Haverhill Street, built in 1974, contains state-of-the-art bodybuilding equipment and a six-lane swimming pool. Its goal is "to put Christian principles into practice through programs that build a healthy body, mind and spirit for all." It sponsors a vast array of programs for all ages, including an after-school program. It boasts sixty-four hundred members.

As the century ends, the trend in clubs has been toward inclusiveness—barriers are coming down. Therefore, nobody missed a beat when Christie Cunningham walked up to the registration table for Andover Youth Football in the autumn of 1993. Christie's coach, Andy Ellicott, says his wife was working the table and was delighted. Christie was issued equipment, then went home because she had a cold. Ellicott took the opportunity to ask her teammates if they knew there would be a girl on the team. He recalls, "There was absolutely nothing unusual about this to any of the players, many of whom played with her in school. They said, 'She plays like a man.'"

Christie, who is 5'2" and weighs ninety-eight pounds, remembers it a little differently. She says, "It was hard at the beginning for the boys to consider me a teammate. But once I started playing, they thought I was all right."

In fact, Christie's team had not won a single game the season before. The year she joined, it went undefeated and won the town championship.

"I just like to play football," says Christie Cunningham, aged thirteen. "I play with my friends and stuff. I just wondered what it would be like to play on a real team. One evening my Mom found an article in the newspaper about signups for football tryouts. 'Can girls play?' I asked. When I went to sign up, they didn't have any problem with it."[11] Cheryl Edwards photo

Route 128 was built in 1950, Route 93 opened in 1959, and Route 495 in 1965. The highways had a profound influence on Andover, something like the rivers in the early days. In the 1600s the rivers were the main transportation routes and a source of revenue. Later, mills were built along the rivers, harnessing their water power. Rivers were hard to cross so boundaries were often defined by them. Our superhighways are today's rivers. They are a source of revenue and help us to get where we want to go. Industries like to build along the big roads. But they are hard to cross, cutting off one section of town from another. Whether their coming has been for better or worse, they have brought us into the modern era and they have surely changed us. Aerial Photos International, 1986

Chapter Five

Entering the Modern Era

The July morning was fresh and warm with a blue sky dome over Binney Street in Shawsheen Village. Neighborhood mothers had finished their chores, hung out the laundry, and pulled their lawn chairs together overlooking the field out back. Children played happily in the summer sunshine. It was 1950. "What's that man doing down at the bottom of the field?" asked one of the women lazily. The man bent over a tripod then reached for a pad to scribble down numbers. The women got up from their chairs and strolled down to investigate. Louise Roberge remembers that he asked, "Whose house is that?" pointing directly at her house. "It's mine," she said. "We're going right through your parlor," he said. This was the first she heard about Route 495.

Louise (Eldred) Roberge, one of nine children born in Andover, quit school at sixteen to work at Tyer Rubber Company. She finished high school at night in Lawrence. When she married Roger Roberge in 1939, the young couple moved to an apartment on Essex Street, Andover. After three babies, Marilyn, Patricia, and Roger, were born, their families suggested that this would be a good time to buy a house. They found what they needed at 15 Binney Street where Barbara was born.

Three days before Christmas in 1957, Roger Roberge died suddenly of a heart attack. He was thirty-nine. "One day after my husband died, two men from the state came to our door and asked me to sign a paper saying we'd get money enough to buy a comparable house when they took ours to build the road," Roberge recalls. "I took the paper to a lawyer and he got me $1000 more, but it still wasn't enough to buy a new house. I had been paying a mortgage for fifteen years, and I had to start over again. The town did nothing to help us."

It was twelve years from the time the first surveyor appeared in the field until the houses actually were taken. Then the state came to the door again. "Here's a dollar," they said. "The state owns the house now, you just have to pay interest." Louise finally found a house in South Lawrence, across the street from her sister-in-law. "I didn't want to live in Lawrence, but it was the only choice," she said.

She was bounced from one low-paying office job to another. The children, aged eight to seventeen, learned to come home to an empty house and to look after each other. Town policy could not permit them to continue attending Andover schools. Through the intervention of two School Committee members, they were allowed to finish out the year. Roberge's son, Roger, an art student at the School of the Museum of Fine Arts in Boston, was not allowed a card from the Andover Library. Her youngest child, Barbara, had to go to Lawrence High School. "I prayed a lot, and after the children were in bed, I would draw the blinds and cry," she recalls.[1]

"We had a nice neighborhood on Binney Street," says Louise Roberge. "That road disrupted our whole lives, but there was nothing you could do when you got your dollar and they said your house was theirs." EMR photo

Karl and Louise Marshall saw the situation as an opportunity. They bought up houses from the state for a few hundred dollars apiece, moved them onto new sites, and fixed them up for resale. They moved three houses from Andover to Weare and Sylvester Streets in South Lawrence and another from South Lawrence to Greenwood Road in Andover. The venture was profitable for them. "You didn't have to pay the power company to move the lines in those day," remembers Louise Marshall.[2]

Longtime Andover teacher Adeline Wright quips:

In the old days, you had the Hill, the Till, and the Mill. The Hill was the academies; the Till was the business district, but has also been used to describe our extensive farmlands; and the Mill was the industries. Once the population started to grow, lots more people flooded in: the Kill was the war industries— Tyer and Raytheon; the Pill was all the new doctors moving to town; the Will was the lawyers; the Fill was the dentists.[3]

Preserving Andover's character during precipitous growth required foresight. The town was no stranger to planning. In 1845 the Essex Company had bought a precinct of Andover and a section of Methuen. Instead of transforming the existing towns, they had put the two parcels together to form the planned city of Lawrence in 1847. In 1848 Ballardvale Machine Company under John Marland planned a small community in Ballardvale. Likewise, Shawsheen Village had been meticulously planned by William Wood.

Virginia Hammond, on the Planning Board from 1955 to 1965, recalls:

Zoning was ancient and ridiculous then. It was simply residential, commercial or industrial. You could build a house anywhere on 10,000 square feet.[4] *After the war, developers started taking advantage of that. The town was alarmed by the*

Construction proceeds on the post office building, 26 Essex Street. In 1927 the town's first planning board drafted an interim Zoning Ordinance. In 1936 Town Meeting passed the Andover Zoning Bylaw. The bylaw created restrictions around Main Street and Shawsheen with the greater part of southern and western Andover residential. Newman photo, 1917

growth and we had some good state aid. In the mid-fifties, we adopted an interim zoning plan which was fairly primitive—we drew concentric circles around the Town House. The farther from the Town House, the bigger the lots had to be. Ten years later, we had enacted a fairly decent bylaw and had hired a consultant to develop a Master Plan.[5]

The consultant they hired in 1957 was Roland Greeley of Adams, Howard, and Greeley in Cambridge. Hammond continues:

Roland Greeley suggested cluster zoning and advised us to keep it simple and make it attractive to developers. If they gave 30 percent of the land they were developing to conservation, they could reduce their frontage and houselot area by one-third. They could put unbuildable land that was swampy or hilly into that one-third. The result was that they would preserve the natural drainage system intact. Conservation land was given to AVIS or the town or put in a homeowners' association. I can hardly remember a developer that didn't take advantage of this, because it reduced their expenses.

In 1956 industrial zones were established between the railroad and Andover

After World War II developers eyed the open spaces of West Andover hungrily with visions of cul de sacs and "colonial" houses. At the same time, farming became less and less viable as a living. Newman photo

Street, in the Lowell Junction area, and in the farmland off River Road in West Andover.

Arthur Peatman watched the transition away from farming at close range. The son of English emigrant parents, he was born in 1914 and raised in Ballardvale.

The Wright Farm, 125 Lovejoy Road, displays its equipment. Newman photo

He remembers working on Sid White's farm at age ten or eleven washing beets for three cents a bunch. "Parents were tickled to death to see their kids go to work on farms or in the mills. The kids paid room and board to their parents as soon as they started working," Peatman observes. He graduated from Essex Agricultural Institute with a specialty in poultry farming and in 1934 married Dorothy Lewis, whose family ran a farm at 221 Lowell Street. The Lewis fields are the site of Andover Animal Hospital today.

As a young man, Peatman decided to become a chicken farmer. He describes poultry farming as he first knew it:

While I was at Essex Aggie, I worked for Nick Zock, a German poultry farmer in West Andover. In the spring we had eight to ten brooder stoves with one hundred chicks each. When they were big enough, we would put them out to range in a summer shelter. In the fall we selected prime pullets for the laying houses. The males we sold as broilers.[6]

Cows meander freely at the Abbot Homestead, 9 Andover Street, about 1890. The loss of its farms has been the single greatest change in Andover this century. The 1920 directory listed 206 farmers. They grew apples, strawberries, and asparagus. They raised chickens and dairy cows, and built greenhouses. They were Armenians, Greeks, Yankees, Scots, Irish, and Italians.

Charles Newton, owner of Sylvan Hollow Poultry Farm on Boutwell Road, gathers eggs about 1920. "There was a great deal to know in poultry then," says Arthur Peatman. "You had to be almost a vet. When we moved the chickens indoors, we'd have to give them a worm capsule and inoculate them for chicken pox. Since it was the Depression, we'd have to tattoo the chicks because destitute people from the city would come out and steal them. We'd clip their beaks to prevent cannibalism."

Roger Lewis, as a boy of twelve, first became interested in strawberries working on the Rennie farm (pictured), 61 Argilla Road, trimming plants after school.

Gradually, farmers began to specialize. Peatman says smaller farmers could no longer compete with larger producers and could not afford the equipment to enter the modern market. The availability of mill jobs at American Woolen and later Raytheon offered their children an easier lifestyle than the long hours of farming.

Peatman, building his own house and raising a family, left farming because he needed more income. He worked his way up to superintendent of Doyle Lumber and after that, served as town building inspector from 1961 to 1978. For him, carpentry was a natural step from farming. "If you needed a chicken coop or a barn, you had to build it yourself," he said. He saw the effect of the new highways firsthand:

There was a slight surge in building before, but nothing like after the highways were built. Route 28 had been the main route from Boston to New Hampshire. When there was a race at the Rockingham track, Broadway in Lawrence was backed up solid.

Industry wanted West Andover. They offered more money than any farmer would make in a a lifetime. My brother-in-law on River Road was one of the first to sell. One by one, the others sold too. Some market gardeners with smaller parcels outside the industrial zone turned to greenhouse farming. Industry didn't want their land. Konjoians still have several greenhouses on Chandler Road.

Roger Lewis, Peatman's brother-in-law, never left farming but he did move his farm out of Andover. He too attended Essex County Agricultural School. "I had what was called modern ideas," he reminisced.[7] He never stopped studying or trying new methods.

In 1939 he bought the one-hundred-acre Bailey Farm on Laurel Lane in West Andover. Starting with just one acre of strawberries, Lewis gradually expanded to twenty varieties on fifteen acres. His big market was in plants. He tried one new variety after another and went to school to learn how to control viruses. In order to get his plants certified, he had to undergo rigorous inspections by county agents. He published an annual catalogue expanding his market. In the early 1960s, he instituted the pick-your-own system for strawberries, one of the first to do so.

He would hire high school boys to come after school or those who preferred farming to school. Eventually, he was approached by the Puerto Rican Labor

Department with a plan to import Puerto Rican workers. This system worked out well for Lewis since many of the men returned year after year. He provided them with sleeping quarters and a place to cook and paid their airfare north in the spring, which the men reimbursed as they earned money in the summer.

Vegetables occupied forty-five acres with twenty-five acres devoted to carrots. The rest went for spinach, parsnips, cucumbers, sweet corn, and asparagus. Again, he went to school to study carrot pests, learning to control underground toads. He took his vegetables to markets in Cambridge, Boston, and North Reading.

In 1958 Route 93 cut across one side of his farm. Business was expanding. He said:

I had reached a point where the demand was greater than what I could produce—a good problem. I simply didn't have enough land. I was in an industrial zone and knew there was a demand for it. Mrs. Shattuck's husband had died, but she wouldn't lease me more land next door. I was ready to go out of business, but people started writing me letters, saying, "Start somewhere else, and we'll stay with you."

So Lewis sold ninety-seven acres in 1968 to Arkwright-Boston for $506,000. In 1969, he bought a five-hundred-acre farm near South Deerfield for a tenth of the price he received in Andover. "And it was a better farm," he said. He ran it for fifteen years.

The Lewis Farm on Lowell Street (pictured), where Roger Lewis grew up, is near the Andover Animal Hospital today. By 1994 there was only one farm stand in Andover, the Loosigians' on Lowell Street.

Lewis helped pass legislation to save agricultural land in Massachusetts. The Agricultural Restriction Law provided funds to keep farmers from selling to developers. The applicants' land was appraised first for its farm value then for its development value. The farmer was paid the difference between the two figures in return for putting a restriction on the land that it would be farmed forever. He could sell it, but with that restriction. Lewis observed, "We were a long time getting it through. We weren't able to save any farms in Andover, but we did save some in North Andover and a lot more around the state."

The Colombosian (Colombo) family showed another ingenious direction that a farmer could take, given a lot of patience. Rose and Sarkis Colombosian moved to Argilla Road in 1927. Their son, Bob, remembers that in his childhood, the family had a couple of cows, some chickens, and a small market garden on their five acres. But there was not enough money to feed their four children, so his mother got them started in the yogurt business:

My parents were Armenian. Mother knew how to make cheese and yogurt on the stove. So she started making yogurt from our extra milk and we would hand deliver it in the local area—maybe a dozen quarts or so. In the early 1930s, word was getting around. Yogurt wasn't known among the Yankees, but my father would drive into Boston in a car that had been made into a truck to sell the yogurt to ethnic food stores. By the late 1930s, they were also making cheese.[8]

On March 2, 1939, the Colombosians suffered a major fire, losing their barn and house. Abbott Batchelder was driving home that night about midnight on his motorcycle. He heard fire sirens in the distance behind him, but thought little about it until he came around the bend by the Colombosians. Then neighbors across the street, the Sheehys, shouted to him, "They're in there, they're in there." Suddenly, he realized the house was on fire. He ran in the door and up the stairs. Tucking the twins, Johnny and Mary, each under an arm, he ran out of the house. The Sheehys helped the others to escape. Bob and his father, away on a delivery to New York, returned to find the house in ashes.

With the help of friends and relatives, the Colombosians built a new house, still standing at 51 Argilla Road, and a big new garage where they moved the

About 1951 Dr. Gaylord Hauser wrote an article for *Reader's Digest* about yogurt, and suddenly, everyone wanted to know where they could get the "wonder food." The Colombosians added to the garage, building more refrigeration space, and a special yogurt room with tile walls. There was also an incubator room with electric heaters, pasteurizing vats, and a homogenizer. Pictured is John Colombosian pasteurizing and bottling yogurt. Courtesy of Robert Colombosian

yogurt-making operation. They began to buy excess milk from other farmers. Bob remembers:

In the 1960s yogurt became more popular, but not popular enough. When my father died in 1966, we were still manufacturing from the garage. We needed more space and the town fathers would not let us expand. I wanted to stay in Andover. Some land was available at the back of Ballardvale, but I wasn't interested in a plant there. Finally, the Planning Board said, "Just move out of town if you want to build a plant." That hurt me.

Colombosian had little encouragement from Andover. Instead he found a good site in the Methuen Industrial Park. He signed over his house, his mother's house, and his brother's house to get the necessary bank loans; building a new plant in 1971. His brother John handled the distribution. He hired a marketing expert, sales doubled the first year and continued to double each year thereafter. He plowed profits back into the company. But a loss in 1975 due to a couple of bankrupt distributors compelled him to sell another 20 percent of the business.

Not wishing to jeopardize family assets, he sold the business in 1976. After working for Colombo as a consultant for several years, he started an ice cream and frozen yogurt shop in Salem, Massachusetts, called Sweet Scoops.

Colombo was a pioneer on several fronts. It was the first yogurt company in America, founded in 1929. It sold yogurt to the Boston area's first supermarket, Star Market in Newton, in the 1950s. It was the first to develop a mix for frozen yogurt in 1968. It was the number one plain yogurt company in America in the 1970s.

During the World Wars, most of the farmers were protected from the draft because agriculture was a vital industry. But for those that stayed on the farm, many more Andover men and women served overseas. They traveled around the world bringing back new ideas which would change the town.

Memorial Tower at Phillips Academy, a town landmark, was given in memory of the eighty-seven Phillips Academy alumni who died in World War I, the Civil War, the Mexican War, the War of 1812, and the Revolution, by eight descendants of Samuel Fuller, first rector of Christ Church. The 159-foot tower, dedicated in 1923, contains one of the few full carillons in the country.[9] Memorial Auditorium, adjacent to the present town offices, was built in 1935 to honor Andover residents who served in World War I. Fourteen Andover women served as Red Cross nurses. A plaque in the vestibule lists those who served with stars beside the names of fourteen who died.

At home in the 1940s, World War II permeated the lives of everyone. The second floor of the Town House was partitioned into offices for the rationing board, draft board, and Office of Price Administration. Citizens received ration books to qualify for purchasing limited food supplies. Meat, sugar, and butter were practically nonexistent as food was sent to the troops. Candy disappeared from the shelves and the only cigarettes bore unfamiliar names. Babies went unphotographed as film was unavailable. Tires, new automobiles, bicycles, typewriters, gasoline, and heating oil were rationed.

Social habits changed. People pooled their ration stamps for a dinner party, swapping meatless recipes. Dance halls foundered without gas; the bands and the dancers could not travel. Sidney White delivered milk with a horse and wagon. People hung heavy blackout curtains over their windows at night.

Families displayed service flags in their windows with one blue star for each son or daughter in the service. A gold star meant the supreme sacrifice. Every night people scanned newspapers for the names of friends. Veterans' service agent Frank Markey helped families in need while their men were away.[10]

Phidias Dantos was a child at the time. He remembers flag-draped caskets being unloaded from the train at the depot. He was in sixth grade on D-Day, June 6, 1944. All the children at the schools were escorted into Memorial Auditorium, where an adult explained what was happening in France. A radio sputtered in the middle of the stage. "We were asked to pray," says Dantos.[11]

There were weekly air raid drills and a Junior Warden course. Women went to work in previously male occupations. The 1943 playground report states, "The care of smaller children, especially those of wartime mothers, proved to be a real benefit to those concerned." The word "babysitter" came into use for the first time.

On VJ Day, September 2, 1945, the town went "slightly and justifiably crazy," with paper streamers, fireworks, sirens, bells, and an impromptu parade.[12]

Less than five years later, the Korean War began. Of the Korean War, Claude Fuess writes:

During World War II, 1,750 Andover residents served, including forty-one women. Army nurse Irene Curtis was the only Andover woman to participate in the Normandy invasion. The GIs were sent to Fort Devens, then scattered into different units. Those who served and the twenty who gave their lives are listed on plaques at the entrance to the town offices.

An aluminum parade by eight hundred children collected nearly two tons of scrap metal townwide. Look photo, circa 1943

*The country, led by President Truman, undertook what was described as "a police action under the United Nations," but which was actually another catastrophic war, carried on in far-off and little-known places. For the third time in a century, Andover's young men were sent off to fight a war, this time a war for which nobody felt any enthusiasm. Once again Andover mothers waited anxiously from one mail to another, wondering when the letters from their sons would cease.*13

Four Andover men died in the Korean War: John P. Andonian, Frederick H. Graves Jr., Donald W. Lee Jr., and Samuel E. Turner. It lasted from June 1950 to July 1953. Seven Andover women served.

The Vietnam War, the least popular war of this century, began by degrees in 1965. American involvement dragged on for eight years. While previous wars had seen women rolling bandages and men raising Liberty Loans, the Vietnam War saw confrontations between veterans and draft dodgers on the steps of Memorial Hall Library. Richard Graber, raised a Mennonite and conscientious objector in Indiana, recalls that time in Andover:

It tore up the Unitarian Church. Friday night coffee hours became devoted to political discussions. I remember attending a dinner party where a Vietnam vet was present. I was determined that we were going to keep our mouths shut. Everything was going hunky-poo until the hostess says to this guy, "How do you feel about people at home who are against the war?" He started muttering things about traitors, etc. My wife Rachel became enraged. I got involved. It destroyed the dinner party.[14]

At the 1969 Memorial Day Parade many people wore black armbands in protest. Afterward, three women wearing armbands were refused service at the Coffee Mill on Main Street. The *Andover Townsman* quoted William Hood, proprietor, as saying, "We don't wait on any commies." A boycott ensued, and by August, the shop was out of business.

Marchers rally at the Unitarian Universalist Church for the IRS Protest April 15, 1970. "The first protest here was in 1967 and I took pictures," says Richard Graber. "About thirty people marched around Lawrence Common. We were scared we were going to get beat up—there were workmen that gathered and sort of glowered at us. We were thankful there were a couple of police around. In 1969 we held a candlelight vigil in the Park and a protest at the Town House in Andover." Richard Graber photo

"Now I think they had a right to protest the war," says Vietnam veteran John Doherty. "They just treated the warriors shabbily. Many were drafted and after they served, returned home to be treated as war criminals." Doherty (pictured) is at a Gulf War rally. Composite photo by Richard Graber, 1991

Vietnam veteran John Doherty saw things differently. A classics major at Harvard, he joined the Reserve Officers Training Corps (ROTC) because in those days everyone either volunteered or was drafted. The Doherty family had a proud tradition of military service. His father had served in World War I, his uncles Joe and Jim Doherty had served in World War II, and a family cousin, Philip Sheridan, had been a Civil War General. He said, " 'My country right or wrong' meant something to me."15

Doherty was commissioned a second lieutenant the day before graduation in 1963. After training, he requested Vietnam duty. He was not shipped to Vietnam until 1966. His second year was spent in Hue as an advisor to a South Vietnamese reconnaissance company:

The night the Tet Offensive began was January 31, 1968 at 3:40 a.m. I was at ground zero, driving around in a jeep at midnight, not knowing there were already seventy-six hundred North Vietnamese troops inside the city. That night I was sprayed by an exploding rocket. When I was leading a patrol on February 24, we were ambushed and a grenade exploded close to me. The medics saved my leg, pulling out twenty-two pieces of shrapnel—there's still metal in me. I got out on a chopper, then we had a wild ride down the river, potshotted, and sniped the whole way. Just before I was due to go home I was wounded for the third time. Physically and mentally I was a mess.

I was still on crutches when I voted for the first time since returning to Andover.

A nice young lady was out in front of the Baptist Church carrying a placard, saying, "End the slaughter, bring the killers home." I made a fool of myself calling her names. She started crying and said, "Don't take it personally." "How can I take it any other way?" I asked her.

Six Andover men died in Vietnam: George H. Belanger, Joseph P. Candiano, Gerald F. Currier, Warren C. Deyermond, Richard Gilbreath, and Brian R. O'Connor.

The Gulf War in 1991 was truly a media war. From January to March, Andoverites were glued to their television sets. Twenty-one Andover people served in the Gulf War, but fortunately none were lost.

Patriot missiles made at Raytheon in Andover were used defensively to intercept Iraqi Scud missiles during the Gulf War. When Saddam Hussein invaded Kuwait, only three Patriot missiles had been produced at Raytheon. At the request of the Army, production was speeded up and Raytheon employees worked round the clock for five months to produce three hundred more for the war effort.[16] Their effort was so extraordinary that it prompted a visit from President George Bush on February 15, 1991.

Ironically, wars have brought prosperity to Andover. World War I produced a tremendous demand for cloth from American Woolen Company. Tyer Rubber profited from rubber contracts in World War II. Raytheon gained national recognition in the Gulf War. In addition, veterans from World War II took advantage of the GI Bill, one of the most significant pieces of legislation in this century. The bill provided returning veterans with a free college education; government loans for homes, farms, and businesses; and job counseling and placement. Many would never have had the opportunity to attend college otherwise. As these college graduates went to work, they created a technological boom which put the United States in the economic lead among nations.

This economic revolution led directly to a domestic revolution. As Bill Dalton so aptly points out in his book, *Local Touch*:

If you're under thirty, you probably don't remember what things were like before the supermarket . . . Prior to supermarkets, people shopped at "markets" or "grocery stores" but most of the shopping was done at home . . . When I was a kid, the milkman was in the neighborhood every day. The bottles and cans on the truck made a jingling sound as they hit together and we'd usually hear the vehicle before we saw it . . . A couple of times a week the Cushman Bakery truck would come by selling breads and pies . . . On Fridays, the fruit and vegetable man came around in his big, multi-shelved truck. [Bill was born in 1943.]

The Golden Family, from left, William, Frank, and Fannie, cultivate a cornfield on Holt Road. Shawsheen Plaza on North Main Street, Andover's first shopping center, was built in 1958 on the fields of "Golden Gardens."

Well, most of that is all in the past. The affluence of the postwar period allowed many families to acquire a second car which gave mobility to the housewife. That was the end of home food delivery businesses and the real beginning of the supermarket era.[17]

The relative peace and prosperity of the 1950s was a welcome relief after two world wars and the Great Depression. Women in the postwar era were glad to have their husbands back. Many had gone to work while the men were away. Now they considered it a privilege and a luxury to stay home.

However, in the general revolt against authority that came with the Vietnam War and the consciousness-raising of the Civil Rights Movement, some women began to feel their roles had become too stereotyped. They were well-educated and felt unfulfilled. Gradually, the feminist movement took hold. Women entered or re-entered the work force and competed for leadership positions. Inflation, an increased cost of living, and a cultural emphasis on material possessions contributed to this trend. In 1960 only 15 percent of married women in Andover with children under six worked outside the home. By 1990, 56 percent of women with children under six and 68 percent with children age six to seventeen worked outside the home.[18] If the milk deliverer came today, chances are he or she would find nobody home.

As we entered the modern era, we became more conscious of what we were doing to the earth. Back when Andoverites were still throwing trash out the back door, there was less of it and plastic had not been invented. Milk bottles and Coke bottles were recycled. Tin cans rusted away. By the 1960s trash had climbed to frightening proportions and much of it was not biodegradable.

Andover began garbage collection of food wastes in 1947. Residents took the rest of the trash to the town dump, starting in 1896 on High Street, then after 1942 on Chandler Road. Selectman William Downs remembers playing in the High Street dump as a child, then driving the family car around the old dump before he got his license. Dump day was the social event of the week. Husbands gathered up the children to give wives a break and wives warned husbands against bringing home more than they left with. One enterprising dump supervisor even started serving coffee. Political candidates who didn't show up at the dump were less assured of election. On the first Earth Day in 1970, a group led by Elaine Katz decided it was time for recycling. Barrels were set up at the dump staffed by volunteers from Phillips Academy and Andover High School. Federal funds paid a man to supervise.

By 1970 it was clear that a new dump was needed. A site was recommended on Woburn Street in Ballardvale, which provoked a "not in my back yard" response. League of Women Voters member Dana Duxbury concluded that the dump was either polluting or would pollute the town water supply and campaigned for closing it altogether. It closed in 1973. Arrangements were made for curbside trash pickup and debris was ferried out of town in bright red bags to an incinerator or "waste to energy recovery plant" in North Andover. This solution is not without problems of its own.

The other waste stream from Andover, its sewage, was dumped untreated into the Merrimack River from 1894 to 1977. New state and federal regulations required that this practice cease and the state advised Andover to go in with Lawrence, North Andover, and Methuen. The incentive was 90 percent funding—70 percent in federal funds and 20 percent in state funds. If Andover built its own sewage treatment plant, it would pay the whole cost. Town Meeting voted to join the district in 1967 and the treatment plant went on line in 1977. Today, swimming in the Merrimack is possible in some areas and continuous improvement is anticipated.

During the 1950s large sums were voted annually at Town Meeting for expansion of the water and sewer systems and in 1957 the possibility of using the Merrimack as a water supply was first proposed. In 1974, a new water treatment plant was built at a cost of $12.6 million, making purification of Merrimack water possible. Today, more than 50 percent of town drinking water comes from the Merrimack River.

Curbside recycling was included when curbside trash pickup began in 1973. Seven years later, the Recycling Committee formed a nonprofit corporation that could contract for services more cheaply than the town. The committee had many adventures trucking glass to Connecticut and finding buyers for plastics. The nadir was when one rebellious trucker delivered a load of recyclables with a dead pig in it. After fifteen years of nearly full-time work, the Committee gave responsibility back to the town in 1990 and Town Meeting declared recycling mandatory.[19] Today, the willingness of homeowners to recycle has outstripped the willingness of industry to reuse the materials. Serigraph of Elm Square police booth by Janvier Lange Miller

Ballardvale was named for Timothy Ballard, who owned a saw and grist mill, blacksmith shop, cider mill, and fulling mill around the pond at the end of the eighteenth century. John Marland and partners built a woolen mill on the site in 1836, planning a village around it. When Marland went bankrupt in 1857, company treasurer J. P. Bradlee took it over, renaming it Bradlee Mill. Bradlee was conservative and efficient and paid off all company debts by 1866.

Chapter Six

Yesterday's Mills to Today's Industry

While the newer resident may think of Andover as organized by roads, it was actually oriented toward the Shawsheen River. Main Street did not exist until 1806, and Central Street, the main thoroughfare to Boston, paralleled the river. Water powered the early mills, so population centers grew up along the Shawsheen: Ballardvale, Abbot Village (around the present Dundee Park), Marland Village (near the main post office), and FryeVillage (now Shawsheen Village). The story is a tangle of genealogy and geography as several families jockeyed for position along the river. But the mill buildings, all active well into the twentieth century, leave a visible record. Let us travel from south to north along the Shawsheen.

Ballardvale

At the Chicago World's Fair in 1893, the Massachusetts Board of World's Fair Managers reported of the Ballardvale Mill:

The product of this mill stands easily first among the mills of the United States in fineness and elegance of its manufacture of flannels, both where wool alone is used, and where silk is used in the warp. Their superior is not to be found in this or in any foreign country.[1]

At the time, the mill was managed by William H. Hodgkins, former mayor of Somerville, and William L. Strong, mayor of New York City. But they were building on a foundation that went back to 1794. Josiah Putnam Bradlee, owner of the mill from 1857 to 1887, and his sister, Helen, did much to benefit the village although they lived in Boston. In Bradlee Hall on the corner of River and Andover Streets, they sponsored entertainments and offered classes for adults. They had a library in the former Marland house, 228 Andover Street, from the 1870s until 1914. The school and fire station were also named in Bradlee's honor. The company owned a boarding house on Dale Street, and purchased houses where employees paid low rental. They could buy their coal at cost.[2]

Upon Bradlee's death, the business was taken over first by Hodgkins and Strong (1887), then by Phillip French (1927). The old brick mill was occupied briefly from 1930 to 1933 by Northern Rubber Company. In the late 1930s, it was purchased by Francis Leland, who bought wool from all over the world, reselling it to mills in the area. Leland's business continued until about 1960. The Ballardvale mill continued to attract investors. C. Lincoln Giles bought it in 1962, renovating it and renting space to small businesses including Colonial Pre-Built Homes, Air Conditioning and Equipment Service Company, and Francis Reilly, contractor. At that time, the smokestack was taken down. After Giles, Dundee Properties of Andover, Deane/Lyman Partnership, and Marland Mill Associates of Boston owned the mill in succession.

In the late 1980s George and Sandra Schussel, founders of Digital Consulting Incorporated, purchased the property. Their company runs seminars and educational conferences for the computer industry. In 1992 the Schussels won an

In the building next to the railroad tracks, Ballardvale Machine Company made locomotives, and later Whipple File Company produced machine-cut steel files. In 1883, after the building stood empty for a number of years, Craighead and Kintz began manufacturing kerosene lamp fixtures, bronze plaques, and other decorative objects. Pictured are pattern and mold-making operations in the 1890s. The factory was destroyed by a sensational fire in 1898. Newman photo

Historic Preservation Award for their restoration of the old brick mill. Just to the west, P. W. Moody bought the two buildings on Dale Street in 1929, where he processed flax from Belgium, France, Russia, and Egypt. It was sold to large textile firms for use in blends with polyester and cotton. In 1959 it affiliated with Coulter Fibers which continued in business until 1978.

On the eastern side of the old brick mill, Shawsheen Rubber Company bought the wooden mill in 1943 from Wool Warehouse Corporation. Fifty years later, Shawsheen Rubber continues to occupy the structure, manufacturing and applying adhesives to cloth and paper. Ballardvale Stoneware Manufacturing Company bordered on the railroad tracks. Founded in 1880 by Lewis Willard of Boston, later joined by Jeremiah Sullivan, the company handpainted blue decorations on their jugs and crocks, which bear inscriptions such as "Willard and Sons," "Willard & Weston," and "Ballardvale Stoneware Manufacturing Company."[3] They are collector's items today. The business moved to Lawrence in 1892.

The oldest industrial building in the district is the 1814 Abbot Mill, near the intersection of Red Spring Road and Essex Street. EMR photo

Abbot Village

Ruth D. Redman purchased the Abbot Mill building in 1945, leasing it to her husband, Frederick, who moved his company from Lowell to this location, to manufacture carding and napping wire for the textile industry. Today, the Redmans' son, George Frederick Redman, and grandson, Charles Frederick Redman, continue to manufacture these products. The Redmans are the last family in the once flourishing textile business in Andover.[4] Abbot Village is named for Abel and Paschal Abbot, who set up a spinning factory there in1814. In 1837 Scottish brothers John and Peter Smith and their countryman, John Dove, bought the Abbot buildings and began processing flax into linen yarn, twine, and sailcloth. They had previously operated downstream at Frye Village. Smith & Dove prospered, purchasing the stone Howarth Mill across the river in 1847. By 1880 three hundred operatives were processing two million pounds of flax per year. From 1894 to 1925, new buildings were added and others enlarged. The long structure on top of the hill, now known as No. 2 Dundee Park, was built in 1905.

Baker's Lane was part of Abbot Village.

In 1908 Smith & Dove opened a boarding-house for female workers on Shawsheen Road, downhill from the intersection with Cuba Street. The *Townsman* advises, "The house is very pleasantly situated, and is provided with forty bedrooms . . . reading and sewing rooms, sitting rooms, lavatories, shower bath, bowling alleys, pool and billiard tables, and everything that can in any way contribute to the opera-tives' comfort. The dining room overlooks the Shawsheen River; the house is heated by the Smith & Dove plant and electric lighted. The prices are: for two in a room, $3.50; one in a room, $4.00 [per week]. Single meals: break-fast 15 cents; dinner 30 cents; supper 20 cents."[6]

Smith & Dove imported many laborers from Scotland, surrounding their factories with a village. Abbot Village Hall, built in 1830 on the northeast lot next to the river, served as a community center. The Indian Ridge Mothers' Club, Order of Scottish Clans, Abbot Village Coal Society, Andover Burns Club, Abbot Village Checkers Club, and Andover Cricket Club all held meetings there. It was demolished about 1935.[5] The mill built playing fields and sponsored bowling, football, cricket, soccer, and baseball teams.

"Forest Hill," residence of Peter Smith, circa 1850, was demolished in 1948, but the wall remains at Shawsheen Road and Stevens Street.

Free Christian Church, founded in 1845 by John Smith and Thomas Clark, was nearby on Railroad Avenue. A residential area developed on Cuba Street and four Abbot Village schools were built there in succession.

In 1906 Smith & Dove built comfortable houses on Brechin Terrace, named for their hometown, Brechin, Scotland.

Vera Downs Daly, of Cuba Street, decided to go to work in the mills when she was fourteen. She remembers:

I went down to Smith & Dove and signed up for a job. At first I was a doffer in the dry flax mill up above. The wet mill was below by the river. When the spinner's bobbins were full, she would knock on her machine and the head doffer would blow a whistle. We'd take a canvas bin, about the size of a recycle bin, and take the full spools off her machine. Each basket was weighed, then taken to another part of the mill.

Jobs were so plentiful then. Anybody could get a job. There would be four or five doffers. Then I became a spinner. You'd have to put a big spool on top, then thread the machine. The room had about ten machines on each side and we would stand in the middle to watch two machines. Sometimes you'd get a big lump in the thread and you'd have to stop the machine or fix it running. If you didn't, there'd be a terrible mess.[7]

When she started working full-time at age sixteen, Vera paid room and board to her family. After ten years, she left to marry Francis Daly in 1927.

Smith & Dove was taken over by a firm in Ludlow, Massachusetts, when they closed and many personnel moved to Ludlow. They sold the buildings in 1927 to the Stevens Mills which used them for wool storage. When Stevens pulled out in 1972, Augustine Sheehy and Paul Cronin purchased the complex, renovating

Vera Daly, aged ninety, remembers Smith & Dove fondly: "We loved to go to work. We'd go over to the store on Essex Street to buy cream pie and pickles. There was a house at the far end of the upper mill called Howarth House where we had parties. The girls gave a shower there for me when I left to get married. We did have a lot of fun down there!" EMR photo, 1994

and renaming it Dundee Park. Sheehy bought out Cronin in 1974 and rented to small businesses for about ten years, then sold to Jordan Burgess in 1983. Burgess continued to lease office and retail space but did not enjoy the same success as Sheehy. In 1994 the complex was purchased by a group of investors sponsored by Pentucket Medical Associates, to create a medical office campus with comprehensive outpatient services.

Marland Village

Following the river just a short way downstream from Abbot Village, we come to Marland Village on Stevens Street across from the main post office. The first major mill in town, Samuel Phillips' gunpowder mill, was built here in 1775. It was later converted to a paper mill, then purchased by Abraham Marland.

Marland Village was named after Abraham Marland (1772–1849), whose 1830 woolen mill (center) survives today in modified form. Marland Manufacturing Company produced waterproofs, cloakings, and cassimeres (suit worsted, sometimes a twill weave). Stockholders were his two sons, John and William of Ballardvale, and his son-in-law, Benjamin Punchard. After Marland's death, the company became "financially embarrassed" in 1879, selling out to Moses Stevens of North Andover. Marland Street became Stevens Street and the mill became M. T. Stevens and Sons, the Marland Mills.

Moses T. Stevens (1825–1907), who bought the mill in 1879, was one of five brothers, all of whom followed their father, Captain Nathaniel Stevens, in the woolen business. They were descended from the first settlers of Andover. A powerhouse like Marland, Stevens was president of both the Andover National Bank and the Andover Savings Bank, and a director of Merrimack Mutual Fire Insurance Company. He served in both branches of the state legislature and two terms in Congress.

Sarah Loring Bailey reported in her 1880 history that Moses Stevens had "connected these Marland Mills and the Haverhill mill with the mill at North Andover by a telephone."[8] Since Alexander Graham Bell had only invented the telephone in 1876, this was undoubtedly the first telephone in Andover. Samuel S. Rogers, great-grandson of Moses Stevens, started training in the family business in 1948, working in every department:

First there was sorting and storage. The wool was shipped into the Dundee Warehouse from all over the world—Australia, New Zealand, South America, and Texas. The higher grade wool was used for fine worsted cloth and the lower grades were used for things like carpets and seat covers. Then it went to the dye house where wool was dyed before it was spun into yarn. That's where we get the expression "dyed in the wool."

Then there was the card-room, where wool was brushed, smoothed, and washed. In the spinning rooms, the roving was spun into yarn for the warp, the lengthwise threads, and the filling which made up the weft, or crosswise threads. These colors were varied to produce plaids. Every girl had a plaid wool skirt in the 1950s.

The weaving room was on the top floor of the saw-toothed building. There were 150 looms and it was very noisy. Then it was taken downstairs to the burling and mending room. Fifty women would pull all the knots to the back side and invisibly reweave any mistakes.

Finally the cloth was taken to the wet finishing room which was the modern equivalent of the old fulling mill. Raw wool was harsh to the touch. Here it was washed, scoured, and shrunk. Burrs remaining in the wool were burned out and the fabric was brushed to bring out the nap. The finishing determined what kind of cloth you ended up with. In the late 1930s, we started working with Dupont's synthetic fibers like nylon and rayon to add strength.9

Abraham Marland built housing along Stevens and North Main Streets, pictured in this 1946 photo. Stevens built a chimney stack and office building in 1880, and a carding mill on the west side in 1883. The rear building with the saw-toothed roof was completed in 1925. Moving clockwise, one sees Tyer Rubber Company, Smith & Dove mills, and Brechin Terrace. In the foreground is Golden Gardens, future site of Shawsheen Plaza and Washington Park Apartments. Look photo

In 1964 J. P. Stevens closed the Marland Mills and moved south, putting 450 Andover employees out of work. Rogers attributes this to several factors. There were labor problems. The mills were built on three or four stories, which made material handling difficult. In the south where land was cheaper, they could built large plants all on one floor. The wool process required a lot of water, which polluted New England cities downstream. Water treatment plants and filter beds again required large amounts of land.

During World War II, it was a seller's market, but after the war, competition increased. The shutdown was blamed partly on Japan and Italy, who could sell their fabric for forty cents less per yard. Moreover, New England sheep farmers could no longer compete with those of the southwest. Vermont had one million sheep in 1880 but only fifteen thousand in 1951.[10]

There were never any unions at the Stevens Mills. But David Reynolds, a former wool sorter at American Woolen Company, says that disagreements with the unions were one reason mills started folding up after the war and moving south.[11] He went to work in a gas station and says that the town "entered a kind of depression." The old buildings were empty for a time until the interstate highways brought a new wave of economic growth. Wood-Ayer Realty, which had renovated two mills in Lawrence, purchased the Marland buildings in 1964 and still owns them today. Bertram R. Paley, a managing partner for Wood-Ayer says:

We had confidence in the old buildings. They had lovely locations. Then problems developed—people began to prefer new buildings. The dilemma was that the old mills had to make sense economically. There were too many columns for open-space use inside. Plumbing, electrical, and sewer systems had to be completely replaced.[12]

DASA Corporation leased the building closest to North Main Street, manufacturing telephone electronic equipment until the early 1980s. In 1984, Dorman-Bogdonoff Corporation began producing tactile keyboards and touch control panels on the west side of the river. Suburban Health Care Clinic opened in the former DASA building a year later. As of 1994 Wood-Ayer Limited Partnership plans to develop the west side of the river into an assisted living complex and Wood Ayer East Limited Partnership plans to enlarge the clinic on the river's eastern side.

Tyer Rubber's steam-powered factory on Railroad Avenue, designed by Charles Main, was built in 1912. This was mainly for auto tires and tubes.

Tyer Rubber Company

Just uphill from Marland Village was Tyer Rubber Company. English immigrant Henry G. Tyer began making rubber cement and overshoes called "Compos" in 1855 in the old Whipple File buildings in Ballardvale. Two years later he moved to North Main Street, the present site of the Andover Public Safety Center. By 1896 Tyer employed 150 hands, producing hot water bottles, fountain syringes, nipples, bulbs, and crutch tips under the "Tyrian" trademark. Tyer was the first to perfect a white rubber compound for pharmaceutical supplies. At the turn of the century, the company diversified into sports equipment such as football "bladders." By 1906 the work force was up to five hundred, with annual sales of $1,000,000. Mary (May) Reynolds of Summer Street worked at Tyer Rubber for about ten years before marrying David Reynolds in 1936. She recalls:

At first I didn't like it. But I came from a large family and my mother said, "You have a job—you stay." She was a cook for Billy Wood. I was making ladies' and children's overshoes and rubbers. You'd pick up a card at the beginning of the day which said how many pairs you had to make. They were all different sizes and colors. They were held together with cement and benzene so you had to be careful—there was no smoking. It was hard on my hands at first, and I got blisters and cracks. But my hands hardened and I liked it better after awhile. There was a real rubbery smell. It got into your clothes and hair and you'd be glad to get home and have a good bath.

You made the shoes on a wooden last, putting together the uppers and innersoles first, then the counter and the outersole. Then you'd give it to the finisher. The men made knee high and hip boots because the lasts were much bigger. I worked in the Railroad Avenue building. On the first floor they made big sheets of rubber. On the second floor they made water bottles, tubings, enema bags, and other pharmaceutical items. The third floor was all overshoes and rubbers, and the packing department. The Main Street factory mostly had boxed shoes.[13]

During World War II, Tyer Rubber received the Army-Navy Production Award for its pneumatic floats, reconnaissance boats, army raincoats, and rubber footwear. Governor Saltonstall came to Andover for the ceremonies. The Korean War created another market for rubber products. Tyer Rubber was up to eleven hundred

In the 1920s, Tyer stopped producing tires, concentrating instead on player piano tubes, tobacco pouches, and large rubber rolls for the paper industry.

Frye Village was named for Samuel Frye who built a saw and grist mill in 1718 where Haverhill Street crosses the Shawsheen. In 1824 John and Peter Smith began producing machinery there for cotton manufacture. Joined by John Dove, they started the first flax mill in America in 1837. Another Scot, William Donald, built an ink factory on North Main Street. Donald was an ardent abolitionist, later serving in the state legislature and on the town's 250th Anniversary Committee. 1888 map by John Morrison, surveyor

employees in 1956, pulling in sales of $7,000,000 per year. In 1961 it was bought by Converse Rubber and concentrated on canvas footwear. It was also the sole supplier of hockey pucks to the National Hockey League. But the company was cutting back. North Main Street buildings were razed in 1963 and 1967. A 1963 article in the *Townsman* cites high labor costs in New England, workers' unwillingness to learn a second skill, and lack of program assistance from the state as causes for the decline.[14] The company stopped shoe manufacture on Railroad Avenue in 1977. A group of employees headed by longtime treasurer Arthur Ermer bought the business and buildings from Converse in 1978, continuing production of rubber rolls. A year later, they sold the 1912 building to Corcoran Company and in 1981 sold the business to JFB Holdings of England, who transferred it to New Hampshire. Corcoran Company converted the Railroad Avenue building to low and moderate income and elderly housing in 1981. Today, "Andover Commons" provides attractive, sunny living spaces.

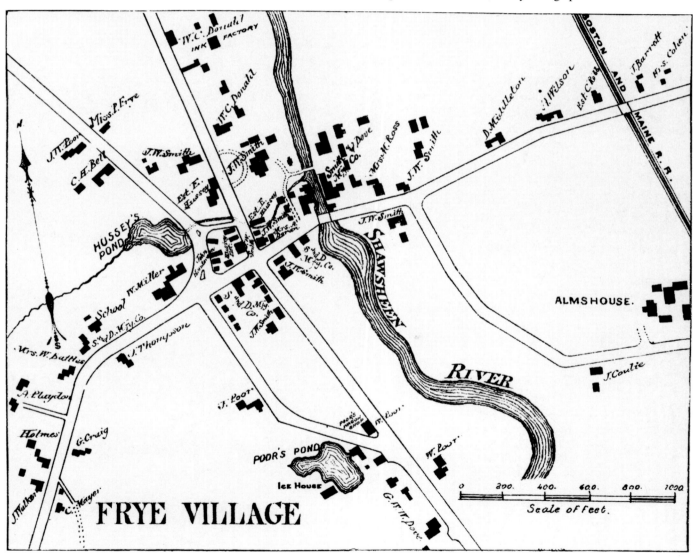

FRYE VILLAGE

Frye Village (1718–1919) renamed Shawsheen Village (1919)

Frye Village no longer exists. In its place is the planned community of Shawsheen Village. The former Smith & Dove buildings in Frye Village were bought by Frank Hardy (1871–1946) from American Degreasing in 1909. His obituary[15] states that when Hardy was nineteen, he returned from Boston by train one day, and stepping out at the station told his father he was tired of working for other people. He started the Hardy Brush Factory which produced textile brushes for woolen mills in a little barn in West Andover in 1890. When William Wood came to Frye Village, he built Hardy a new factory at 16 Haverhill Street after razing the old Smith & Dove building. Hardy served the town on the Board of Selectmen from 1923 to 1935 and headed the building committee for Memorial Hall Auditorium and East Junior High.

William Poor operated a wagon factory near Poor's Pond. He drove many an escaped slave to a way station in Salem, New Hampshire, in the dead of night.[16]

Shawsheen houses were designed without garages. Central garages on North Main Street (pictured) and Haverhill Street housed all automobiles.

The company that William Wood brought to Andover was the largest woolen company in the world and it changed Frye Village beyond recognition. American Woolen Company was an innovative company that had been extremely profitable from the beginning of the Wood-Ayer partnership in 1885. As the First World War approached, Wood won a large contract of fabric for uniforms, increasing capital even more. At the end of the war, Wood was ready for another daring innovation: the development of a model corporate community in an agrarian setting.[17] He had been buying up land in Frye Village since 1906, amassing a total of fifteen hundred acres. On the northwest corner of the village were neat blocks of executive housing, brick and slate dwellings each of a different design. In the southeast quadrant were the "white houses," for lower echelon managers and clerks. Laborers in the mills came from surrounding towns by automobile, trolley, or specially scheduled trains to the mill's railroad station. Wood ordered a fireplace for the station's waiting room, "so that people will be warm and feel welcomed." In this formal era, the workers called him "Billy Wood" to his face as there existed mutual esteem based on common origins.

William M. Wood built Shawsheen Village from 1919 to 1926. Adopting brick Georgian Revival architecture, he constructed the administration building (foreground) and a distinctive flatiron post office in the central square. They faced a bowling green, with a small stone replica of a Scottish crofter's cottage. Across the green stood the Balmoral Spa, an elegant drugstore and soda fountain with an outdoor dance floor. North on Main Street were an office building and a hotel, "Shawsheen Manor," formerly the John Smith mansion. East on Haverhill Street rose the immense Shawsheen Mills (upper left), measuring one million square feet. They employed twenty-seven hundred workers. Across the street was a cafeteria (center). Near the mills were a warehouse, dye plant, laundry, power plant, and a creamery (left foreground) supplied by company-owned farms in West Andover. Look photo, 1947

Wood planned recreational facilities for young and old. There were the Balmoral playing fields, tennis courts, and a putting green. Hussey's Pond was lined with cement and staffed with lifeguards. An eighteen-hole championship golf course, later Andover Country Club, was laid out near the brick section. The Crystal Ballroom was available in winter for dancing and there were facilities for cinema and live theater. Wood wanted the community to be entirely self-sustaining. It was largely self-governed by the Shawsheen Civic Association, and the Shawsheen Homestead Association controlled housing rentals.

The experiment was in its prime only from 1919 until 1924. Family losses, poor health, and business problems caused Wood to resign from the American Woolen Company in 1924. His successors were not impressed by Shawsheen and were appalled at the cost. They moved the headquarters back to Boston in 1925 and to New York in 1931. But Shawsheen continued to be the company's most profitable mill until it ceased to exist in 1957. Shawsheen Village thrived and was named a National Register Historic District in 1979.

The "white section" had been the fields of the town's Almshouse, which Wood did not get easily. Although the town sold the land at public auction, there were unwritten rules unknown to Wood such that bidding was suddenly cut off at $15,000. It was purchased by Hovenes and Vartar Dagdigian on July 11, who then sold it to George Dufton, who sold it to Wood on July 26. Thus Wood had to pay a lot more. At a special Town Meeting November 1, 1921, citizens voted to sell the brick farm building and the remaining ten acres to Wood.

The 251 houses were purchased in 1932 by F. M. and T. E. Andrews of Methuen, who sold them off over fourteen years. The administration building was converted into Sacred Heart School in 1946. In 1974 it was converted to condominiums. The playing fields were purchased by the town as conservation land in 1978. American Woolen Company's successor, Raytheon, was the leading producer of radar tubes and systems during World War II. The company, founded in 1922 in Cambridge, purchased the Shawsheen Mill complex in 1956. When Raytheon found the buildings no longer adequate, it sought a site for a modern plant. In the controversy over Raytheon, Andover outgrew its textile mill town identity and entered the era of high technology.

Raytheon sold Shawsheen Mills to Shetland Properties in 1972. Space was leased as low end factory mill complex property, with Modicon as its major tenant. In 1986 Andover Mills Realty Limited Partnership purchased the property to develop "Brickstone Square," managed by Brickstone Properties. This partnership manages several former mill buildings. It upgraded the facility and now leases to twenty-three businesses, with Marshall's the major tenant. Others include John Hancock, Andover Controls, Germanium, FTP Software, the Network, Northeast

Document Conservation Center, and PictureTel.[18] At Christmastime, people come from miles around to see the giant lighted tree at Brickstone Square.

As Andover began to convert mills in the 1950s, it created the Development and Industrial Commission. Its task was to attract industry, to serve as a liaison with the community, and to solve problems. Lawrence Spiegel observes:

Wolf Berthold, a retired AT&T engineer, was really the father of the whole thing. We would all get down on our hands and knees in his living room crawling over big maps. We worked with Peggy Keck and Dave Erickson, chair of the Planning Board. When Berthold died, the Commission foundered and Maynard Austin, the town manager, asked me to take over. In the early 1970s and 1980s things were really exciting. Under Dukakis, the state mandated that each town develop a growth policy plan. Ours was to attract clean industry and we did; the 1960s zoning determined where it would be. We turned some big industry away. They were pouring up Route 93 into Andover.

I remember getting heavily involved when the Sacred Heart Brothers wanted to sell their school to create the Balmoral Condominiums. We learned that a zoning variance was better than a bylaw change, because with the variance, we could control the specifications. That was how we saved the authentic windows in that building. We lost that control on Shawsheen Plaza—it was supposed to be brick colonial but once we changed the bylaw, they could do whatever the zoning laws permitted.[19]

By 1993 Raytheon was the nation's seventh largest defense contractor. But a year later, in the face of national defense budget cuts, the company laid plans to close three plants in Massachusetts, moving two thousand employees to Andover.

Industrial Zones

On July 31, 1968, Andover held its largest Town Meeting ever. The issue was whether to change the zoning in a residential area bounded by Lowell Street and Route 93 so Raytheon could develop an industrial site. Phidias Dantos and John

Davidson, owners of the land in question, each brought their mothers to the meeting, afraid they would not get a quorum. When they arrived, they could not even get near Memorial Auditorium. Fred Stott, then secretary of Phillips Academy, remembers:

Memorial Auditorium was full and still people were arriving. They called me up to the podium and asked whether Phillips could put this on the next night in the Cage. I said I would arrange it. We carried a lot of chairs that next day. The rostrum was in the gym with events internally broadcast to the cage. It was the biggest Town Meeting ever—there were at least three thousand people there. It was a big issue and a real landmark.[20]

Richard Bowen, then town manager, observes:

Raytheon had a chance to buy a big piece of land next to Route 93, but it was zoned residential. The abutters were fighting the change. The new plant was important for the town tax base, and provided income for those who worked there. Some people felt that the town had entered into a covenant with the abutters. They had built their homes knowing the zoning was residential. Now a major industry was about to relocate in their back yards. They were afraid it would bring land values down. People were angry, upset, and unforgiving. But it was approved by a big margin. Raytheon has been a good neighbor.[21]

After several hours of debate the vote was taken shortly after midnight. The article was approved by 1,863 votes to 615.

The Internal Revenue Service, less controversial than Raytheon, was built on industrially-zoned land at the east side of Route 93 in 1966. The center, built to handle seventeen million returns yearly, would serve the Boston/New York area and employ one thousand full-time and two thousand part-time employees. It was the first to use computers for processing the returns and was the largest facility of its kind in the world.

River Road Industrial Park

The Development and Industrial Commission continued working to attract appropriate companies to Andover. Hewlett-Packard Medical Products Group in Waltham began a search for larger quarters in 1972. Management explored several sites including the former Shattuck and Lewis farms on River Road. Dean Morton was general manager for the division at the time. He says Andover attracted Hewlett-Packard for the following reasons:

It fit the Hewlett-Packard model. There was room for future development and growth—the site is 114 acres. There was good access from Route 93. It was a beautiful and attractive place for our people to work. It was not too far from the airport or our existing operations in Waltham. Moreover, we had access to a community with good schools that cared about its own development and housing stock with growth potential. We kind of fell in love with it—the river and the topography. And it had already been zoned for industrial use.[22]

There were still certain agreements to be worked out with the town. One was extending the sewer system to West Andover. A bond issue for $2.5 million was voted 1,270 to 84 at the 1973 Town Meeting. The Board of Selectmen took a proactive stance in protecting the Merrimack riverbank from development. Selectman Alan French was designated to negotiate with Hewlett-Packard's Burton Dole. If the sewer extension was granted, Hewlett-Packard would create a 100-foot strip along the river with 50 feet open to the public and 50 in conservation. Dean Morton continues:

We began to talk about the river long-term. Harold Rafton persuaded the developer, Arkwright-Boston, to donate a strip of their land along the river for conservation, eight acres total. Milton Greenberg, chairman of the Board of Selectmen, was an industrialist, the founder of GCA Corporation, and while he was not a strong advocate of development, he was not opposed to it. He balanced the interests of the town. It's a good example of positive collaboration when you have a community that wants to protect its historical values and yet provide jobs and economic growth. When you have a company that is sensitive to those issues it really works out wonderfully.

Hewlett-Packard erected two more buildings in 1982, and a fourth in 1993. Today it is a leader in cardiac ultrasound imaging, patient monitoring, and clinical information systems. In late 1994 the Waltham Division moved to Andover and employees totalled twenty-two hundred. William Sousa is facilities manager for the plant. He saw the development of the Industrial Park close-up.

We leased the property from Arkwright-Boston at first, even after we built our building. The official opening was in 1976 but we did not purchase the land until 1980. Arkwright-Boston had assimilated about 540 acres in all four quadrants around Route 93. We were the first tenant in the Tech Center so we had our choice of properties.[23]

Andover Tech Center on River Road includes ISI Systems Incorporated, Compusource Incorporated, R. M. Bradley, Bailey Controls Company, Computer Associates International Incorporated, Ascom-Timeplex Incorporated, Siemens, Inchcape Testing Services, and Ford Motor Credit Corporation. A typical site is pictured. Courtesy of Andover Tech Center

Businesses in the River Road complex later included Digital Equipment Corporation, Physical Sciences Incorporated, Andover Companies, Sun Micro Systems, Mast Industries, Eisai Corporation, GCA Corporation, MKS Instruments, and AT&T.

Lowell Junction

Lowell Junction, Andover's third major industrial area, brings us full circle back to Ballardvale. Lowell Junction is Andover's oldest industrial park. The Ballardvale Lithia Company located there in the 1880s, selling mineral water from Ballardvale Spring. Watson-Park Chemical bought the Lithia Spring building in 1927, manufacturing dyestuffs and textile-related chemicals through the 1940s. Howell F. Shepard, part-owner of the company, served as town selectman for nine years. Watson-Park was succeeded by Reichhold Chemical Company in 1952.

Gillette Toiletries Company moved to Lowell Junction in 1969, the first large industrial factory complex in town. The $11 million plant today employs 589 people producing anti-perspirants, deodorants, and shave preparations. Other companies in Lowell Junction are Genetics Institute, Wetterau, Industrial Materials

Genetics Institute completed its Burtt Road facility in 1988. Genetics is engaged in the discovery and development of human pharmaceuticals through recombinant DNA and other technologies. The Andover plant produces a blood clotting factor, "Recombinate," for people with hemophilia. Its advantage is that it is not derived from human plasma with its attendant risk of viral contamination. The company is also developing treatments for anemia, cancer, bone damage, heart disease, inflammatory conditions, and immune system disorders.[24] Morse Photography

Technology, Harris Environmental Systems, Dec-Tam Corporation, Standard Duplicating Machines, Wyeth-Ayerst Labs, Celus Fasteners, Central Industrial Labs, Crusader Paperboard, and Mystic Warehouse.

Companies at nearby Dascomb/Frontage Road include Smith & Nephew Dyonics, Allied Chemical, Brockway Smith, Digital Equipment Corporation, and Vicor.[25]

A Century of Change

The disappearance of the family-owned mills and the arrival of industry changed the character of Andover. Sam Rogers observes:

The old mill families—Marland, Sutton, Stevens, Wood— lived the life of country squires before the days of income tax. During slack periods, mill owners would send men up to their estates to build houses rather than let them go. They were philanthropic—my great-grandfather and great-uncle were both president of the bank. They kept the towns going, and put in time as volunteers.

They were kind of benevolent despots. Uncle Nat Stevens knew half the employees by their first names. He would ask after members of their families. It was a very personal relationship. Eighty percent of the Marland Mill workers lived in the neighborhood. There would be picnics, outings, and Christmas parties. They all took care of each other. If somebody was sick, we'd all pitch in and work a few extra hours. The boss's wife would send flowers when a baby was born. Skills were passed down in families. I remember the four Hilton sisters in the mending room, chatting away, having a grand time.

The rise of the unions changed all that. The boss had to talk to the agent, not the worker. Gripes were not brought to the superintendent of the mill anymore, but to the union agent. He'd go to the superintendent and say, "You fix this or we'll strike."[26]

Presidents of the large corporations today are not household names. These industries benefit Andover tremendously in their tax contribution, but the contribution is not personal. Access by highway is easy and it is not necessary for workers to ever see the center. Peter Smith of Smith & Dove gave the town Memorial Hall Library. Benjamin Punchard gave the high school. Abraham Marland gave the Christ Church rectory. The present industrialists give too, but are removed from the tangible results.

Family foundations remain in silent testimony to the old order, helping community causes throughout the Merrimack Valley. The Stevens Foundations are three trust funds set up by family members, men and women, in the early part of this century, which have quietly contributed to the South Church steeple renovation, the library addition, and a wing at Lawrence General Hospital. The Rogers Family Foundation, founded by Irving E. Rogers Sr., has donated anonymously to many community projects, as have the Wood Funds. The Smith-Purdon Fund, at West Parish Church, has been used to help the very young, the very old, and those in crisis in the region. Another of Purdon's donations funded the research center at the Andover Historical Society. Susanne Smith Purdon was a descendant of the Smiths of Smith & Dove.

The Marland Mills on Stevens Street in 1960, four years before the Stevens Company closed them.

In this 1912 photograph the South Church was painted brown.

Chapter Seven

Faith Communities

In 1646 we had just one church, "The First Church of Christ at Cochichawicke," today called North Parish Unitarian Church in North Andover. By 1827 we had three and at the 250th Anniversary we had ten, still all Christian. As of 1994 we have twenty-six religious organizations, no longer just Christian. All have regular meetings, rites of passage, religious education, and community outreach. In this chapter, we will touch briefly on what makes each unique.

The first two churches in what is now Andover were organized as geographic subdivisions of the town—South Church in 1711 and West Parish in 1826. South Church of Andover was characterized by long, stable ministries. Its first minister, Samuel Phillips, served sixty years. It had strong ties with Andover Theological Seminary from its founding in 1808 until its departure a century later—South Church's Rev. Justin Edwards was also president of the seminary. Andover's tradition was proudly orthodox. While the seminary sent 248 missionaries from Andover out into the world in the nineteenth century, South Church sent many missionaries well into the twentieth. An essay by Joan Patrakis depicts one:

Mary Louise Graffam began as a teacher at Sivas, Turkey, in 1901 . . . Soon after World War I broke out, the Turkish government issued a plea for help at Erzerum where typhus was rampant . . . [Graffam] was appointed head nurse at the hospital . . . On her return to the mission she learned of the Turkish decree to deport Armenians from Sivas . . . she decided to accompany the Armenians into the desert. Her futile attempts to prevent the atrocities that occurred there exposed her as a dangerous threat to the Turks . . . She was ordered back to Sivas and kept under close scrutiny. Undaunted she opened a hospital and relief center for war refugees and ran the local orphanage. With relief funds she established a textile factory and developed industries in agriculture, carpentry, and other trades . . . For her outstanding humanitarian service she was awarded the Turkish Red Crescent and the International Red Cross in 1917 . . . She died of complications from surgery in 1921 at age 50.[1]

South Church still continues its missionary work close to home. In 1980 parishioners founded Covenant Housing in Lawrence, where members converted a fire-damaged building into twelve units of cooperative housing. The church received the Immigrant City Award from the International Institute of Lawrence in 1981 for sponsoring refugees from Hungary, Cuba, and Vietnam.

The present meetinghouse, the church's fourth built on Central Street was designed by architect John Stevens in 1861. An educational building was annexed in 1956. In 1987 structural damage was discovered in the 160-foot steeple and in

1990 it was lifted off with a crane. Restoration was completed in the fall of 1994 and a town landmark was preserved.

West Parish Church was established in 1826 for those west of the Shawsheen River. The oldest church building in the area in continuous use, it was fashioned with stones from Andover fields. The 1856 vestry on the green was moved across the street next to the church in 1908. A new vestry was built in 1927 and enlarged in 1948. West Parish, too, had steeple problems. Soon after Rev. Joseph LaDu arrived in 1988, the building inspector pronounced its steeple unsafe, prohibiting services until it was removed. A new steeple was built duplicating the old one.

The character of West Church was a bit different from South Church. Harold Tyning Jr. observes:

West Parish was really a farmer's church. When there was a supper, all the farm wives would come in and cook. When my wife Priscilla Batchelder and I got

West Parish Church

married, my mother-in-law gave the women's group $100 to put on a dinner reception. She told them to keep any money they had left over for the church. It was a family-style meal, but it was good and I'm sure they had money left over.

Tyning has organized West Parish bean suppers for years. He continued:

We used to have a couple in the church who did bean suppers for the Boy Scouts. Then they moved away. We hired a caterer and cleared $10. I couldn't ask the boys to work that hard for a measly $10 so I said I'd run it myself. I went to Chef Coakley at the Voc Tech School and he told me how to figure the amounts. It wasn't bad cooking, but we ended up with about two inches of beans on the floor. The supper was over at 7:00 but we didn't leave until midnight.

Now two of us can do all the cooking and preparation. We use fifty pounds of pea beans and kidney beans. We serve about two hundred people at a dinner, but make beans for three hundred. We can always sell leftover beans on Sunday, or give them to the Lowell Shelter for the Homeless.[2]

West Church was not only farm folk. Manufacturer Peter Smith of the Smith & Dove Manufacturing Company was a longtime deacon. American Woolen Company's William Wood built a garden cemetery with an arched granite entrance and a chapel with Tiffany windows in 1908. He also paid for a new church roof, so durable that when it was removed in 1990 and underpinnings repaired, the same red tiles were returned to their places.

Cochran Chapel, designed by Charles A. Platt, was erected at Phillips Academy in 1932 to replace the Seminary's 1876 stone chapel. Daily attendance was required for Phillips students until they rebelled in 1966. In May 1971 all compulsory religious services were abolished. Chaplain James Whyte wrote, ". . . from a worship perspective, required chapel is an insult to the participant and to Him whom all is to celebrate. It is the kind of praise I don't think God needs."[3]

Cochran Chapel. Thibault photo

One of the most fundamental changes in Phillips Academy this century has been its attitude toward religious training. Thayer Warshaw recalls:

When I entered the school in 1929, there were a half dozen Jewish students, most of whom didn't want to be known. When I left, there were upwards of thirty. I worked with the chaplain from 1937 on, arranging for students to attend Passover Seders in the community. They gave us a room in Graham House. Our services finally became an option to the big chapel service.[4]

A Jewish alumnus donated the three-way Sylvia Kemper Memorial Chapel in the basement of Cochran Chapel in 1963, and since 1977, Protestant, Catholic, and Jewish chaplains have been available for celebration and support, but not for indoctrination. Rabbi Everett Gendler makes arrangements for students with needs beyond Christian and Jewish. The chaplains participate in the school's ceremonial occasions. One year, Rev. Philip Zaeder and Rabbi Gendler spoke the final blessing alternating in English and Hebrew. Now it has become a tradition.

A second group of churches was founded as church and state began their separation. In Massachusetts individuals were exempted from taxation by churches where they were not members. Formal separation of church and state was official in 1834.

The Andover Baptist Church was founded in 1832. It differed from other town churches in its practice of adult baptism. In 1834 the congregation constructed a handsome brick Greek Revival structure on Central Street. To finance the venture, members mortgaged the lower level for 999 years, and grocer T. A. Holt and Company long occupied the site, but unclear title to the building plagued the congregation for years. Ministers came and went in rapid succession, and at times the congregation ceased meeting altogether, but the Baptists survived.[5] They provided a meeting place for Abolitionists. Professor C. H. Dufton wrote in a 1992 memoir, "We take pride that several of our families were among the few Andover descendants of the Underground Railroad." By 1923 the church was able to buy out the basement lease and build Sunday School rooms. In 1971 they renovated the cellar into a pleasant space with two large windows.

Andover Baptist Church

Once Andoverites were no longer required to support established churches, there was an explosion of new ones. The Methodist Episcopal Church[6] at Morton and Main Streets was founded in 1829, but dissolved in 1841. The First Universalist Church at Punchard and Main was founded in 1837, but only lasted until 1865. Its building was reused as a public school, then moved to 9 Bancroft Road and converted into a barn. It was demolished in 1986.

The Episcopal Society (later Parish of Christ Church, Andover) was founded by Abraham Marland in 1835. A number of Anglicans at South Church had been

Christ Church, 1887

waiting for Massachusetts law to change. In 1837 they built a Greek Revival structure on Central Street where the parish house now stands. The present rectory was built in 1845. The first building burned in 1886, but fortunately John Byers had already offered to donate a new stone building. Dedicated in 1887 with Rev. Phillips Brooks preaching, it is a Byzantine Romanesque Revival structure designed by Boston architects Hartwell and Richardson. Under the pastorate of the Rev. Edson Pike (1959–1980), a nursery, professional preschool for the handicapped, and refugee resettlement program were begun. An education building was completed in 1966. The present rector, Rev. James Diamond, brought the church to full sacramental worship including weekly communion and midweek healing services.

The history of Christ Church observes, "During Civil War years the National Episcopal Church of America attempted to maintain a low profile to avoid what might have become a permanent separation between North and South dioceses."[7] The Association of Congregational Ministers issued a pastoral letter forbidding the discussion of slavery. Andover Theological Seminary likewise forbade any discussion of the question, for fear of splitting the student body and alienating benefactors.[8]

On April 9, 1846, seventeen members of West Parish, including John Smith and John Dove, withdrew to form the Free Christian Church which outspokenly favored freeing slaves. The name had three meanings—the Free Church in Scotland was the counterpart of Congregational churches in America; it was

The second Free Christian Church building was dedicated on September 19, 1908.

against slavery; and members were free of town taxation for its support. Its covenant read:

Rule 4: This church will fellowship all who love our Lord Jesus Christ, who have witnessed a good profession before men, and practically honor Him. All such are most cordially invited to unite with us in commemorating His death. Believing that . . . slaveholders and apologists for slavery do not practically honor Christ, they are not included in this invitation.[9]

John Smith moved the former Methodist Episcopal building to Railroad Avenue in 1850 for the Free Christian Church. The Abbot Village congregation was strongly Scottish. By 1905 membership had grown to nearly one thousand and B&M Railroad was eager to buy the land. So the building was sold and a bigger church built at 31 Elm Street in 1908. In 1941 the church was heavily damaged by fire, but restored. By 1971 membership had shrunk and there was talk of closing. It had always been a workingman's church, and most of the mills had left town. But under the ministry of Rev. Jack Daniel, it has grown again to a congregation of nine hundred adults and children. The church affiliated itself with the United Church of Christ in 1961 but later withdrew. Today it calls itself a Bible-oriented church centered in the Evangel, good news, and is strongly pro-family and pro-life. It supports many missionary families and projects, both abroad and locally.

The Methodist Episcopal Church in Ballardvale was organized in 1850, at the corner of Tewksbury and Marland Streets. A parsonage was built next door in 1884, which survives today although the church is gone. In 1885 a vestry was

Methodist Episcopal Church, Ballardvale. Courtesy of Bernice Haggerty

created in the lower level of the parsonage. Church historian Steven Byington wrote that at Andover Theological Seminary, "under the old charter the professors must promise to fight as hard as they could against the Methodists." The formation of the Ballard Vale Union Society one month after the Methodist Episcopal Church was a "counterstroke to take Ballardvale for the Congregationalists."[10] In 1854 the Society was renamed Union Congregational Church of Ballard Vale. Byington wrote:

Union Congregational Church of Ballard Vale and parsonage

Thus the church began its life with a ready-made feud with the Methodist Church. Everybody agreed that there ought to be only one church in Ballard Vale but each church thought that it had been there first and had the best rights, and the others had broken in and robbed the henhouse.[11]

The first Congregational minister, Rev. Henry S. Greene, stayed twenty-five years, while the Methodists saw eighteen ministers come and go. Yet the Congregationalists did not erect a building until 1875, at the corner of Andover and Church Streets. A parsonage was added in 1893. Both survive today, but the church has been converted to an apartment building.

The 1930 Congregational ministry of Marion Phelps anticipated the participation of women in the ministry. Phelps' wife, also named Marian, was a trained minister. The Sunday School thrived under her leadership and Vacation Bible School was instituted. The team ministry was considered a great success.

Steven Byington, church historian, decided at age thirteen to translate the Bible. A proofreader for Ginn and Company, he worked sixty years on it, mostly on the train to Boston. After his death in 1957, it was published by the Watchtower Bible and Tract Society of New York. Ruth Sharpe former Ballardvale librarian says Byington was prevented from becoming a minister by a speech impediment. As teenagers, she and her friends would wait during the sermon for Byington to clear his throat. The minister would pause while Byington struggled to form his words: "I believe that you would find that incorrect," he would say politely. Then the chastened minister would continue the sermon.[12]

In 1937 Union Congregational Church received an invitation from the Methodists regarding merger. The vote came back from the tiny but proud Congregationalists: nine to seven against. In 1949 Congregationalists were for merger, but the Methodists dragged their feet. Finally in 1955 the churches became one, with "dual" membership in the two denominations.

The Ballardvale United Church erected a new building at Clark Road and Hall Avenue in 1967. On Dedication Day Rev. Robert Bossdorf led people from

Ballardvale United Church. EMR photo

the Congregational Church on Andover Street up Clark Road, singing all the way, to the first service in the new church. Like other churches in town, it has worked to help those in need, and has also engaged in a partnership project with the Henry K. Oliver School in Lawrence. It has sent missionaries to Jamaica and Maine.

Roman Catholicism came to Andover in 1852, when St. Mary's Church in Lawrence founded St. Augustine's, a mission church, on Central Street near

Phillips Street. By 1866 it became an independent parish, growing rapidly. In 1883 a new church was built on Essex Street, which tragically burned in 1894. Members set about building a new church, dedicated in 1900. The rectory was added in 1904. Today St. Augustine's comprises thirty-one hundred families. Cooperating with others on such projects as Bread and Roses and Habitat for Humanity, it also supports three Catholic charitable organizations—the Catholic Daughters, helping unwed mothers and widows; St. Vincent de Paul, assisting the poor; and the Catholic Mothers, helping young parents. The church also sends missionaries to South America.

In 1914 the Tyer residence at the corner of Central and Chestnut Streets was purchased for the Sisters of Notre Dame. The convent was home to St. Augustine's Parochial School for four years, before the school building was completed in 1918.

One priest with a strong influence in both parish and town was the Very Rev. Henry B. Smith, O.S.A. He arrived as a curate in 1935, serving the parish twenty-eight years. Under his leadership, the church built a new parking area, renovated the lower church, modernized the rectory, built a new convent, and added nine rooms to the school. A sign under Route 495 on North Main Street will tell you

Free Christian Church on Railroad Avenue, left, and St. Augustine's 1883 building, with its cross, stand out in this 1880s photo.

that the overpass is named for Father Smith. Selectman Stafford Lindsay once said, "This man was equally loved by people of all faiths and was the most wonderful man I have ever known . . . Why, Father Smith was Andover!"[13]

In 1881 St. Augustine's Parish founded its own mission church, St. Joseph's, on what is now Highvale Lane in Ballardvale. Since 1866 Mass had been

St. Joseph's Church, Ballardvale

celebrated in the hall over the B&M Depot. Millowner J. P. Bradlee donated the altar to the new church. St. Joseph's remains a mission church today. In 1981 in celebration of its One Hundredth Anniversary, a stained glass window was commissioned for the wall behind the altar, designed by Ted and Ann Traver of Andover and donated by the John Cronin family. Made from one thousand pieces of glass, it features at its center a flaming heart pierced by an arrow, symbol of St. Augustine.

St. Robert Bellarmine Church. EMR photo

Andover's twentieth-century religious communities have fallen into three categories: those "planted" following demographic studies, those moving to Andover from neighboring towns, and those founded by individuals seeking a particular kind of worship.

St. Robert Bellarmine Church, 198 Haggett's Pond Road, completed in 1961, was planned by Cardinal Cushing, who foresaw the growth in West Andover. By 1963 the parish had 260 families and today has 850. The number of children per household has been steadily growing, so the church is largely focused on children. In May 1993 it celebrated the ordination of its first native-born priest, Rev. James Daley. A parish profile by Rev. Arthur Driscoll describes two waves of migration. The 1970s brought urban residents out Route 93 from Medford, Malden, Revere, and Somerville, along with more affluent families from Lawrence and Lowell. The 1980s brought employees of high tech industry from all over the country. St. Robert's has initiated programs to draw these groups together.

The church land once belonged to Millie and William Flint, aunt and uncle to parishioner Warren Kearn. Rather than grieving for the family farm, Kearn rejoices in the positive effect the church has had on his family:

A Catholic church in West Andover! Thank God for answering my mother's prayers . . . It has been a wonderful blessing for our family. Our twin sons, Stephen and Ronald, were the first altar boys . . . They were taught all the responses in Latin and can still recite them thirty years later . . . When our sons Ricky and Charles were old enough they in turn became altar boys . . . Our daughter Louise helped out in the rectory by cooking meals for Father Fitzgerald, Father Malloy, Father Smyth, and Father Martin. In addition, my daughter Jane cooked for them on occasion . . . my son Ricky tended the grounds . . . I myself change the lightbulbs in the church and have done so for twenty years, especially the tricky ones over the altar. It's getting a little risky at nearly seventy years old to climb that ladder which is resting on the beams in the ceiling by only 4 or 5 inches . . .[14]

Fourteen Sisters moved from crowded quarters in an old Lowell firehouse to the new Monastery of St. Clare on River Road across from St. Francis Seminary in 1960. Sister Veronica Foley, historian, explains that they are "enclosed Sisters," who only leave the monastery for doctor or dentist appointments and family funerals, and do not go home for vacations. Self-governing, their chapter meetings are led by an abbess elected every three years. Their principal work is prayer. People from outside fill in enrollment cards so the Sisters can say prayers for their deceased loved ones. They also make memorial vestments and distribute communion breads by mail.[15]

Faith Lutheran Church was founded in 1962 following a telephone survey of families entering Andover from other parts of the country. Services began in

Faith Lutheran Church. EMR photo

1962 at Pike School and later moved to Peabody House at Phillips Academy. Gordon Edgar was the only member "native" to Andover. In 1964 the congregation purchased land from Marian White on South Main Street, erecting a building designed by Royal-Barry Wills in 1967. An addition was completed twenty years later.

Several engineers in the congregation ordered an electronic organ kit, taking various components home to garages and workshops. Parishioner Sally Thoren remembers:

We were meeting for services at Peabody House at Phillips Academy at the time. Every time the organ made a funny noise, we all would look at our husband that had a part in building it, wondering what went wrong. This particular Sunday, the organ was making many different noises. I kept nudging Dan asking what was the matter. After the service was over, it was discovered that birds had built a nest in the chimney of the fireplace and each time music was played, they began to do their thing! [16]

In 1979 the church purchased an 1845 tracker organ built by Henry Pilcher in Cobleskill, New York. The church has sponsored a Vietnamese family, hosted a Christmas School for children of the town, and held Lenten programs for adults. Suppers are enhanced by the German, Scandinavian, and Cambodian heritage of members and the church has published two cookbooks drawing on their international recipes.

New England Bible Church, an independent, nondenominational Bible church, was also a "planted church." As its pastor, Rev. M. E. "Chip" Thompson III contemplated an area for his ministry, he saw a need in the Andover area. The congregation first met at Heritage Green in 1982, moving to 16 Haverhill Street

This barn first functioned as a Universalist Church, circa 1838, then as the Central Grammar School and was located on Main Street at Punchard Avenue. The church-school was moved to 9 Bancroft Road and reused as a barn until its demolition in 1986.

in 1987. In 1994 they built a new church at 60 Chandler Road. The building was funded by selling bonds to members which will be paid back with interest. "So the people actually hold the mortgage," says Rev. Thompson. In addition to Sunday services, the church holds Bible training classes and home fellowship groups. It also sponsors an AIDS ministry led by Linda Murdock, an AIDS patient who has spoken at area schools as well as to the Massachusetts State legislature.[17]

New England Bible Church. EMR photo

Chabad Jewish Center of the Merrimack Valley was established in 1992 after a survey of Jewish families by its parent organization, Chabad Lubavitch, in Brooklyn, New York. Rabbi Osher Bronstein remarks, "Andover said yes they had more Jewish families than the other towns, but that they didn't think Chabad Lubavitch would be successful here. We decided that if Andover was the worst area to move into, then it was the best area to move into."[18] Chabad Lubavitch seeks to educate Jews about their heritage and to bring them back to practicing Judaism. Its publishing house, Kehot Publication Society, is the largest Jewish publishing house in the world. Andover services are held in different locations.

The arrival of the Unitarian Universalist (UU) congregation and Faith Lutheran Church in the 1960s wreaked havoc in the Andover Council of Churches. When the UUs applied for membership, the Lutherans felt that the "introduction of a congregation outside the orthodox Christian family made a formal statement of the organization's essentially Christian aims a requirement for continued Lutheran membership."[19] The bylaws committee drafted a preamble stating, "We, the churches of Andover, Mass., desiring to work together in areas of common concern and to declare in unison that Jesus Christ is Lord and Saviour, do hereby adopt this constitution and solemnly pledge ourselves to be governed by its provisions." The Unitarian Universalists were unable to sign what they called a Trinitarian creed. West Parish resigned in protest to the way the UUs had been treated.[20] Newspapers referred to Andover as a "Religious Selma." The Andover Council of Churches was disbanded. Today's Andover Clergy Association welcomes all clergy, Christian and nonChristian. The turmoil in the Council of Churches was but a microcosm of the town's increasing religious and ethnic diversity. More and more groups were moving in from neighboring towns.

Unitarian Universalist Congregation in Andover, Locke Street building, formerly the November Club. EMR photo

The UU Church of Andover (now Unitarian Universalist Congregation in Andover) was a child of the First Unitarian Society (1847) and the First Universalist Church (1847) of Lawrence. After the churches merged, membership declined. Demographic studies showed Andover as the best site for a new church. Architect Joseph J. Schiffer designed the contemporary structure at 244 Lowell Street with glass, concrete, and redwood, featuring a 40-foot ceiling in the sanctuary. After the building was completed in 1965, the energy crisis hit. Nancy Mulvey later wrote:

Many of my memories of this church are rooted in that inspiring and depressing building—a true love/hate relationship. It was beautiful and impressive, but it was also cold, dysfunctional, and impossible to keep clean without a full-time custodian. Volunteers struggled valiantly to keep those walls of windows looking clean.[21]

Joseph Zahka recalls:

From the first day, we felt comfortable here . . . But it wasn't until the furnace failed, the pipes buried in the floor burst, and the building flooded with six inches of water, that I knew I had found my church. Religion and plumbing problems, a chemical engineer's heaven![22]

In 1981 the Unitarian Universalists sold their building and in 1985 bought the November Club on Locke Street. Today the congregation teems with children. Gay, lesbian, and bisexual members are welcome. Religious diversity is celebrated with festivals of Eastern and Western religions throughout the year. In 1994 the name was changed from "church" to "congregation" to reflect that diversity. During past summers, it has hosted a six-week Summerstart program for preschoolers from Lawrence.

Andover Bible Chapel met in Methuen for a hundred years, but by the early 1960s, they needed a larger, more accessible building. They purchased a portion of Sidney White's Wild Rose Farm at 266 Lowell Street, building an A-frame chapel in 1963. In a 1981 history of the chapel, correspondent Robert A. Watters described their philosophy:

Theologically, we are undenominational and evangelical in our understanding and presentation of Christianity . . . Our communion service each Sunday is open to all born-again Christians who wish to remember the Lord in this manner in accordance with New Testament simplicity. The preaching services have speakers from within the lay leadership of the chapel and are open to the public. Qualified persons are available for anyone requiring Christian teaching or fellowship.[23]

Andover Bible Chapel. EMR photo

Like runners carrying the Olympic torch, members of Temple Emanuel in Lawrence carried the Torah six miles to their new home at 7 Haggett's Pond Road, Andover, in 1979. The tradition goes back to the Old Testament when King David carried the Ark of the Covenant to his new capitol in Jerusalem. One runner, Joel Labell, remembers:

Temple Emanuel. EMR photo

At the last service in Lawrence, Rabbi Roth asked for volunteers. As the sun was setting a few days later, older members Paul Goldman and Walter Wertheimer carried the Torah down Lowell Street to Broadway. Then Jerry Silverman, now a selectman in Andover, and his son, Michael, ran with it to Lowell Street, Andover. At West Parish Church we met the children who took it down Lowell Street. I helped the youngest ones carry it down Bellevue Road to Haggett's Pond Road. The sun had set by that time and it was dusk. The building was all lit up and members of the Temple greeted us. We handed the Torah to Rabbi Roth, who put the scrolls into the ark for the first service that weekend.[24]

Temple Emanuel's 1940 cemetery in Andover was founded by Thayer Warshaw's father. Thayer, whose baby daughter is buried there, says, "The live ones moved to be near the dead ones. It was not a cause, merely a coincidence."[25] The Lawrence building was inadequate and there was a parking problem. The observance of their religion had begun to change in subtle ways. For example, it was no longer necessary for the temple to be within walking distance of members. Many already lived in Andover. Temple Emanuel's 620 families today include many third- and fourth-generation members. It is now a Reform congregation, affiliated with the Union of American Hebrew Congregations.

When Temple Emanuel invited the conservative Jewish congregation across the street to come with them in 1979, Tifereth Israel (meaning "Pride of Israel") said they would stay. Ten years later, however, the congregation did some self-searching and set three goals: attract new members, move to Andover, and start a religious school.

In 1990 they began weekly Shabbat services in rented space at St. Augustine's Church. The next year, they moved to Christ Church, bringing their Torah and Ark from Lawrence, and in 1995 bought a building at 510 South Main Street. Co-president Don Lasser says the congregation is rooted in four congregations, Children of Abraham (1889), Sons of Israel (1895), Anshai Sfard (1900), and Tifereth Israel (circa 1935), which all merged at various times to form "Tifereth Anshai Sfard and Sons of Israel." In 1992 they shortened their name, taking the first and last words, Tifereth and Israel. It was not until they researched their past that they discovered one of their parent congregations had also been named *Tifereth Israel.*[26]

North Boston Korean United Methodist Church. EMR photo

North Boston Korean United Methodist Church bought the Unitarian Universalist building on Lowell Street in 1981, moving from Methuen. Pastor Dr. Young Bok Rha said of his congregation:

Many of them do not have a sufficient command of the English language to benefit from a service in English. Also, an ethnic church provides a religious and social setting in which they can adjust to a new language and new customs while honoring their native identity and traditions.[27]

The building which had been one

congregation's burden became another's blessing. The parking lot accommodated one hundred cars and the playground was large. Two additions expanded the kitchen and classrooms. A Korean School was established to help children maintain contact with the language and customs of their native land. Pastor Sung Kim began bilingual services and added an English class in 1986. Many second generation Korean-Americans felt more at home with English, and membership grew to include Caucasians as well as Koreans. A special invitation was extended to adopted Korean Americans and their families. Each year, the community is invited to a fall festival, with exotic delicacies of homemade Korean food.

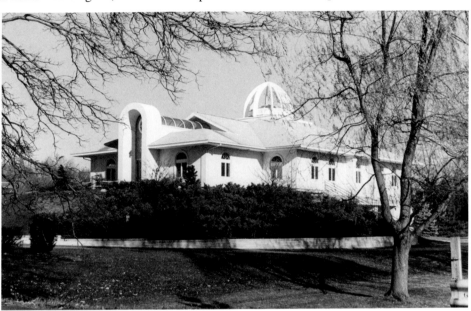

Saints Constantine and Helen Greek Orthodox Church. EMR photo

Saints Constantine and Helen Greek Orthodox Church is also famous for its fall festival featuring music, dancing, Greek items for sale, and lots of delicious Greek food served in a tent. The church purchased Doyle Lumber's property at 71 Chandler Road in 1985, building a Byzantine revival church designed by John Brennan and Associates. Charles Matses of North Andover, a lifelong member, was general contractor. Founded in 1917, the congregation built a church on Essex Street in Lawrence in 1936 but by 1985 it could no longer accommodate the influx of new families. The Andover church seats 350 and allows space for other activities. Father George Karahalios, who led the congregation to its new home, ended his twenty-two-year pastorate in 1993, and was succeeded by Father Paul Pantelis.

Victory Free Methodist Church, once called the Spanish Free Methodist Church, moved from Lowell in December 1992, to be closer to members living in this area. Space was found at the Andover Baptist Church. Pastor Juan D. Grullon says the church is changing to reach more youth and to make the church bilingual, and changed its name to become more inclusive. "Many young people don't like to speak Spanish. We need to accommodate and understand what they are going through. Also we want to tear down the barriers and open our doors to the Anglo community."28

Some religious groups were planted in Andover by design, some came from neighboring towns, but a third group grew out of the hearts and minds of individuals. One was the Christian Science Church. In 1949 Andover people attending Christian Science services elsewhere decided their numbers warranted a church in Andover. They held their first service in 1949 at the November Club. In 1950 they formed the "Christian Science Society of Andover," and by 1965 were ready for a building of their own. Nancy Morehardt recalls:

The committee asked Muriel and Cornelius Wood whether they would consider selling us a piece of land on North Main Street. They thought about it for a little while, then invited us to their house for tea and cinnamon toast. The Building Committee was astounded when they told us they would give us the land. I'll never forget it.29

Although the Woods were not members in Andover, Muriel was a longtime

Christian Scientist. "They were interested and generous," says Morehardt. The Woods also helped retire the mortgage. The church at 278 North Main Street, designed by Royal-Barry Wills, was dedicated in 1968. A Christian Science Reading Room was opened at 66 Main Street in 1949 and today is located at 36 Main Street. The congregation has no clergy. Two members are elected to read from the Bible and *Science and Health with Key to the Scriptures* by Mary Baker Eddy during the Sunday services. Nancy Morehardt says of Christian Science and the health issue:

We've had some bad publicity on that. It's not true we don't "believe" in doctors. I had a doctor (required by law) when both my children were born and they were wonderful and understanding people. As a rule, Christian Scientists don't go to doctors but nothing forbids us. It's a very individual thing. For years we have turned to God in prayer, and it's been very workable and spiritually rewarding. So if something works, you do it.

Joanne and Alfred Dahlgren, husband and wife, founded Andover's Siddha Yoga group in 1977. They had met in college and discovered a common interest in Eastern religions. They traveled to India to seek out a teacher they both admired, but found she was not the right teacher for them. After moving to Andover, Al found a book in Memorial Hall Library by Swami Muktananda, who spoke of experiencing the divinity within through meditation. When Swami Muktananda came to this country, the Dahlgrens met him. "It was an instantaneous recognition that he was our teacher," says Joanne. After a year of study, Joanne was invited to join in a meditation course through Andover Community Schools. It was so well received that the group continued at the Dahlgrens' home and Siddha Yoga Meditation Center of Andover was born. At weekly meetings, the group chants in Sanskrit and meditates together, accompanied by Indian instruments, the harmonium, a mrdang (drum), and a tamboura, a stringed instrument which provides a background hum.[30]

In 1979 Anne Avery and Jane Griswold decided they needed a Quaker Meeting in Andover, wishing to raise their children as Quakers. "We went from being simply a group who met and worshiped in the Quaker manner to a Worship Group of Cambridge Meeting with our own tax exempt number, Sunday School, and potlucks," says Griswold. "We are just getting big enough for social outreach." About five years ago, the Quakers began meeting in Phillips Academy's Graham House. They have no clergy. Children are still an important part of the congregation. Griswold explains:

Quakers meet in silence and we wait on God in that silence. I can attend another church and appreciate its service and gain great strength from it, but it's not the same. I have Quaker family background, but I was not raised a Quaker. It is like coming home for me. There is a sense of being whole—to sit in the silence— to be together and work with each other.[31]

Havurat Shalom was formed by a group of Jewish parents who wanted their children to have religious training on a less rigorous schedule than area temples. Once the school was established, parents began gathering for holidays and group discussions. ("Havurat" means friends or group discussion.) Each member works on a committee for at least one holiday. Religion School is professionally led by Janice Skolnick. An active group for youths who have been Bar or Bat Mitzvah'd meets monthly. Members of Havurat Shalom wanted to preserve Conservative Jewish tradition, but adapt the observance of Judaism to the present day. Marsha Cohen, former president, gives the example, "If you have to work on Saturday,

Christian Science Church. EMR photo

not doing so may mean the loss of your job. This does not make you a bad Jew. You have to observe Judaism in a way that suits your life."[32] Four years ago, Havurat Shalom joined the Jewish Reconstructionist Movement. Current co-presidents are David Hastings and Linda Vasconcellos.

In 1988 Bill Watson and a few friends started a church for people who didn't go to church. Watson, a pastor and Bible teacher, had sponsored a 1970s coffee house at Backstreet Restaurant. One of his friends started asking people why they didn't go to church. "The answers were always the same," says Watson. "It's irrelevant, it's boring, you're made to feel guilty, and they're always begging for money. Those issues a church can and should address." They rented space at West Elementary School and in 1988 the interdenominational BrookRidge Community Church was born. In 1995, they moved to 16 Haverhill Street. They engaged a part-time drama director along with a music director and pastor. Watson felt drama was key to presenting the issues of the day. He says:

The drama director leads a troupe which writes and performs scripts every week. Drama puts people into situations they can relate to and say, "That's happened to me." We use a lot of humor. After all, drama had its roots in the church. It's just that most churches have the same theater every week. You have to use different lingo for unchurched people. We try to mirror the Creator by being creative. Music is contemporary, with guitars, drums, and synthesizer. My part is to address the issue of the morning and talk about what the Bible says to that issue.[33]

Sixteen Haverhill Street, meeting place of BrookRidge Community Church. EMR photo

Chau Dang, at left, and his wife, Linh My Ho (not pictured), have two children, Long, right, and Linda, center. Their niece, Thuy Ho (standing), also lives with them. Dang found work assembling computer parts and entering numerical data, while his wife worked at Polo Clothing Incorporated in Lawrence. They moved to Andover in 1988. EMR photo

Chapter Eight

Our Ethnic Heritage

Chau Dang poured tea at the dining room table in his immaculate home on High Plain Road. Pictures of the Buddha and the goddess Quan The Am adorned the mantel. Dang's son, Long, helped his father now and then with English words while Dang told of his escape from South Vietnam in 1980:

I served two years in the military fighting the Communists. I was captured and put in jail by the North Vietnamese in 1975 and came back to South Vietnam in 1977. I wanted to escape to freedom, and my future wife, Linh My Ho, had the same idea. We already loved each other. So with friends we put all our money together to buy a little riverboat. The first time, we lost the ocean's map on a small island. The second time, we were captured on the high seas, and imprisoned in an upstairs room. We climbed out a window and started saving for another boat. The third time, there were forty-six people on a boat about 14 meters long. We were at sea for three days and nights until we were picked up by an American ship.[1]

Carefully, Dang memorized the address in Lawrence of a former neighbor from South Vietnam, who agreed to be his sponsor. After three months in a Thai refugee camp and six months on an Indonesian island studying English, the Dangs were transported to Lawrence through a Catholic relief agency. Dang carried just one small bag with him to the U.S. They flew to Logan Airport, where he says, "I met the family of my sponsor and they took me home."

Andover is blessed with a rich ethnic heritage. For the first two hundred years, almost all townspeople were of English background, but the mills brought in a diverse labor force. The federal census of 1880 lists 22 percent of Andover residents as foreign-born—10.5 percent Irish, 5.3 percent Scottish, 3.5 percent English, 1.6 percent Canadian, and 1.3 percent from other countries. These figures show why St. Augustine's Church prospered here among the Irish Catholics who came to escape the potato famine of 1846. We can see the presence of the Scots who founded the Smith & Dove Mills in the 1830s and Free Church in 1845. By 1920 Scots (691) outnumbered the Irish (532).

"The Scots were king," says Pete Loosigian, who grew up in an Armenian family in the 1960s. "It was as though everyone else was using 'their' town. The police chief was a Scot, and the fire chief was a Scot. One day a Jewish man came by the stand and thanked my father because his cousin had sold them land for their temple. Nobody else would."[2] Police Chief David L. Nicoll and Fire Chief Henry L. Hilton were not only both Scots but cousins. The Scots were not faced with the cultural barriers of other groups. Like the Yankees, they spoke English and practiced a Protestant religion. They came mostly from the east coast

Clan Johnston performs a Scottish rite. Such ceremonies were common in Andover. On another occasion, the *Townsman* reported, "They piped in the haggis at Free Church Friday evening, and had a good time doing it. John Whyte provided the bagpipe accompaniment while Robert V. Deyermond bore in the haggis, carrying it aloft on a platter so large that it must have been especially imported for the occasion. Then Bob read a Scotch—very, very Scotch—grace . . . The supper was the main feature of the two-day Caledonian fair."[3]

towns of Dundee, Brechin, and Arbroath, bringing some new customs with them. James Batchelder, whose family were of Scottish background remembers:

You could always tell a Scottish household. They polished the brass on the front door the first of every month. There were a lot of festivals during my childhood such as Hogmanay on New Year's Eve. "First Footing" meant the first person across the threshhold. He had to have a piece of coal in his hand. Then there was Robert Burns night, when everyone gathered in the Square and Compass Club to read Burns' poetry and to perform Scottish music.[4]

May (Shorten) Bell's parents emigrated from Ireland:

My mother attended the Church of England School. My father was born on a farm in County Cork. They played together as children, then my father went off in the Navy and came to America. They continued writing back and forth though, always on postcards. The postman would come to the door and give her the news every time. Finally she said "Let me read my own postcards." Eventually, Father sent for Mother. She came second class and thought that was pretty good. Father opened his own business in Andover when I was five—the Park Street Garage, where the town parking lot is now. He was thirty when he bought it and sixty-four when he died at work.[5]

Joan Patrakis reminisces, "I was never taught Arabic, but my mother, aunts, and relatives spoke it. When any of us kids got into mischief we knew we were in big trouble when the adults discussed our fate in Arabic. My great-grandmother lived to be 101. Even in summer she dressed in layers of clothing. Where she came from, women always covered their heads and bodies. She only spoke Arabic." EMR photo

Many immigrants got their start in Lawrence, which had an insatiable demand for labor. By the turn of the century, people with more varied backgrounds began to arrive. Joan Silva Patrakis, a resident of Chandler Road, remembers her Lebanese grandfather with affection:

Joan Patrakis says of her grandfather, " Giddo raised produce—tomatoes, corn, celery, squash—and sold it from a stand or trucked it to Boston. In early spring, Giddo covered the hotbeds with worn Persian rugs to protect the young plants from frost. An aerial view of that scene would have been a dazzling sight."

His name was Elias Nicholas. We called him "Giddo," the Arabic word for grandfather. In 1896 he came to Lawrence where he worked in the mills. Four years later he married my grandmother, Barbara Skeirik, who had emigrated from the same village. They bought the nineteen-acre farm on Chandler Road in 1904. My parents, aunts, and uncle had homes on the property. There were nine of us cousins growing up together. Now Route 495 runs through what used to be the farm.[6]

In the early twentieth century a number of Armenians purchased farms in West Andover. Alice Loosigian recalls:

I was born in Armenia. My father came to this country with his father and brothers to earn enough money to bring their mother over. He attended high school and the University of New Hampshire here, then returned to Armenia where he taught and studied at the American College. By then he was an American citizen. He was married and I was a baby. We lived in Ankara when the Turks started rounding up intellectuals. One night, there was a knock on the door. They asked for my father and took him away. We never saw him again. My grandmother, mother, and I went to Switzerland. We got a ship from Bordeaux about 1916 and landed on Ellis Island.

Alice met Peter Loosigian of Andover at a dance in Boston. His family had come from Armenia after the first massacres by the Turks in 1898. In 1917 Peter's parents, Ohan and Anna, bought the Lowell Street farm in Andover. Peter remembers:

Our farm was the worst one. It was not level, quite stony, and of variable texture. My father didn't work the farm. He had various jobs, the last of which was digging graves at West Parish Cemetery. The farm was my mother's pride and joy. She raised and sold all kinds of animals and even sold gasoline. Billy Wood owned three fancy dairy farms and would make the rounds every day in a

Armenian farms near Chandler Road were owned by the Harry Loosigians, Asoians, Bolians, Arekalians, Hagopians, Krikorians, Mararians, and Jacobsons. The Sarkisians and Konjoians are still active in the greenhouse business there. Near Haggett's Pond were the Al Loosigians, Asoians, Vartabedians, Kasabians, Ozoonians, and Tateosians. The Garabedian and Dargoonian farms (pictured) are still active there.[7] The Colombosians were on Argilla Road.

The last farm stand in Andover, Strawberry Hill Farm, belongs to Peter and Alice Loosigian at 406 Lowell Street. Their son, Pete, commutes from New Hampshire to work with them. EMR photo

horse and buggy. He never drove a car. He would always stop here and try to buy this farm. He'd keep sticking money in my father's pockets and my mother would keep taking it out. She loved the outdoors and would never sell the farm. That must be where I get it.

Loosigian spent two winters at Essex County Agricultural School after returning from World War II. He worked for a while at Watson-Park Chemical in Ballardvale, but preferred farming. "He's an excellent grower," says Alice. When asked why he is still in farming when all the others have quit, Loosigian replied:

Maybe I should have my head examined. One day during the real estate boom we were having lunch when we heard a knock on the door. It was a guy with a brief case. "I'm not selling anything. I want to buy your farm," he said. I told him, "It's not for sale," and headed for the door. But my son Pete was curious and wanted to kill time before going back to work. "Do you have a million dollars?" he asked the man. "I'm prepared to spend that kind of money," the man replied. I heard him say that just as I was stepping through the threshhold. I was picking beans that day. It was very hot and the stones were cutting into my knees.[8]

Back in the town center, upper Central Street was the Black district, according to Cornelia Yancy Lawrence who lived at number six, a triple decker razed in 1950 to enlarge the BayBank parking lot. The seven Yancy children lived with their parents on the third floor, while Edith Saunders Latham lived on the second. Lawrence does not recall where her family came from originally. For as long as she can remember, they lived in the Andover area. She says:

My mother, Anna Murphy, was raised on Burnham Road in Shawsheen, where her mother, Fanny Shephard, was a beautiful dressmaker. My father came from Five Points in Methuen. He worked as Mr. Searles' valet and traveled with him to places like Newport. He developed very expensive taste that way. He always wore Pendleton shirts and handmade Romeo shoes. He was Mr. Got Rocks with no rocks. Later he worked in Waltham at the Shoe Shop. I was born in 1926. We attended South Church.

The Sweeney sisters owned our building. Miriam married late and became Miriam McArdle, the music teacher at the High School who organized the All Girls' Band. We would sew the uniforms in home economics class—light blue with gold braid. They were so pretty. I wanted to be a majorette but Mrs. McArdle informed me that a Black girl could not be a majorette.[9]

Most Black families lived in houses (right) along Central Street between the Rose Cottage and Main Street including the Saunders, Gordon, Murphy, Yancy, and Rich families. Edith Latham remembers that cars came down Central Street about once an hour and children would rollerskate up and down the middle of the road. The Yancys later moved into the white house at left, demolished in 1989. Newman photo

Cornelia Lawrence remembers, "When we walked to school, my older brothers would make me walk from Central Street through Roger's Brook culvert under Main Street and we'd come out at the Park. If we had fallen in, they'd never have known where to look for us. In winter, we'd do it on the ice." EMR photo

Connie Lawrence says, " My father, Frederick R. Yancy Sr., played sax, my mother played piano, and my brother played drums. People would drive up to Pete's Andover Spa on Elm Street for ice cream, then come park near our house with the car windows open. They'd holler up, 'Mrs. Yancy, play Bye Bye Blues.' My father played for the Boston Pops and at the Balmoral Spa. I'd think nothing of it when Skitch Henderson would drop by our house. Once my father took me into Boston to audition as an obbligato singer with Duke Ellington." Courtesy of Cornelia Lawrence

Edie Latham's parents, George and Annie Williams Saunders, came from Halifax, Nova Scotia, to Andover, where she was born in 1916. She chimed in:

Remember how we used to go down to Balmoral Spa and dance on the sidewalk, Connie? They wouldn't let us into the dance floor, even though your brother, Gayton, played in the orchestra. They'd let us into the ice cream parlor to spend our money, though. For poor people we sure had beautiful times. We had a lot of fun with nothing. They can't take that away from us. We'd walk to Lawrence to go to the movies without giving it a thought. We loved to go to the Andover Guild on Brook Street. There would be dances. Thursday night was Black people's night and people would come from all over—from Boston, Winchester, Woburn, and so forth, and remember the time you set off that basket of fireworks, Connie?

Both women went off into gales of laughter. Lawrence explained:

My parents were out at the movies. There was a picnic basket of fireworks sitting on the porch that they'd bought for the Fourth of July. I was just a kid and I dropped a lighted sparkler into the basket by mistake. That set off a Roman candle and that set off everything else. One rocket flew across the street, right through a stained glass window in the Baptist Church, then exploded inside with all kinds of beautiful colors. It left just a little hole in the window. I don't know if they ever noticed it.

Ruth Sharpe's mother, Elizabeth Trautmann, was born in Berlin, Germany, and arrived in the U.S. aged three months. Her grandfather was an ivory engraver in Germany, but worked for German manufacturers Craighead and Kintz in Andover. The company brought a number of expert German workmen with them, some of whose descendants still live in Ballardvale. "We're very proud of our German heritage and love the town as our ancestors did," says Ruth.[10] EMR photo

By 1920, 25.6 percent of Andover residents had been born in other countries. Mary Furnari, of Italian ancestry, lives on the River Road property where her husband's parents farmed about thirty acres. She says:

My mother, Grace Arena, was brought to Lawrence by her parents from Italy when she was a child. As she grew into her teens a neighbor became enamoured

"Sebastiano [pictured] and Maria Cavallaro Furnari were wonderful people and they worked so hard," remembers daughter-in-law, Mary. "Two brothers married two sisters, and the four of them bought the farm at 279 River Road in 1917. Neither Sebastiano nor Maria could read or write. My mother-in-law did a lot of wonderful baking from recipes she had memorized. They spoke Italian and they went to church at Holy Rosary in Lawrence, an Italian parish. There were not many other Italian families in Andover." Courtesy of Mary Furnari

and asked her parents for her hand. They married her off at sixteen and went back to Italy. My father, Vincenzo Ronsivalli, was thirty-two. My mother had to grow up in a hurry. She had six children but one died. My father was as romantic as his name. They were very poor, living in Lawrence during the Depression and working in the mills when there was work. But they'd sit out on the stoop on summer evenings and he would play the guitar and they'd sing to entertain the neighbors.[11]

Mary met Fred Furnari at Tyer Rubber Company. Both their fathers were born in the same town in Italy in 1890. They came to America separately and did not see each other again until their children met and married in 1958.

World War II brought its own immigrants. Herta Stern and one sister, Hildegarde Lebow, came in 1938 and 1940 respectively. Stern recalls:

There was no future for Jews in Nazi Germany. We had an uncle in New York who sponsored us. We left behind a successful hosiery mill founded by my great-grandmother in 1865 and a comfortable lifestyle. My husband, Julius, brought some machines over in 1938 and started a family-run hosiery factory at the Everett Mill in Lawrence. People needed work so badly, they almost knocked the door in at the factory. We lived on Arundel Street in Andover. I had two small children and washed with a scrub board. This new start was the most exciting time of my life. I saw that I helped and we were successful in the business. I didn't miss the old lifestyle.[12]

Herta's twin sisters, Hildegarde and Margot, their parents, and their grandmother, were still in Germany on "Kristallnacht," November 9 and 10, 1938. Hildegarde describes the experience:

We were still in bed. They came into our house and destroyed so much, and kicked and pushed us around. I still have a silver sugar bowl that they flattened. They humiliated my father by sending him out to sweep the street in front of his factory as his employees arrived. After that, we couldn't go out on the street. Friends had to bring us food. We had to go through all kinds of officials and permits and passports to leave. We got to Holland in February 1939, then spent about a half year in England before coming here in February 1940.

Even in America, life was not always easy. Ironically, their German background gave them trouble. One weekend, the family left on a skiing trip without getting the proper permission to travel more than twenty-five miles. Hildegarde says they made the mistake of speaking German loudly with a Swiss man they met, and were taken into custody for two weeks at a detention center in East Boston. Members of the Rotary Club and friends in Lawrence came to Boston to vouch for them. "The officials must have thought we were Jewish Nazis," says Hildegarde wryly.

Herta Stern remembers the day they arrived at their rented house on Arundel Street. Their furniture had been delivered and neighbor Joseph Mulvey came over to help them move in. He politely asked, "Come essen mit us." Her husband Julius replied, "Thank you very much, we've had dinner." EMR photo

By the 1980 census in Andover, 30 percent of those who reported their ancestry declared themselves to be Irish or part-Irish; 27 percent English; 12.7 percent Italian; 11.4 percent German; 10.4 percent French; 5.4 percent Polish, and 2.2 percent Russian. The Scots had slipped to 2.1 percent, although the numbers are misleading because the census did not list those who considered themselves part-Scottish.

Between 1980 and 1990 the most dramatic increases in the foreign-born population were Asian, African, Ukranian, Arabic, and Hispanic as our population diversified. In 1980 these groups made up 1.3 percent of Andover's population, while in 1990 they represented 7.5 percent.

Elsie and Peter Wu and their children moved to Andover in 1978, looking for a school system with a gifted and talented program for their son, Steven. Although Peter had come to America from China as a student in 1957, Elsie's family had come much earlier. She explains:

My parents came from the Kwang Tung Province in Southern China in the early 1900s. The corrupt government and poor crops combined to make farming fruitless. The men came first. My father came to Boston in the 1920s to work in a laundry owned by his uncle, then returned to China to marry my mother, an arranged marriage. They lived about a year in the Village of the Floating Moon until he had to return to the U.S. to earn a living.

My mother came to America in 1936, but Immigration would not allow her to bring my older brother. She left him with his grandparents when he was only nine, and he was not able to come until he was twelve. I was born in New York in 1945.

We grew up in Manhattan in the laundry which my father ran. There were very *few businesses open then to Chinese. I knew I wanted to go to college but was not really encouraged as the youngest of five and a daughter. There were not many options for me: nursing, secretarial work, or teaching. I chose teaching. After jobs in other places and ten years off to raise a family, I came to teach at Bancroft School in Andover, where I have taught fourth grade for seven years, loving it very much.*13

Madhu Sridhar, from India, left a prestigious job as director of the actuarial department at Blue Cross/Blue Shield in Boston to raise a family. She and her husband explored the suburbs, and when a friend at Blue Cross invited them for dinner and showed them Andover with its old houses, academy, and fine school system, they began to be interested. "What do you think I'm going to do here in the country—grow vegetables and raise chickens?" Madhu remembers asking her husband. But the library finally convinced her this was the right town. Madhu's journey to America was not as hazardous as some:

*I came to the U.S. in 1974 from New Delhi. My two sisters had both come here before me. Unmarried daughters were more protected than sons but my sister got a scholarship at MIT, so she paved the way. She had a wonderful host family in Winchester, who visited us twice in India, offering to help if any of the other children wanted to come to America. I remember saying, "I will never go to the U.S.," but once I came to visit my sisters, I never went back. I met my husband in Boston at his brother's wedding. I am from New Delhi, in the northern part of India and I speak Punjabi and Hindi. My husband is from Madras, from the South, and speaks Tamil and Telgu. Our only common language is English.*14

Madhu was on the board of her older daughter's nursery school, then served on the Shawsheen School PTO Board. She followed her daughter to South School, where she was vice president of the PTO for the 1991–1992 school year and president from 1992 to 1994. In 1994 she successfully led the campaign to pass Andover's school construction article for $40.5 million through a proposition 2 1/2 override question. She serves on the townwide PTO and on the Equity Coalition Task Force, which works for acceptance and celebration of diversity. She has spent considerable time in the classroom presenting study units on India. She believes:

The world is becoming a smaller place. We need acceptance and mutual respect, not just tolerance. I want my children to be proud of their heritage and at the same time to blend in and be proud of the country that we have chosen to live in. I want to make a difference and give them an example of civic responsibility.

And what of our Native American population? Bailey notes in her *Historical Sketches of Andover* that "no descendant of an Indian is now [1880] known to live on the soil sold by Cutshamache. Some persons now living remember a woman named Nancy Parker, who is said to have been the last Indian."15 In 1991, Richard Meyers, a member of the Class of 1993 at Andover High School, protested the revival of the Indian as the school mascot at football games. Meyers' mother is an Oglala Sioux from South Dakota, while his father comes of an Irish-heritage family in Andover. He says:

I came back from South Dakota at age four to attend school here. In ninth grade, I went back to South Dakota, and spent time in Mexico and Nicaragua. I had experiences that were very different from those of my classmates in Andover and it helped me to see things they didn't. Andover had stopped using the Indian as a symbol in the 1970s and brought it back in 1991. It bothered me deeply to see people dressed as Indians running up and down the sidelines picking up

Madhu Sridhar observes, "My accent actually worked for me rather than against me. My clients could identify me because of my accent. They would call and say, 'That woman with an accent did an excellent job.'" EMR photo

pennies. What would they have thought if it was a Rabbi? They stopped while I was there, but have started again now that I have left for college. The Native American population in Andover is not large enough for people to even have to notice.[16]

From Andover's beginnings new families have been emigrating to town. David Abbot's ancestor, George Abbot, came to Andover from England in 1643. An original proprietor, he received a grant in the South Parish from England in 1660, and bought an eighteen-acre parcel at what is now 56 Central Street. There he built a garrison-style house. When George died in 1681, he left the house to his eldest son John. The house was owned by five successive eldest sons named John. The last of these taught at Bowdoin College in Maine, so the house on Central Street passed to his brother, Ezra. The homestead at 56 Central was replaced by newer houses, the latest being the 1797 house which occupies the site today. In 1944 David's father and uncle inherited the two properties. David says:

Ezra Abbot bought a 1790 house for his son at 72 Central Street about 1810, where Louise and David Abbot live today. Their house has been in the family for 184 years. EMR photo

My uncle wanted very badly to live in the old homestead at 56, so my parents came to live at 72 in 1945. They lived here until they died— my mother in 1984 and my father in 1985. We spent our first winter here in 1987–1988, moving in full time about 1989. My cousins sold 56 Central Street after my aunt died in the early 1980s to the Edward Coxes and it went out of the family. I had two brothers. One died in infancy and the other in World War II. He survived the sinking of one destroyer in the South Pacific, went home, married, and soon afterward went back to the Pacific. On June 25, 1945, the destroyer Twiggs *was sunk and this time he did not survive.*

I have three sons. The oldest, John Radford Abbot, was living in this house when his son, Gregory, was born, the twelfth generation of Abbots in Andover. But now they are well settled in Yarmouth, Maine, and my other two are in West Newton [Massachusetts] and Madison, Wisconsin. I don't imagine any of them will come back to live in this house.[17]

Main Street about 1897 shows the Andover National Bank building at right. The Masons occupied the third floor, with Merrimack Mutual Fire Insurance Company on the second. The bank shared the first floor with Arthur Bliss' drugstore and Andover Savings Bank. The 1890 building was enlarged in 1910 and remodeled in 1942 and 1981. "Electric car" lines to Lawrence were installed in 1891, to Reading in 1900, and to Haverhill in 1901. The tracks caused havoc for sleighs in winter. The last trolley made its run in 1934.

Chapter Nine

The Face of "Main Street"

The size of Andover's downtown has not changed radically since 1896, but its character has slowly altered. Annual business listings indicate a slow evolution of goods and services. The composition of Main Street itself was transformed from gravel to macadam to granite paving blocks and finally asphalt. Trolley tracks came and went. The railroad, thriving at the turn of the century, was superseded by the automobile. Old buildings were replaced and residences commercialized. Sons took over from fathers, and daughters from sons. Andover worked hard to preserve its strong downtown.

1897

In 1897 Andover already had 191 businesses serving a population of sixty-five hundred. A graduate of Punchard Free School in 1897 might send word to W. H. Higgins at Park Street Stables or J. H. Adams at Elm Street Stables for a "depot carriage" when he left for college. He would travel down Main Street between stately elms with the gravel crunching under the carriage wheels, while workers paved the west side of the road. "Hair dresser" John Soehrens, stepping out his door at 33 Main Street, might look up, as traffic was infrequent. Soehrens would cut miles of hair for Andover men and boys between 1877 and 1937. Charles H. Newman took their photographs, and W. J. Burns sold them their suits. The Andover Bookstore provided their textbooks and the Andover Press published their weekly newspaper, the *Andover Townsman*. Playdon Florist at 60 Main Street kept their sweethearts in flowers for fifty years.[1]

Crossing Roger's Brook, one saw Jacob Barnard's 1883 brick building on the right where John Edward Whiting, jeweler and optician, might be standing in his doorway, polishing a pair of spectacles in the autumn sunshine. The business was more than fifty years old when he sold it in 1918. Whiting was followed by George Homer, John Blackshaw, and Walter Billings, who ran it for more than forty years before selling to Dino Artigiani.

Next, the carriage would pass the Town House, erected in 1858. Across the street was Omar Chase's paper store and the new Andover National Bank building. Andover Bank (now BayBank), the oldest bank in town, was founded in 1826. Several generations of the Stevens family served on the board of directors and three served as presidents: Moses T., Nathaniel, and Abbot Stevens. Until it became Andover National Bank in 1863, the bank was authorized to print its own money, including three-dollar bills. The bank merged with Merrimack National in 1956 and was joined a year later by Methuen National, forming Merrimack Valley National Bank. The latter was taken over by Baystate Corporation of Boston in

When spring fever set in, students walked down to Allen Hinton's on South Main Street. A former slave, Hinton started his ice cream business about 1877, the first in town, moving to Hidden Road (pictured) in 1901. His daughter Alice carried on the business from 1912 until 1929.[2]

ANDOVER
MASS.

1964 and the name became BayBank Merrimack Valley in 1976. It was the first bank to install a drive-up window (1965) and the first to offer an Automated Teller Machine (1978).

Andover Savings Bank, organized in 1834, became a tenant of the National Bank in 1853. Its hours were Saturday afternoon from 2 to 5. The Savings Bank erected a handsome building on the northwest corner of Main and Chestnut Streets in 1924. In 1983, it acquired Valley Cooperative Bank and in 1994 the Community Savings Bank, simplifying the name in 1991 to "Andover Bank." Today it is the only locally owned bank in town. Residents fondly remember presidents Louis Finger (1958–1963) and Robert Henderson (1963–1991). Henderson served as chair of the Finance Committee, member of the Conservation Commission, and director of the YMCA and Andover Endowment for the Arts. Current President Gerald Mulligan, former commissioner of banks for Massachusetts, is a member of the Finance Committee and active in the town's 350th Celebration.

The Merrimack Mutual Fire Insurance Company was founded in 1828 by citizens concerned with the lack of fire protection in town and it, too, rented space in the bank building. It acquired Cambridge Mutual Fire Insurance Company in 1913 and Bay State Insurance Company in 1955, when the name was changed to The Andover Companies. It grew dramatically under the leadership of Burton S. Flagg, president from 1914 to 1959. He was succeeded by Edward C. Nichols, who greatly expanded the company's advertising and investment activities from 1959 to 1979. Nichols' son, William E. Nichols, now serves as president, treasurer, and chief executive officer.

In 1933 the insurance company moved to the Post Office Building in Shawsheen. When it again became cramped for space in 1951, it purchased the former Balmoral Spa. Continued growth necessitated a move to 95 Old River Road in 1989, where the company employs 240 today.

Back in 1897, approaching the convergence of seven streets and a trolley track around the giant tree in Elm Square, one would be struck by the new Musgrove Building, built in 1895. The Elm House had been purchased by John Flint and dismantled in 1894. The Post Office occupied a spot in the rear of the new edifice, hence Post Office Avenue. Flint's in-laws, heirs of Henry Tyer of Tyer Rubber Company, invested heavily in the new building and named it in honor of Sir John Musgrove of England, who left their family a large bequest. The building was soon filled with tenants—Herbert F. Chase's bicycle store; Barnett Rogers' real estate office; American Express Company; and Allen Brothers' Drug Store.

Householders had a wide choice when it came to buying food. Close to Elm Square were Valpey Brothers at 2 Main Street; P. J. Daly & Co. at 4 Main Street;

T. A. Holt in the Baptist Church; and J. H. Campion and Smith & Manning on Essex Street. Florence Abbot, writing of her childhood in Andover says, "I remember Mr. Smith, white haired and bearded, who always had a candy for wee folks, and Mr. Manning, more conventional and business-like."[3] John Hutchinson at 87 Summer Street offered fish and oysters, while W. G. Brown at 63 High Street and John P. Wakefield at 16–18 Main sold meat and provisions. Wakefield's granddaughter, Betty Bodwell Stevens, recalls that Wakefield was the richest man in town until the 1929 stock market crash. His double chimneyed building next to the Town House was leveled in 1910 to build the Barnard Block.

Ice was cut during the winter and delivered by grocers or by B. F. Holt and Henry Hayward. People's Ice Company would open in 1899. Homes were warmed with coal from Cross Coal Company of Lawrence starting in 1864. In 1907 Cross opened an office in Andover. The business stayed in the family through four generations: Captain Jerome Cross, John Sargent Cross, Jerome W. Cross, and Jerome W. ("Jerry") Cross Jr. Jerry sold it to Whaleco in 1988.

1908

A woman walking downtown in 1908 might notice that three stores were advertising corsets and Elite Millinery offered hats on Barnard Street. Physicians Charles Abbot, Jeremiah Daly, and William Walker were available should she need medical attention, as was Andover's only female doctor, Emma Sanborn, M.D.

Elm Square after 1910 shows, from left, the Baptist Church, library, Musgrove Building, Valpey Block, and new Barnard Block. There were two stables: Higgins on Park Street and Morrissey on Main Street, but Higgins was already converting space for automobiles. A. M. Colby made harnesses, F. E. Gleason sold hay, and three blacksmiths offered services on Park Street: Morrison & O'Connell, Anderson & Bowman, and Dennis Sweeney. James E. McGovern was a horse undertaker.[2]

Ballardvale residents had their own drugstore, run by Charles Shattuck, M.D., on Andover Street next to the railroad crossing (pictured). They could buy groceries from Green & Woodlin or F. G. Haynes, and meat from J. S. Stark in the old schoolhouse.

135

Several laundries vied for business: Andover Steam Laundry on Post Office Avenue; W. J. Burns; W. C. Crowley; Charlie Howe; and the Chinese laundry, Chin Dang & Company. The laundries suffered when automatic washing machines came in after World War II. Newman photo

A new face on Park Street was Buchan & McNally Plumbing, looking after residents who had installed running water. A telephone exchange opened in 1899. Lawrence Gas and Electric bought out the 1888 Andover Electric Company in 1901, joining the telephone company in the Musgrove building.

In 1906 John N. Cole moved the Andover Press from the old Draper building at 35 Main Street to a new building on the northeast corner of Chestnut and Main. Lowe's Drug Store occupied its prime retail space facing Main Street. Formerly the site had been occupied by the Darius Richardson residence.

The Andover Press was started by Ames and Park on Academy Hill in 1798, becoming publisher for the Andover Theological Seminary in 1813. That same year, Timothy Flagg and Abraham Gould took over, and Moses Stuart published the first Hebrew grammar in the United States. By 1829 Flagg & Gould was producing tracts in Mahratta & Tamil, Arabic and Syriac, Armeno-Turkish, Arabo-Turkish, Chinese, Japanese, Hebrew, Cherokee, and Choctaw.[4] Missionaries traveled around the globe to work with indigenous peoples, learning their languages and inventing alphabets to record them. They would return to Andover and "occasionally made the type with their own hands,"[5] in order to print sacred works using these alphabets.

The Press also stimulated women's place in American literature. Six wives and daughters of professors issued books which sold more than a million copies

The Andover Press pictured here in the 1930s specialized in academic publications. It printed all Harvard football programs and even National Geographic magazine. Dino Valz taught college students how to produce their yearbooks. A native of Italy, Valz landed the job at the Press in 1925, right after graduating from Harvard, and stayed until 1943. The Press and the *Townsman* passed to Cole's son Philip in 1922. In 1938 they were purchased by editor Elmer Grover, who changed the name to Townsman Press. Grover sold it to Josiah Lilly, who sold to Irving Rogers in 1949.[6] The Andover Press ceased operations in 1960 but the *Townsman* survives. Note the cobblestones on Main Street.

each: Harriet Beecher Stowe, Mrs. Elizabeth Stuart Phelps, Miss Elizabeth Stuart Phelps, Sarah Stuart Robbins, Harriet Woods Baker, and Margaret Woods Lawrence.

On February 19, 1853, an "Association of Gentlemen" published their first issue of the *Andover Advertiser*. It was taken over by Warren Draper in 1854 and published weekly until 1866. In 1887 a corporation of businessmen, including John N. Cole, purchased the Press from Draper, and Cole started the *Andover Townsman*.

John N. Cole built the Arco building next to the Andover Press at 56 Main Street in 1907. Arco stood for Andover Realty Company. The first tenant was Herbert F. Chase, who moved his bicycle store there from the Musgrove Building. He sold out to William Poland in 1929. Omar Chase moved in his newsstand, and Cross Coal also took a space.

In 1927 Carl Elander moved to the Arco Building, where he sold menswear for twenty-five years. Grecoe Jewelers occupied the front portion of his store. Elander and Stanley Swanton bought the building from Philip Cole in 1946, and in 1955 took over the storefronts on either side of them: Western Union and Joseph Mulvey's Arrow Cleaners. In 1959 Swanton bought the business, operating it with store manager Al Legendre until selling out to William Long in 1967. The building was taken over by CVS pharmacy in 1973. Today, Royal Jewelers occupies the space.

Andover's first movie theater, the Wonderland, opened at 7 Elm Street in 1909.

Colonial Theater on Essex Street opened in 1912 and was bought by Sam Resnick in 1918. Sunday movies would not be permitted until 1933, and the Colonial was off limits for Phillips Academy students. The building, later named Andover Playhouse, was razed to expand library parking in 1985. Note the Capitol diner at right.

1918

A wartime visitor in 1918 might stay at the Phillips Inn in Stowe house on Chapel Avenue. From the window they would see Phillips boys drilling on the parade ground. Eighteen nurses offered their services in the *1918 Directory*. While men were away, many women had gone into business—eight had opened boardinghouses. Ten were teaching music; and Annie Donovan, Marion Abbot, and Ella Onasch would have long careers. Olga Sjöstrom later joined their ranks. Bessie Hiller purchased Miss F. M. Porter's dry goods store at 6 Main Street which she sold to Irma Beene in 1935. Everett Lundgren had opened his undertaking business at 1 Elm Street in 1913.

The transition from horse to automobile was evident. Park Street Stables was offering automobiles to rent. John Morrison advertised "automobile sundries" in addition to blacksmithing. The town supported two cattle dealers, Daniel Donovan and Thorndale Stock Farm, and there were 148 farmers. Meyerscough and Buchan moved their garage to 90 Main Street in 1913; their building would be taken over by the A&P in 1940. Three chemists appeared on the scene: Ballardvale Chemical and Lyster Chemical in the Vale, and Beaver Manufacturing at 10 Pearson Street.

By 1918 Horace Eaton had opened a pool room at 4 Bartlet Street and by 1919 the elm was gone from Elm Square. Food stores abounded: Franz Groceries at 195 North Main Street, Andover Pork Store at 7 Barnard, Gustave Yunggebauer at 10 Main, Andover Fish Market on Post Office Avenue, S. K. Ames at 50 Main, Bridget O'Brien at 40 Essex, and two A&P's at 7 Elm and 68 Main. Amos

Loomer's meat wagon and Poor & Riley at River and Andover streets served Ballardvale Residents.

On certain afternoons, Abbot students could visit the Marlands' Rose Cottage Tea Room at 2 Chestnut Street or a "tea garden" at the old Abbot Homestead on Andover Street. Then they could browse at William Allen's, 4 Main Street, where they marveled at the talking machines and records.

Next to Allen's was the big new Barnard Block. The Barnard family was a vital force on Main Street. Jacob Barnard, descended from a 1644 settler of Andover, opened a shoe shop in the bank building about 1856. In 1883 he erected a brick building on the corner of Barnard and Main Streets and in 1895, built a shop at 19 Barnard Street. By 1895 the company employed two hundred making hand-sewn "Ankle ties in goat, dongola, kid, and patent leather; men's slippers; ladies' toilet slippers and lace gored buskins; ladies' congress boots; and children's and misses oxfords."[8]

Barnard's son, Henry, built the Barnard Block at Main and Park Streets in 1910. Tenants over the years have included First National Stores; Irma Beene's

Jacob W. Barnard was a poor but respectable boy from Ballardvale, who delivered blueberries to Benjamin Punchard in his large house at the intersection of High, Elm, and Main Streets. Once he said to Mr. Punchard, "I'm going to own this house one day." Punchard just laughed. But one day Barnard did own that house and a good part of Main Street too.[7]

Ladies Shop, Charles Buchan Furniture, a pharmacy owned in succession by Crowley, Lowe, Dalton and Hughes, Ford's Bakery/Coffee Shop and Cole Hardware.

Jacob's grandson, W. Shirley Barnard, opened an insurance and real estate office at 13–15 Barnard Street in 1931, moving in the early 1940s to 36–42 Main Street. On his wall hung a huge aerial photograph of Andover where Shirley could point out each house. When Shirley died in 1951, his grandfather's trust included the Barnard Block, the Jacob Barnard Building, 43 Main Street, all the buildings on Barnard Street, the Wilbur Block on Maple Avenue, eight buildings on Temple Place and thirty acres on Sunset Rock Road.9

Hairdressers divided into barbers and beauty shops in the 1920s. Pictured is hairdresser Edwin Eastman in 1927. Raven Beauty Parlor, founded in 1928 at 30 Park Street, still crimps and curls today on Stevens Street. Courtesy of Edith Eastman

1928

In June of 1928, the height of prosperity before the stock market crash, Thomas Cochran was beginning to convert the former Andover Theological Seminary campus into the new Phillips Academy campus. Only two blacksmiths remained. One was Joshua Lawrence Paine. His granddaughter Beatrice Hall, now of North Andover remembers, stopping by the shop of her grandfather on her way to third grade at the Samuel Jackson School, and watching him bang horseshoes on the forge. Paine, a native of Eastham, moved in 1892 to Andover where he opened a shop at Park and Bartlet Streets. He died at work in 1936.10

Percy Dole opened his trucking business on Washington Avenue in 1920. A star athlete at Punchard and Central Catholic, Dole was known to carry pianos upstairs on his back. He fathered thirteen sons, and even his wife, Retta drove a truck when necessary. Dole was active in the community and provided floats for many parades. The firm moved to Methuen in the 1950s to be carried on by his sons until 1983.

Ice companies were slowly replaced by "Frigidaires," available at the Electric Shop. Two "filling stations" were pumping gas for shiny new Model A Fords: Fred Broadley's on South Main Street, and John Snyder's and Marie Thomas' on Woburn Street. Three nurses started "sanatoriums" where many little Andover citizens were born: Anderson Sanatorium at 13 Maple Avenue; O'Donnell Sanatorium on Center Street, Ballardvale; and Snow Sanatorium at 12 Florence Street. Snow's moved to the town Almshouse in the 1930s.

A visit to Andover in 1928 would surely mean a drive to see Shawsheen Village. Corporate headquarters had moved back to Boston, but business was thriving, with Shawsheen Hairdressing Parlor, Shawsheen Laundry, Shawsheen Manor, Shawsheen Market, and Shawsheen Garage(s). Shawsheen Spring Bottling Company, Shawsheen Dairy, Shawsheen Co-operative Bank, Shawsheen Pharmacy, and Shawsheen Tailor. Helen Reilly remembers:

My mother loved it here in Shawsheen. Both our parents were working but she never had to worry about us. Billy Wood was a great old man. I remember the Shawsheen Market opening. He was there in person and handed every child a box of candy. 13

Company support systems were gradually absorbed by the village. The garage on Haverhill Street became Shawsheen Motor Mart in 1936. The garage on North Main Street became Woodworth Motors which survives today. The Post Office building became a symbol first for Merrimack Mutual Fire Insurance Company, later for Lawrence Savings Bank.

Several major buildings were erected between 1923 and 1924: Andover Savings Bank, the K&D Block, 66–68 Main Street, and "Caronel Court" at 98–100 Main

George and Peter Dantos (pictured at right) opened the Andover Spa at 9 Elm Street in 1921, offering fruit, candy, and homemade ice cream. John Auchterlonie is delivering ice. George's son Phidias tells how one Memorial Day, Mrs. Basso,11 who operated a fruit store near the bank, had five coconuts for sale. When a child asked what it was, she replied, "A coconut." "How much?" "A nickel." When his friends saw the coconut, they ran back to the store and bought the rest. The next year, children asked, "Are you going to have coconuts for Memorial Day again?" She bought more and the Spa stocked up too. Before long, a coconut on Memorial Day was like a tree on Christmas. "Andover was the only town in the nation to celebrate Memorial Day with coconuts," chuckles Phidias. He says, "The last year I ran the Spa in 1969, I sold sixteen hundred coconuts before noon." Dantos sold the Spa to George Dukas and George Angelicus in 1970. 12

Hartigan's Drug Store boasted a marble fountain, stained glass, and a mahogany phone booth.[14] They advertised in 1924, "The fountain is equipped with a 'Frigidaire' using no ice, and under this system the creams can always be kept in proper condition."[15] Hartigan's closed in 1978. At right is Andover Consumer's Co-operative grocery store.

Street. The K&D building (Merchants' building), today the Shawmut Bank, had a significant impact on the appearance of the street. Hartigan Drug Store occupied the corner spot, with neighbors Polly Prim Beauty Shoppe; Emma Knox Millinery; Andover Art Studio; Herbert Fischer, real estate; The Clothes Shop; William Fleming, dentist; and Temple's Electric & Radio Shop.

In 1928 W. R. Hill bought out Morse Hardware at 31 Main Street, becoming chief supplier to Andover residents until 1970. Norma Gammon remembers, "You'd ask Rod Hill to match a little bolt and he'd go over to his warehouse on Buxton Court and be gone about a half hour. Then he'd come back and sell you the new bolt for three cents. That was personal service."[16]

1937

Times were hard during the Great Depression. The 1937 Directory listed thirty-seven men as "carpenter"—presumably many of these were out of work elsewhere. Phillips Academy campus was complete and building was modest on Main Street—the new Post Office in 1931, the Simeone Block in 1933, and the Woolworth building at 44 Main in 1936. James Greeley bought J. H. Campion's grocery store at 22–26 Essex Street (founded in 1886), and carried many a family through the Depression. In Ballardvale Dick O'Brien and George Cheyne provided groceries and other necessities. Cheyne also helped families during the Depression. Despite the economy, a few new businesses quietly opened up. Some had to fight their way in. In 1931 W. Shirley Barnard dared to challenge Burton S. Flagg's monopoly. Flagg, president of Merrimack Mutual from 1914 to 1959, was also a partner in Smart & Flagg Insurance, president of the Andover Savings Bank, a

Simeone Drug Store operated twenty-five years in the Musgrove building (pictured) before building its own block in 1933 at Main and Post Office Avenue. The store closed in 1994. Newman photo

Main Street in the early 1940s featured, from left, Shirley Barnard's office in the Jacob Barnard building, the 1936 Woolworth building, and Grecoe Jewelers. In the background is the firehouse tower.

director of Andover National Bank, a trustee of Phillips Academy, and a fifty-eight-year trustee and treasurer of Abbot Academy. In his day, Flagg was the most powerful man in Andover. Richard Lally remembers:

Nobody could get his hands on the town insurance. Burton had it all locked up. Shirley would get Lynn Mutual to represent him and Burton Flagg would hear about it. So he'd call the Lynn Mutual and he'd say, "Hey Claude—B. S. Flagg here. Have you gone into Shirley Barnard's office? What's he giving you? $1,800 a year in premiums? How'd you like $5,000?" It was the Depression. As fast as my mother-in-law could type up the policies, Shirley would get a notice of cancellation. Of course everyone wanted his insurance in the Merrimack because they paid a dividend. It's probably one of the best-run companies in the United States—still. So it was Harvey Abbot from the Hartford, who disliked Flagg, that told Shirley, "I'll take you on and I won't cancel you. A fellow named Bevington with a big agency in Lawrence didn't like Mr. Flagg at all. So he started brokering for Shirley.[17]

William Doherty broke into both the Yankee and the insurance establishments when he opened his insurance office in 1934. He was joined by his brother, Jim, in 1937 in a successful partnership which lasted for fifty years. Three of Jim's children, Mary, Sheila, and Jay, now run Doherty Insurance Agency.

Jack Driscoll took advantage of the town's 1934 vote for a liquor license to open a package store at 5 Post Office Avenue in 1936. The store later moved to 42 Park Street, then the corner of Barnard and Bartlet. Today Driscoll's is approaching its sixtieth year. Likewise, McLellan Gift Shop opened in 1933 and survived until 1971. Elm Street Service Station opened in the early 1930s and is owned today by Ron Abraham on Lupine Road. The Gulf Super Service Station on the southwest corner of Chestnut and Main opened in 1936, managed by Charles Baxter. The building was carefully designed "to blend with colonial Andover." John Murray took over in 1940, and David Reynolds in 1962. The next year, it was taken down and rebuilt. From 1972 to 1992, William Tynan managed the station, then Hussein Damergi. Today it is owned by Cumberland Farms.

In 1938 a group of citizens formed the Andover Consumer's Cooperative, Incorporated, patterned after the first co-op store in Rochdale, England, dating

William Reinhold bought out Henry Miller's shoe store in 1939, where youngsters could put their feet into the x-ray machine and see green bones. Bennie's Barbershop opened at 9 Main and survives today at 17 Main as Andover Barber Shop. The present owner, John Freitas, bought the shop in 1993 from Charles Torrisi. Before that, Joe Mazza operated the shop (pictured), having bought it from Steve Balsama, who bought it from "Bennie" Ventura.[18]

from 1844. Principles were: open membership, democratic control, prevailing market prices, and refunds from earning on the basis of purchases. One became a member by buying at least one share for $5. Cornelia Fitts wrote:

Many Andoverians will not yet have forgotten the January frantic cash-slip-gathering for the Andover Consumers Cooperative rebate. The slips had to be tethered, totals at one end, with an elastic band, and the curly tops forced to fit the envelope; and always after a hasty search of purses and pockets. Then two months later, almost forgotten, the check for about one week's food bill would arrive as a bonus. This, the supermarket presided over by a smiling Mary Angus and the Annual Meeting gorge on roast beef, were what the CO-OP represented to most members.

To some, however, and certainly to the founding members, the CO-OP was a movement, an ideal democracy-in-action . . . the motives were both idealistic and practical, for they grew out of discussions on social ethics at the North Andover Unitarian Church and out of the demand for inexpensive food in the midst of a deep depression.[19]

After several homes, the CO-OP moved to the K&D Block at 68 Main Street in 1943. It added to the building in 1954 and 1960, purchasing land around the store for parking. The CO-OP peaked at three thousand families and nearly $2 million in sales by 1968 but in the 1970s, sales declined and the store was sold to the Barcelos brothers in 1975.

FIELDSTONES LUNCHEON AND DINNER
ROUTE 28, MAIN ST., ANDOVER, MASS.

1947

By 1947 the town was entering the postwar boom. Many returning soldiers had opened small businesses. Andover's 1947 Directory shows an epidemic of enterprises "off Railroad Avenue": Andover Manufacturing Company producing leather, Colonial Spinning Mills producing yarns, Murray Tire & Supply, Sealskin Gasket & Packing Company, Harry Stephenson turning out textiles, and Walbuck Crayon Company.

Sally Bodwell opened "Fieldstone's" tearoom in 1937 at 430 South Main Street. Bodwell left during the war, but returned in 1947 with her husband Leon Houghton, to conduct a thriving restaurant business in a quaint atmosphere. It was a favorite spot for anniversaries or birthdays. Betty and Edward Romeo bought Fieldstone's in 1960, selling again to the Andover Elks in 1970. A more modest choice for food was Ann's Andover Cottage across the street. At the other end of town, Kirkshire House tearoom at 174 Lowell Street and Scanlon's Inn at 420 North Main were also popular.

The Musgrove building was home to Donald Look's photo shop in 1943, even while he was still in high school. After a tour of duty which included landing on D-Day, Look reopened his shop, taking photos for the *Townsman* and the *Eagle-Tribune*. In 1954 he moved to Colorado, selling to employee Carlton Shulze, who operated the shop until the mid-1970s. In 1978 Richard Chapell bought into the business, which he moved to Barnard Street.[20]

Andover News at 54 Main Street was run by LeRoy Wilson and his father, Penry "Pop" (pictured). This town nerve center handled the *Boston Globe*, the *Herald*, and the racing sheet, and carried magazines, cigarettes, and school supplies. Alan Wilson remembers his father drove to the depot daily at 3 a.m., where newspapers were thrown off the train onto a truck. They were sorted and ready for the paper boys at 6. "Almost every boy who went through the Andover school system in the 1940s worked for my father as a paperboy," says Wilson. When both LeRoy and "Pop" died in 1957, the family sold the store to Kenneth P. Thompson.[21] Photo courtesy of Alan Wilson.

Off Essex Street were Andover Silver Company and Andover Weaving Company. Merrimack Card Clothing Company at 14 Buxton Court had competition from Redman Card Clothing Company on Red Spring Road. In Ballardvale, P. W. Moody added wool batting to his cotton batting business. Shawsheen Rubber bought the two-story wooden mill building and Watson-Park completed its second decade producing chemicals in Lowell Junction.

New words had entered the language: "baby-sitter," "cafés," and "convalescent homes." Bay State York was advertising "air conditioning." Woolworth's moved into the downtown and Howard Johnson's took over the corner of Routes 28 and 125. A town boasting nine tailors in 1918 was down to just one in 1947. But dressmakers had increased from five to seven. Andover even boasted its own furrier: Robbie's at 15 Barnard Street.

Women of Christ Church established the Andover Thrift Shop in 1941. Borrowing $50 from the church they rented a small space on Post Office Avenue. After three moves the shop ended up at 10 Park Street, which the church bought in 1972. Proceeds have since repaid all mortgages and loans. During its first fifty years of operation, the shop donated $663,111 to the church. Unsold goods are donated to the needy.[22]

Charles Dalton bought Lowe's Drug Store at the corner of Main and Park in 1943, and in 1958 bought the block from the Barnard heirs. Life in the drugstore had its moments. Dalton's son Bill wrote:

One day . . . a man walked into the store and asked for change. He wanted to weigh himself on the penny weight machine. He got his change, walked to the machine, took off all (yes, all) his clothes, put a penny in the machine, got his accurate weight, got dressed, and left. It was all done in a business-like, efficient manner, and was over in a flash.[23]

Dalton sold the pharmacy to Alan Hughes in 1967.

While businesses evolved, the surface of Main Street changed too. The trolley tracks were donated to the scrap metal drive during World War II as were the Civil War cannons in front of the library. In the summers of 1949 and 1950, the 1922 cobblestones were paved over with macadam.

The Rogers family purchased the *Andover Townsman* in 1949. Barnett Rogers, emigrant from Scotland, was an auctioneer, real estate dealer, travel agent, insurance broker, and Andover correspondent for the *Lawrence American*. His son, Alexander, a reporter for the *Lawrence Daily Eagle*, formed a partnership with *Evening Tribune* manager H. Frank Hildreth in 1898 to buy both newspapers. Alexander's son, Irving, worked his way up, taking over as publisher when his father died in 1942. He moved his family back to Andover in 1947. Irving's son, Allan, was managing editor from 1956 until his untimely death in 1962. Another son, Irving Jr., followed his father as publisher in 1982.[24]

In March 1988 the paper won a Pulitzer prize for investigative reporting that revealed serious flaws in the Massachusetts prison furlough system and led to statewide reform. Irving Jr.'s son, Irving "Chip" E. Rogers III, is presently General Manager of the *Eagle-Tribune*. Although the Rogers own both the *Andover Townsman* and the *Lawrence Eagle-Tribune*, they are run by separate staffs. *Townsman* editors David Young, Marcelle Farrington, Robert Finneran, and Perry Colmore have become well-known voices in Andover. In 1992 the *Townsman* moved into a new building at 33 Chestnut Street.[25]

Leaving the downtown and moving south toward the academy, Leon Davidson operated "Leon's Spa" for a number of years at 125 Main Street, which the teenagers nicknamed "Doc's." Davidson leased the front left portion of the building to Langrock's men's store. (The structure was the former South Center schoolhouse, moved to the site by Ovid Chapman). In 1948 Davidson's son, Charles, and son-in-law, Virgil Marson, opened the present Andover Shop. The Birdsalls opened the Coffee Mill restaurant at about the same time in the right side of the building. The store has hardly changed in forty-six years. As Marson says:

We established a positive identification with traditional clothing and stayed with it. Originally, we sold to students, but after the revolution we switched from the schoolboy business to the commuter business. We go to Europe and order things you can't find anywhere else. We even have mail orders from Europe and Japan.[26]

1950s

In the 1950s new highways brought many families seeking country life and good schools. Station wagons clattered up and down Academy Hill. Radio stations WCCM and WLAW kept people in touch with all the latest happenings. Dial telephones streamlined communications in 1958, using the exchange GReenleaf-5. Fathers gathered up children on Saturdays and took them to the dump. On the way home, they might stop for a newspaper and some penny candy at Rickey's Variety, 53 Essex Street. Rickey's had the best fish and chips in town, on Fridays only, for the crowd from St. Augustine's next door. They could check over used cars at Clark Motor Company or J. W. Robinson's on Park Street, or Shawsheen Motor Mart. Then they dropped the children off at the movies in Sam Resnick's Andover Playhouse on Essex Street. Invariably one stopped in at Cole Hardware in the Barnard Block. It was said of Milton Cole that if you wanted a "whatzis" for a "thingamabob," more than likely he had it. Or, if it was not in stock, he'd have it within a week. Furthermore, if he didn't have it, or couldn't get it, you probably didn't need it.[27] The Coles bought the Barnard Block in 1970, selling in 1984 to William J. Scanlon, who had already purchased Hill's across the street. Today, there is no hardware store in Andover.

Mothers enjoyed the new children's store, Jonathan Swift's at 27 Main Street. They could shop for clothing of their own at Michael Jay's, the Carriage Trade Shop, Lee-Antoine Dress Shoppe, or Ruth L. Hammond. For food, there was Johnny's Supermarket on the corner of Bartlet and Park, but Elm Farm opened at Shawsheen Plaza in 1959. The huge parking lot made it convenient to stop in at

Macartney's took over the corner of Main and Central Streets from Lawrence Gas and Electric in 1952. The men's clothing store operated more than forty years in Andover, through three generations. In March 1993 Bob and Gardner Macartney leased the store to Richard Kapelson, who opened his Andover branch of KAPS Menswear, itself a fourth-generation business. Look photo, circa 1950

Woolworth's, W. T. Grant's, or Liggett's Drug Store all in one trip. DeMoulas took over the supermarket in 1966. Next door, Washington Park Apartments were built in 1963.

Family businesses thrived. In 1955 Douglas Howe Sr. founded Howe Insurance and Real Estate at 52 Main Street. In 1977 Howe's business moved to 4 Punchard Avenue, where today his son Doug manages real estate and son Clifford handles insurance. Doug, an Andover native, expresses the frustrations of some business people in Andover today about "preserving the character of the town":

It seems as though there is an anti-business sentiment in the community. The central business district has not been allowed to grow, the parking bylaws prevent many businesses from expanding, and the unfair tax burden that businesses bear as compared to residences are examples of this anti-business attitude. Historically, elected officials, appointed committee members, and town staff do not come from the business world and they may not appreciate how difficult it can be to sustain a growing business in downtown Andover.[28]

Contractor Fred Doyle began selling lumber on Chandler Road in the 1930s (now the site of the Greek Orthodox Church), but when his son Russell tried to expand in 1979, zoning laws identified the area as residential, and the family business moved to River Road in 1984.[29]

The Lindsay family built Andover Animal Hospital in 1958 on the former Lewis Farm on Lowell Street. Dr. Richard Lindsay was veterinarian and his wife Betty handled the administration. By 1993 they had seven veterinarians on the staff, four of them family members. Today, the hospital sees eighty to one hundred patients a day.[30]

Between 1947 and 1953, eighteen new contractors went into business in Andover. The longest-standing was J. E. Pitman (Building Supplies) at 63 Park Street, opened in 1898, operated later by Lee and Forrest Noyes. The company was sold to Lincoln Giles in 1963. Robert Finlayson developed Park Street Village on the site in 1984. Other contractors of note have included Edward P. Hall & Son, George M. Henderson & Sons (William and Allan) in Ballardvale, Arthur E. Steinert in Shawsheen Village, Hardy and Cole, Perley Gilbert, Harry Axelrod, Jim Hamilton, and Yvon Cormier.

1960s

A proposed 1962 urban renewal project would have leveled all the buildings on both sides of Main Street from Chestnut to Elm. During reconstruction, eighty-seven businesses would have had to close for more than a year and forty residents would have been evicted. Phid Dantos remembers:

I was running my family business, the Andover Spa, and John Davidson was running his, the Andover Shop. He came down to see me one day, saying, "We should do something about organizing opposition to this." We felt that it had taken three hundred years to develop the character of the town, and they wanted to make a cute little Lawrence out of it with concrete buildings and parking spaces. We thought the young people in town could fix up a few blighted areas and the town would be fine. Irving Rogers was supporting us with his newspaper. We won, and after Town Meeting we went back to the Spa to celebrate. Then John said, "Now we should do something about it." Right then we formed Danton Realty Trust.[31]

Davidson and Dantos razed the old Square and Compass Club in Elm Square in 1964, built the Masons a new building on High Street, and erected "One Elm Square" for Standard International Corporation in 1966. Since 1977 the building has been office condominiums. They purchased the A&P at 90 Main Street in 1965, renovating it for the Andover School of Business. Owner Charles Liponis planted a gigantic IBM mainframe in the window and registrations soared. In the early 1970s the building housed shops such as Brigham's Ice Cream. Today Gardenia Boutique and Bertucci/Menucci restaurant occupy the first floor.[32]

One renewal plan called for Town Offices at 85 Main Street, which was purchased by the town in 1944 and converted to a parking lot in 1957. At 77 Main Street Karl C. and Geneva H. Killorin lived and Karl conducted his real estate office for many years. Fearing their land would be taken by eminent domain, they sold to Davidson and Dantos in 1965.[33] Davidson, Dantos, and Nicholas Aznoian moved the Killorin house back, attaching a modern building to the front, home to Aznoian's House of Clean. Thompson's Stationers used the other half of the new building before moving to 45 Main Street, and since 1992, different banks have occupied the space. The renewal plans spurred several builders into action. On the corner of Bartlet and Park, Purity Supreme replaced Clark Motors and Johnny's Supermarket in 1965. The same year, Friendly Ice Cream was built at 16 North Main. The Public Safety Center, was built at 32–36 North Main in 1969. Olde Andover Village was built in 1961.

One of the first tenants in Olde Andover Village was the Andover Bookstore. This was the oldest business in town, linked with the Andover Press and founded in 1808, supplying textbooks for generations of Phillips Academy students. When Jerry Cross, fourth generation owner of Cross Coal Company, and his wife, Ethel, bought the store in 1960 it occupied the front portion of the Andover Press Building. Ethel recalls the bookstore warmly:

In 1961 Lincoln Giles purchased the Hulme house at 93 Main Street, left, and the Scott-Stowers house at 89 Main, which he incorporated into a little mall named Olde Andover Village. Albert E. Hulme practiced dentistry in his house for fifty years. Physician Cyrus Scott and then dentist Nathaniel Stowers, also used 89 Main for offices.

It was not a large capital investment even in those days. The bookstore did not have to serve the same economic aim as Cross Coal which was our livelihood. But it eventually became a very profitable little bookstore. You have to be a little patient. Book buying is contagious. Jerry and Lincoln Giles worked together on the barn that became the bookstore. We tried to make it warm, inviting, and personal. We were Andover people and one of us was there all the time. We were helped by a renaissance of reading in the 1960s and were proud of our children's section.[34]

The Crosses used no cash registers, computers, or sales slips, only a cash drawer, and to open a charge account, one simply left one's name and address. They laugh about one incident:

One night when we closed the store, a little boy was locked in. He was twelve or thirteen, and was embarrassed because he was in the adult books section, so he hid. Police heard him a couple of hours later knocking on the window. Luckily,

it was summer and still light and warm. When they unlocked the door he darted out and ran along home without a word to anyone.[35]

The Crosses sold the bookstore to William and Carolyn Dalton in 1989. They sold to Robert Hugo in 1992. Other stores in the complex have included Sutherland's, Phinney's TV and Records, Yankee Lady, Hiscox Domestic Goods, Susie Sweets Bakery, the Shoe Tree, Vena Coco Collection, Mary Ann's Card Shop, Williams Jewelry, Young Fashions, Home & Abroad, Andover Video, Designing Kitchens, Supercuts, Daher's Shoes, the Lantern Brunch, and What's Cooking? restaurant.

1970s

By 1970 the Musgrove building had fallen into such disrepair that the roof collapsed. Robert Webster of North Andover purchased and renovated it in 1973, selling to the Liberty Group in 1984. Eagle Investment bought it for $2,925,000[36] in 1987. In June 1990 it won an Andover Preservation Award. It is now owned by James White and Stephen Steinberg. Street-level tenants include Enzo's of Andover, Merrill Lynch, Lydia's Hair and Nails, and Josef's Men's Hair Styling.

In 1972 Eugene A. Bernardin III and George Heseltine bought the Andover Press building and Bernardin had moved his offices into the rear space. Bernardin started his insurance and real estate business in 1947 on Park Street. Heseltine, president of the Chamber of Commerce and selectman, owned Dana's Sport Shop in the front portion of the building. In 1975 Bernardin bought out Heseltine.

Main Street was streamlined in 1980, when Andover Bank expanded into two neighboring properties. The bank had to wait for the lease at Millie Vogel's Taylor Shop to expire and Scanlon's Hardware (formerly Hill's) refused to sell, so it had to build around both stores. Culverts containing Roger's Brook made it necessary to raise retail space on a walkway. This 1950s view shows the buildings before change.

Today, Bernardin's daughter, Amy, is president of the firm, and son Daniel is also active in the business. Gene Bernardin, who died in 1989, felt it was his duty to be active in the community. He chaired the Town Planning Board, the Board of Selectmen, the Board of Trade, Visiting Nurse Association, Red Cross, Rotary Club, was trustee of Lawrence Savings Bank, and president of the Chamber of Commerce. He was instrumental in planting trees along Main Street to replace the stately elms.[37]

Across Chestnut Street, Carlos, John, and José Barcelos bought the Andover CO-OP in 1975, establishing Barcelos Market. Residents today still miss this convenient grocery in the town center. In 1990 the Barcelos closed the market and added a second story, matching the 1924 Merchants' Block. CVS and Shawmut Bank are the present tenants.

1980s

In June 1982 the 1910 Barnard Block was placed on the National Register of Historic Places and after its restoration by William J. Scanlon, received an Award for Historic Preservation. Purchased by Tom Belheumer in 1994, it presently houses Bruegger's Bagels, the Coffee Connection, the Chocolate Shop, Athlete's

Corner, Vincenzo's Restaurant, Mid-Asian imports, Christina's bridal shop, and Silverado women's fitness center. Not to be outdone, Merrimack Valley National Bank (now BayBank) renovated its 1890 building in 1982, removing rear portions, adding modern space, and rehabilitating the 1890 façade. In 1982 the building was named to the National Register of Historic Places.

After the change: the Andover Bank addition, left, houses Courtney's, Nazarian's, Waldenbooks, a bank operations center, and Daher's for Kids shoe store. Photo courtesy of the *Andover Townsman*

1990s

In latter years, Andover's choices for banking have greatly increased. In addition to the Andover Bank and BayBank, one may stash one's cash in First Essex Savings at 211 North Main Street (1977) or 71 Main Street (1994); Lawrence Savings Bank at 342 North Main Street (1980); Bank of Boston at 20 Central Street (1986); Shawmut Bank at 68 Main Street (1991); Fleet Bank at 84 Main Street (1991); or First Federal Savings at 77 Main Street (1992).

Andover High School students of today tie on roller blades to skate down to the video store. They buy bagels at Bruegger's, Perfecto's Muffins & Bagels, and the Butler's Pantry. Dunkin' Donuts has three outlets. Pizza is plentiful between Bertucci's, King's, the Depot, Domino's, and My Brother's Pizza Place. Pizza is one thing you can still have delivered to your home, but to find a hardware store, it's a long skate to Reading or North Andover. The nearest movie theater is in South Lawrence. For tapes or CDs, they must drive to suburban malls. There are twenty-four restaurants in town but only one full-service grocery store for thirty thousand people. We no longer live in isolation. Into the modern age we go, like it or not.

District Schools (1795 on)
(some had several buildings in succession)

Abbott 1795-1904 – Chandler Road and Brundrett Ave.
Bailey 1795-1926 – Bailey Road*
Chandler 1795-1828 – Chandler Road (divided into West Center and Frye Village)
Osgood 1795-1930 – Osgood and Bellevue streets*
South Center 1795-1888 – Central St. next to South Church* (moved to 125 Main St.)
Scotland 1795-1902 – Wildwood and South Main (burned 1902)
Holt 1797–1901 – Salem Street and Gray Road*
Frye Village (Richardson School) 1828-1924 - Lowell Street and Iceland Road; razed 1964
West Center 1828-1952 - Lowell and Beacon Streets; sold at auction then torn down in 1952
Phillips 1828-1889 – Highland Road* (moved; now 1924 house at Phillips)
Abbot Village 1828-1952 - Cuba Street (several buildings; one is now a residence at 28 Cuba Street) A
        playground occupies the site today.
Ballardvale – 1837-1889 - Andover Street, Ballardvale;
        later Ballardvale Community Center; demolished 1981
North School 1837-1947 - River Road and North Street; demolished 1984

Centralized Schools (1866 on)

John Dove School 1878-1952 – Bartlet Street (originally Center District School)
Bradlee School 1889-1958 - 149 Andover Street* (now condomiums)
Stowe School 1888-1971 - Bartlet Street (originally Central Grammar School) burned 1981
Indian Ridge School 1893-1952 - Cuba Street; demolished 1958
Samuel Jackson School 1910-1981 - Bartlet Street (demolished 1982)
Shawsheen School 1924-present - Ann's Way* (now an alternative school)
Andover Jr. High 1936-1982; renamed East Junior High in 1968 - Bartlet St.*
        (now School Administration offices)
Punchard High School 1856-1957 – Bartlet Street* (now Town Offices)

Modern Schools (1950s on)

Central School 1952-1981 - 36 Bartlet St.* (renovated and renamed Doherty School, 1972)
West Elementary School 1952 - Beacon Street*
Andover High School 1957 - Shawsheen Road* (now West Middle School)
South Elementary School 1958 - Woburn Street*
Henry C. Sanborn School 1962 - Lovejoy Road*
Bancroft School 1968 - Bancroft Road*
West Jr. High 1968 - Shawsheen Road* (former Andover High School building)
        renamed West Middle School in 1988
Doherty Jr. High 1982 - 36 Bartlet Street* (former Central Elementary School building)
        renamed Doherty Middle School in 1988
Greater Lawrence Regional Vocational Technical High School 1965 - River Road*

Andover High School 1968; Collins Center 1982 - Shawsheen Road*[10]

*Building still exists
Lists compiled by James Batchelder.

Chapter Ten

Andover's Pride in Education

Andover Public Schools

When Carol Winkley Znamierowski entered kindergarten, she little realized she was preparing for her future career as purchasing and transportation coordinator for the Andover Public Schools. It was a time of tremendous population growth. District schoolhouses were closing and sprawling modern buildings were being erected. Carol remembers:

I was brought up at the Livingston Apple Farm on Lowell Street. I entered kindergarten at Indian Ridge School in 1946 and stayed one year. Then I was sent to West School, a two-room schoolhouse at the intersection of Lowell and Beacon Streets for grades one through three. In fourth or fifth grade, they sent us down to the Stowe School on Bartlet Street. By sixth grade, the new West Elementary School on Beacon Street had opened, and they sent all sixth graders there. For Junior High, I came to this building [the present School Administration Building on Whittier Street]. *In tenth grade, I moved next door to Punchard High School, but the following year they opened Andover High School on Shawsheen Road (now West Middle School), so I completed my last two years there, graduating in 1959. I had an awfully long bus ride because there was just one bus for all of West Andover.*[1]

Carol's second school, West Center School, was the last district schoolhouse. Although Carol's memories are vague, her teacher, Isabelle Dobbie, remembers every detail:

Every morning, I had to unlock the door, go down to the cellar, and put my hand in a little closet full of spiderwebs to turn on the urinals for the boys' room. I hated spiderwebs. Then I'd put up the flag. One day a policeman came to the door because I had put up the flag upside down, the distress signal.

You had to plan very carefully to teach two grades at once. I'd have the reading group from one grade at the front of the room. The other group had written work. They knew they were not to make a sound or interrupt unless they

Isabelle Dobbie recalls, "I came to teach at West School in September 1946. One room was seventy-five years old and the other was 103 years old. I taught a class of thirty-six, first and second grades combined. Georgianna Hilton taught third and fourth graders."

broke a leg. We concentrated on reading, language development, writing, math, and penmanship. The physical education, art, and music teachers each came one day every other week. It was like a big family—the children were eager to learn and the parents were very supportive.[2]

Isabelle Dobbie was named principal of West Center School just before it moved to West Elementary in 1952. The school was already too small, making an

Andover built its first schoolhouse in 1701, and five schools were added in outlying areas in 1757. The District System was created in 1795. Prudential committees had autonomy for building schoolhouses and hiring teachers, but a School Committee came around to administer exams.[3] Abbot District School (1795–1904) is pictured here, with Mabel Roxie Bailey in the foreground.

When Andover changed from a district to a municipal system in 1866, many one-room schoolhouses were built with separate entrances for boys and girls, like the Scotland District School. Courtesy of Louise Batchelder

Teachers pose for photographer Charles Newman before Indian Ridge School.

addition necessary by 1956. In 1970 Miss Dobbie moved to Shawsheen School as principal and in 1980 she became principal of Sanborn.

Whenever possible, the School Committee hired teachers from Andover. The Stack sisters lived at 20 Summer Street. Of ten children in the family, five became teachers. Alice taught fourth grade for forty-three years and Eunice taught sixth for forty-six years, both at Stowe School. Rita Stack Cronin taught in Pelham, New Hampshire, and Methuen, then returned to Andover in 1948, teaching twenty-one years at West School. In all, the three sisters taught 111 years in Andover.4 Except during World War II, women were asked to resign from teaching if they married, thus losing the career and the income. School Committee minutes for October 2, 1928, read:

. . . that it be a policy of the School Committee to employ hereafter, unmarried women teachers and that in case of women teachers in service become married, their resignation be requested, policy to become effective after June, 1929.

The first brick school, Richardson School in Frye Village, was built in 1848.

An interesting experiment was the open-air classroom at John Dove School from 1918 to 1919. The School Committee reported:

This school consists of 34 pupils of the fifth grade. The room has windows on three sides which are kept sufficiently opened to keep the temperature between 45 and 60 degrees during cold weather, the steam heat being on continuously . . . the pupils were each provided with a coat, bloomers and hood . . . and felt boots which reach to their knees . . . The teacher was also supplied with a coat, hood and boots by the town . . . So far the results from the fresh-air school have been very satisfactory. There has been scarcely a cough during the whole term and very few other illnesses. The children like the fresh-air room very much.[5]

Transportation was not attempted by the town until 1901, when Holt District school closed and Mrs. C. H. Brownell was hired to drive its students in a horse-drawn barge to Stowe School. Alvah Wright began driving a barge in 1909, and when buses came in, continued driving for fifty years. In 1919 it was voted to bring students by car from the Haggett's Pond area. Previously, many high school students were obliged to take the train to Lawrence and the streetcar to Andover, a two-hour trip, and the Ballardvale students took the Boston and Maine line to the Andover depot.

The 1920s and 1930s were a time of stability. Henry C. Sanborn, a self-made

man with progressive ideas, was superintendent of schools from 1916 to 1939. Nathan C. Hamblin (pictured), a scholar and a gentleman known for his interest in each student, was principal of Punchard from 1910 to 1941. Eugene "Pop" Lovely joined the staff in 1911, heading the science department and coaching football and baseball teams for thirty years. He succeeded Hamblin as principal.

Punchard alumna Frances Dalton taught art at the high school from 1940 to 1968 and headed the Art Department for all schools. Her mother was Mary Dalton of the Metropolitan

Nathan C. Hamblin was principal of Punchard High School from 1910 to 1941. Look photo

Bakery. She studied at the School of Museum of Fine Arts in Boston and at the Sorbonne in Paris. She always dressed flamboyantly. Dalton said:

A stilted, programmed art curriculum can never meet students squarely nor follow them down the unexpected paths they pursue. The unimaginative, uncreative teacher covers them with blanket assignments, exercises, gimmicks, and her own limited sense of all things. She smothers them at birth or worse still, tears the seeds from the fertile soil from which they spring. This is done so she may "control" the classroom and control it she does by producing pseudo-creations with frightening death-rattles. She produces conformity of thought. She is never aware of the damage she is doing; that their imaginations are slowly being "laid to rest." If they are not rescued by some teacher who cares and knows how to care they may be lost forever or worse still, so crippled that they are tormented for the rest of their lives.[6]

Of Dalton's students, 115 went on to higher education in art.

There was a temptation following the successful terms of Sanborn, Hamblin, and Lovely to let the system continue along as it had been. When Virginia Cole moved to Andover in 1952 with her husband, Milton, she was struck by what she saw as an antiquated situation:

When I moved to Andover in 1952 I was shocked to find that my daughter was using the same textbook in first grade that I had used in upstate New York a generation before. The children were seated alphabetically year after year, and teachers were assigned alphabetically as well. If you wanted Adeline Wright and your name was Cole, you were out of luck. When I went to observe in my daughter's classroom I was kicked out. One of my daughters was dyslexic. The teacher would cover her paper with red marks, than hold it up in front of the class for the other children to laugh at, saying, "This is ___'s paper." She never recovered. I hate those teachers.

Punchard Free School, founded in 1856 by bequest from Benjamin Punchard, went from private to public funding in 1901. Endowment was no longer adequate, so Town Meeting voted to establish Punchard High School.7 In 1957 when a new school was built on Shawsheen Road, the name was changed to Andover High School. Pictured is the 1917 school with the 1871 building behind it. 1934 photo courtesy of *Eagle-Tribune*

Punchard's Class of 1935 was the only class without a yearbook, due to the Depression.

Concerned parents persuaded Dr. Milton Meyers and John Sullivan to run for School Committee as reform candidates. Then Barbara Moody ran. She was frank, honest, worked hard, and pushed Superintendent Erickson. I ran and served two terms. We managed to hire a business manager and an assistant superintendent willing to work on curriculum. When Bancroft was built in 1968, I thought it was the most marvelous thing I'd ever seen. The idea of learning at your own speed was wonderful.[8]

The school population quadrupled between 1945 and 1970, resulting in a frenzy of school building. Of these, Bancroft School was the most controversial. Former Town Manager Richard Bowen observes:

It was terribly exciting. There was a critical need for space; we were in double sessions. Bancroft was designed in response to educational specifications developed by the School Committee which dictated an open school design, and was built of the most common materials: wood, cement blocks, and concrete. People called it Early American Hay Barn.[9]

Some said, "It looks like a medieval castle!" Others argued, "But who would love to learn in a medieval castle? Kids, of course." Isabelle Dobbie reckons, "If we had all the money that's been spent on that roof, we could support the whole system for a year." Bancroft teacher Adeline Wright observed:

We went in "trailing clouds of glory" and believing that every child could get all the education he or she needed there. But it wasn't long before we found that certain children needed a more contained situation.[10]

The debate was between traditional education and open classroom. West Elementary added an open classroom wing in 1970. In 1972 walls were removed in Central Elementary. But in 1974 the backlash set in. Huge building expenses and declining test scores caused three conservative members to win seats on the School Committee, ousting liberals. The Committee fired Assistant Superintendent

Punchard students appear eager to learn in Ida Grover's 1954 Latin class.

Technology developed during World War II influenced building styles, which went from vertical to horizontal. New heating systems and insulation made it possible to send heat through long, brick, one-story buildings. Pictured here, clockwise from lower left, are Stowe School, Central Elementary, Punchard High School, Memorial Auditorium, Andover Junior High, and Samuel Jackson School, next to the power plant. Look photo

Bancroft School's imaginative design by architect William Warner earned it a national award from the American Institute of Architects, one of the ten best buildings constructed in the United States in 1970. Richard Graber photo, May 1975

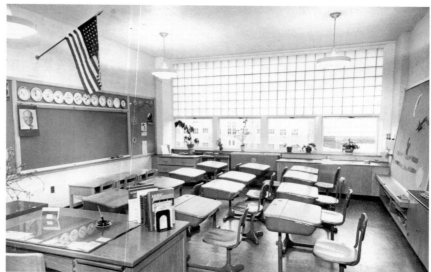

This Eisenhower-era classroom at Central Elementary overlooks John Dove School. Courtesy of James Batchelder

Walls were removed in Doherty School (formerly Central Elementary) in 1972 to create open classrooms.

Edward Regan in order to implement a standard 3R education. Regan sued the School Committee. Although he won, he did not return to Andover.

Dr. Kenneth Seifert was superintendent through the turbulent years 1969 to 1990. In the 1974–75 School Committee report he observes:

In the past decade, Andover students have been on an educational merry-go-round. Community thought dictated continuous progress from 1967 to 1973. From 1973 to the present we have been told the community has a desire for a more structured approach to education with greater standardization . . . During both periods Andover educators addressed themselves to the task and performed well.

In the same report, committee member George Oleson Jr. concluded:

It should be noted that a majority of your School Committee has been the target of media criticism for the abrupt way it attempted to change the educational direction of the Andover Public Schools. In retrospect, we (John Lyons, John Wragg, and myself) might have attempted too much too quickly, but the need was there.

In the 1990s the approach has been to balance developmental needs with structure. Dr. Mark McQuillan succeeded Seifert in 1991. McQuillan was obliged to cut $2.5 million from the school budget due to declining state aid to schools. Thirty-five teachers and several administrators were let go. Although the school population decreased between 1975 and 1990, it was rising again by 1991. Building maintenance and capital improvements had been deferred. "New" schools were now forty years old. McQuillan observes:

Ken Seifert did a fine job of galvanizing resources and establishing Andover's reputation for excellence. I've faced different dilemmas. Budget shortfalls and overcrowded buildings have consumed most of my time, slowing down many of the things I was originally hired to carry out. I have become a standard-bearer

Andover High School, 1968 to the present. EMR photo

for our school construction and renovation program. Despite it all, the students have been wonderful. They are what make the Andover Public Schools the Andover Public Schools.[11]

As early as 1956, residents felt the time had come for a vocational school. Led by Fred Tarbox, they worked hard to make the school a reality. The school was chartered in 1963 and opened in 1965. It was the second vocational technical school in the state, and the building, designed by Korslund, LeNormand, and Quann, became a model for twenty-three other schools. It drew students from Andover, North Andover, Methuen, and Lawrence, supervised by its own School Committee and superintendent. The original name, Greater Lawrence Regional Vocational Technical High School, was shortened to Greater Lawrence Technical School about ten years ago.[12]

The first superintendent, James Booth, managed with limited funds as he waited for grants. The 357 male students were required to wear jackets and ties to school. In 1973 the building was expanded and girls admitted for the first time. Louis Gleason followed Booth from 1976 to 1991, struggling with limitations imposed by Proposition 2 1/2. He was determined to bring computer literacy into the school, from the days of key punch to the most recent keyboard and screen, as a requirement for both students and staff. The present superintendent, Marsha McDonough, has emphasized an integration of academic and technical curricula. The school offers the following "shops": automotive, auto body, allied health, carpentry, CAD/CAM, cosmetology, data management, electronics, food technology, graphic communications, machine shop, metalworking, plumbing, small engines, major appliance/air conditioning, and distributive education. Students alternate a week of shop with a week of academics, receiving a high

school diploma upon graduation. Shop certificates include a state mastery certificate listing the student's competencies. There is a full athletic program. About 36 percent of graduates go on to post-secondary education. Today more than 50 percent of the fourteen hundred students are Spanish-speaking. A transitional program emphasizes English as a second language and offers courses in Spanish until students are mainstreamed. The 1993 Freshman Class contained well over 65 percent minority students including Hispanic, Cambodian, and Vietnamese.

Andover High School Class of 1989 graduates salute the flag. From left, they are: Bobbi Jean Williams, Sheila Marie Wilson, Michael Winters, Wanda Witkowski, Young Juk Won, Jennifer Wood. Senter photo

Andover's Private Schools

Founded in 1914 by the Sisters of Notre Dame in the former Tyer residence (left), St. Augustine's present building opened to eight grades in 1918. Newman photo

Those wishing a Catholic education for their children might send them to St. Augustine's School at 26 Central Street. Helen Reilly remembers:

When St. Augustine's was built, everyone wanted to go there. It was a new school with new books. I had four brothers and three sisters and four of us went:

Barney, Kay, Peggy, and myself. We had to walk there from Shawsheen and we stayed together. The nuns were strict. One day my brother Barney misbehaved and one of the nuns put a dress on over his clothes to punish him. My sister was so mad she went right over and got him. The nuns would carry little wooden signal sticks which they would snap for attention. They would hit you on the hand with them if you were bad.[13]

Archbishop Cushing poses with students at Sacred Heart School, founded in 1946 for Catholic boys in grades four through eight. Brothers of the Sacred Heart purchased the administration building, athletic fields, and later the Crystal Ballroom from American Woolen Company. By 1961 enrollment reached 250, but later declined, obliging the school to close in 1975. Look photo

Between 1959 and 1962 the Cross family's former carriage house was renovated as a convent and a wing added to the school. In September 1962, school opened with a record enrollment of 537. By 1965 fourteen Sisters were teaching 636 children. Today, St. Augustine's has an enrollment of 470.

Although the Catholics were the only religious group to open a full primary school, nursery schools were established at Free Church (1958), West Parish (1959), Christ Church (1969), St. Robert Bellarmine (1970), Ballardvale United Church (1972), Unitarian Universalist Church (1975), and Temple Emanuel (1980). Today both Phillips Academy and Pike School offer extended care for young children, and independent day care centers provide further choices.

While the public schools struggle with funding, they do have the economy of the town behind them. Private schools, on the other hand, are basically business ventures, responsible for raising their own funds, balancing budgets, and pleasing their clientele.

In 1908 Amy Briggs started Briggs and Allen School in the Arco building with five pupils. The coeducational school grew to sixty-two students. When Mrs. Briggs died in 1933, her daughter, Lucy Eaton, conducted the school at 49 Abbot Street until 1941.[14]

The Marland School opened in the early 1940s at 8 Elm Street, later moving to 106 Main Street. Edna ran the school with some help from her sister Charlotte. Robert Monette attended the school from 1958 to 1965 because Andover schools could not handle a child in a wheelchair with spina bifida. Today he is a lawyer and a certified public accountant who prepares candidates for the CPA exam. He remembers:

When I first got there as a very young child, there were other children with normal intelligence. But it evolved into a school for special ed [education] problems and the mentally retarded. I was the only one for a long time with normal intelligence. Now that I am a teacher myself, I can appreciate how hard it was for Edna. She was very religious. Her family founded Christ Church and she started each day with a hymn accompanied on the reed organ. It was a one-room school with old wooden desks with inkwells and a lot of dogs who smelled. Out front on the porch she ran a dusty old curiosity shop, and she also took in boarders—old men who wandered around during the day. They were good people and good to me. Edna talked to me like an adult and made it clear to me that I was intelligent. But the education was nonexistent.[15]

Enrollment in 1959 was twenty students, ranging from pre-primary to eighth grade. The school closed about 1970.

The Pike School was founded in 1926 by Mrs. Cynthia E. Pike on her sun porch at 126 Lowell Street. In 1944 it moved from its second home in Shawsheen Village to 5 Porter Road, where it remained until headmaster William H. Harding and the trustees foresaw the coming population growth. They built a new school on Sunset Rock Road in 1963. Pike educates about four hundred students yearly, from pre-kindergarten through grade nine. It has not grown much since the move to Sunset Rock Road because it has chosen not to, according to English teacher Tony Dyer.[16] Classes average twelve to sixteen students. The faculty has grown considerably, however. While other schools were forced to curtail art and music, Pike added a new Arts Center in 1985, expanding its offerings in chorus, glee club, and instrumental programs. An annual art show exhibits the work of every child. Pike emphasizes athletics in all grades and interscholastic sports beginning in grade six. Today 50 percent of Pike students come from Andover, 25 percent from North Andover and 25 percent from thirty-three other communities. The student body has changed markedly in diversity. Forty-four students speak another language at home. The school is consciously working on economic as well as ethnic and cultural diversity.[17] Nearly all Pike graduates choose private secondary

During the Depression, Pike School rented space in the administration building in Shawsheen. Pictured is the 1928 first grade. Among the back row are Preston Johnson, John Collins, and Gloria Field (White). Among front row students are Constance Cole, Judith Hardy, and Donald Boynton. Photo courtesy of Preston Johnson

education. More go to Phillips Academy than to any other school, with Brooks School in North Andover a close second.

The Academies

Until 1973 Abbot Academy was the choice for girls. Founded in 1829, it was the first academy incorporated in Massachusetts for girls only. Although it always struggled financially, it had its benefactors. Warren Draper, owner of the Andover Press, was a close ally of principal Philena McKeen, donating heavily to the gargantuan Draper Hall built in 1890. Burton S. Flagg, president of Merrimack Mutual, worked closely with principal Bertha Bailey in the 1920s and 1930s. Flagg's careful stewardship of funds kept Abbot afloat through the Great Depression.[18] An Abbot education was once considered complete unto itself, but under principal Laura Sophia Watson (1892–1898), it divided into two paths: college preparatory and the academic course. Teacher Katherine Kelsey expressed nostalgia for "the time when girls read Livy and Horace . . . because they wished to do it, and not because the reading was prescribed by any college for admission to its doors."[19] Emily Adams Means, principal from 1898 to 1911, supported the academic course, while her successor, Bertha Bailey (1912–1935), favored college preparation. Bertha Bailey was a legend unto herself. A graduate of Wellesley, she accepted the low salary offered by the trustees with the qualification, " . . . for the present. Should my value to the school increase, as I trust it may, I am sure the Trustees would recognize the fact."[20] She built physical and psychological walls around the school. Walks to town were prescribed for different days and on different routes than those frequented by Phillips boys. Cathleen Burns Elmer, a member of Abbot's Class of 1935, remembers:

The boarders were very interested in boys and felt as though they were in

Susan McIntosh Lloyd in her history of Abbot observes that the only edifice built under Bertha Bailey was the Merrill Gate (1922), which could be locked on Sundays. Draper Hall and Abbot Circle are in the background. Look photo

prison. Their hormones were raging. There were tea dances which were very closely chaperoned. Life was easier for day students like me. We were connected to the town as well as the school and have remained loyal to the school over the years because of that double bond. The Depression was a period of constant anxiety, while my brothers and I struggled to hold onto scholarships which paid for our education. During the Depression there was always money for those academically achieving, especially at Phillips. The headmasters were brilliant and insightful with strong social concerns.[21]

Bertha Bailey died suddenly in 1935 and Marguerite Hearsey took over. During her nineteen years, which Lloyd calls a "golden age" for Abbot, Hearsey hired the first Catholic teacher, alumna Jane Sullivan, and admitted the first Black students, Beth Chandler and Sheryl Wormley. Her successor, Mary Crane, initiated fall mixers and allowed girls to sit with boys during the second half of football games. But teachers who saw Abbot girls talking with boys on the village street were still required to cut the conversation off at five minutes.[22]

Applications soared through the 1950s, but declined in the mid-1960s. Trustees Philip Allen and Grenville Benedict began working toward a merger between Abbot and Phillips. They hired Principal Donald Gordon, a "missionary for coeducation,"[23] in 1968. The decision was not a simple one. Abbot Alumnae feared their school would be simply "swallowed up."

Phillips Academy was by far the larger. Founded in 1778 by Samuel Phillips, it had a two-hundred-year reputation of excellence. From 1891 to 1913, alumnus Melville Cox Day donated five dormitories and two cottages, beginning the first

At the beginning of the twentieth century, Phillips Academy was still a relatively small cluster of buildings across the street from Andover Theological Seminary.

major development of the campus. Previously most students had boarded around town. From 1924 to 1932 Thomas Cochran and Headmaster Alfred E. Stearns led the second great development, hiring designers Guy Lowell of Boston, Charles Platt of New York, and the Olmsted Brothers in Boston. In the years following, George Washington Hall (1925), Morse Hall (1928), Paul Revere Hall (1929), Commons (1929), Oliver Wendell Holmes Library (1929), Phillips Inn (1930), Addison Gallery of American Art (1931), and Cochran Chapel (1932) were built.[24] Cochran donated a large part of the cost himself. School historian Frederick "Fritz" S. Allis Jr.[25] explains that Cochran's wife died in 1914, and their only daughter died at nineteen, so he poured his energy into his old school.

The school was led by dedicated headmasters. Alfred E. Stearns emphasized academics along with sports and moral values. In addition he served as school chaplain and town moderator. Claude Fuess, English teacher, historian, and author, emphasized intellectual integrity. John M. Kemper, one of the founders of ABC, related intellectual experience to the building of character, supporting Josh Miner in Outward Bound. Theodore R. Sizer presided over the transition to coeducation. He also led the Bicentennial Campaign for $52 million, then the largest amount ever raised by a secondary school. Donald McNemar encouraged diversity, seeking students from many backgrounds to live and learn together.[26] In 1928 the title "principal" was changed to "headmaster." When Barbara Landis Chase succeeded McNemar in 1994, the title was changed to "Head of School."

In 1978 the school commissioned Fritz Allis' *Youth From Every Quarter*, a history of Phillips, and Susan Lloyd's *A Singular School*, a history of Abbot. These authors give the two faculties proper credit for the outstanding job they have done in and outside the classroom over the years, coaching sports and the arts, and monitoring dormitory life for hundreds of bright, healthy, and restless adolescents.

Paul Monette, in his autobiography about growing up gay in Andover, *Becoming a Man: Half a Life Story*, demonstrates how one great teacher could pierce all the pain and confusion of adolescence to bring young minds alive:

All that [senior year struggle] *was secondary, though, when I lucked into Dudley Fitts's English IV. He was the one true Olympian on the faculty. The Sophocles we used in class had been translated by him and Robert Fitzgerald, a feat of erudition that seemed almost Biblical to us. To hear Mr. Fitts talk about Greek theater, how the chorus moved, how it sounded—you were there. The prodigious learning was tempered by a rollicking wit, delivered in an absent-minded drawl, half to himself so you had to crane to listen. Yet more than anything it was the humanness of the questions he asked of a line of poetry, bringing to bear feelings we hadn't dreamed of naming . . .*

He would have us so rapt, or me anyway, that we all forgot that he never rose from his chair or wrote on the blackboard. Because he was brutally disabled, some kind of degenerative muscular disorder, MS maybe . . . 28

When the Seminary pulled out of Andover in 1908, Phillips purchased its two-hundred-acre campus for $200,000.[27] **Here, students enjoy space in front of the old stone chapel circa 1920.**

Thomas Cochran dramatically altered the look of the Phillips campus. Samuel Phillips Hall (center) was built in 1924 and Bartlet Chapel (renamed Pearson Hall) moved back to create the Great Quadrangle." At left and right are Foxcroft (formerly Phillips) and Bartlet Halls.

The issue of coeducation came to a head in the 1960s. Headmaster Theodore Sizer observed that when he arrived in 1972:

They hadn't made a decision. I saw both academies going through the tortures of the damned. Applications were falling off as they were in all boarding schools across New England. It was clear to me decisive action had to be taken by the Boards of Trustees. The only respectful thing was to merge the schools.[29]

The combined school owned 160 buildings and 450 acres. The merger was eased in, first by joint activities, then by coordinate classes. Mary McCabe, Abbot '71, remembers:

In 1969 the German teacher at Abbot got sick and they didn't replace her. Instead they sent three of us up to P.A. It was the first integration of classes. The first day, everyone was sitting out on the steps of Samuel Phillips Hall. Teachers stopped in their tracks, dropped their books on the ground and followed me with their eyes as I walked across campus. The second year, the teacher told us to bring tea and cookies to class. I knew this wasn't right, but we did it. The teacher has since turned around quite nicely.[30]

Ten years later, Phillips commissioned a study of coeducation at the Academy, written by Kathleen M. Dalton as *A Portrait of a School: Coeducation at Andover.*[31] Dalton observes: "In the late sixties and early seventies a wave of coeducation swept up single-sex schools and colleges across the country, in part because students no longer wanted to be cloistered and in part because all of a sudden it seemed old-fashioned and even discriminatory to exclude applicants because of their sex." [32] Today, 8 percent of Phillips students are African or African-American; 5 percent Latino, and 15 percent Asian. Ten percent are from other countries. Forty percent receive financial aid with 10 percent on full scholarship.[33] "This is what it means to be committed to youth from every quarter in the 1990s," says former headmaster Donald McNemar.

Higher Education

By 1900 Andover Theological Seminary had fallen on hard times. Allis and Lloyd attribute some of the decline to the "Heresy Trial" of 1886–1887, when the Board of Visitors tried to oust five liberal faculty.[34] The Board had been set up in

1808 to "guarantee the continued orthodoxy of the professors."[35] In addition, the rising social gospel was based on city life and required additional courses only available in a great university.[36] Allis observed, " . . . the Seminary began to suffer from its relatively isolated position, at one time considered one of its great advantages."[37]

In 1906 the trustees voted "that the interests of the Seminary would best be served by a removal to Cambridge,"[38] completed in 1908. Andover Theological Seminary's library was installed at Harvard. The former rivals did not actually merge, but lived side by side very successfully. When they tried to associate more closely, however, the Board of Visitors objected on the basis of the Andover's 1808 creed. Eventually the Seminary merged with Newton Theological Institution, a Baptist School, in 1931. But Harvard would not give back the library, known today as Andover-Harvard Library.

Andover was not without a theological school for long. St. Francis Seraphic Seminary came in 1930, a minor seminary for Catholic high school boys interested in the monastic life and the priesthood. Built on the former Hood farm off River Road near Tewksbury, the school was owned by the Friars Minor of the Immaculate Conception Province of the United States. It offered college-level courses for ordination to the Catholic priesthood in the Franciscan Order from 1930 to 1946.[39] In 1952 students from St. Anthony's Seminary, a junior college in Catskill, New York, were transferred to Andover, staying twelve years. Every June the seminary celebrated the St. Anthony Festival when pilgrims from Metropolitan Boston converged for Mass, Communion, and sacraments. About five thousand people would arrive with picnics to enjoy the beauty of the grounds, the festival atmosphere, and spiritual renewal. The seminary closed in 1977.

Andover Theological Seminary, founded by Trinitarian Congregationalists to counteract the Unitarian heresy at Harvard in 1808, was the pride of Andover for one hundred years. Seminary Row included, from left: Phillips Hall, Bartlet Chapel, and Bartlet Hall.

At Christmastime, St. Francis Seminary was decorated with sixteen thousand colored lights. One year, an estimated two hundred thousand people came to see them.[40] Father Claude Scrima, a student at the time, recalls, "From September until January the seminarians were involved with the lights after school. Every bulb was stripped and dipped annually. If we hadn't done our homework, we'd just say, 'I was working on the lights.' We trapped ourselves with that excuse because they finally discontinued it."[41]

In 1968 a new building was built and named the Christian Formation Center and by 1990 the Franciscan Center opened. This retreat and education center uses both the former Seminary and Christian Formation Center buildings. Father Claude has returned as a member of the new retreat team.

Merrimack College was founded by the Order of St. Augustine in 1947, responding to the demand for colleges by returning G.I.s. Six Haverhill businessmen enlisted the aid of Archbishop Richard Cushing and raised the money. Land was purchased at Wilson's Corner, and seven Augustinians moved into the Murphy residence on Peters Street. "The Andover-North Andover line ran right through the front door," says Father William J. Wynne, O.S.A., one of the first faculty members. A temporary classroom building was erected to accommodate the incoming class of 165, all male, ninety-nine of whom were veterans.[42] From the beginning, there was a demand for coeducation, but the first president, Father Vincent McQuade, was told, "It will greatly complicate your problems, particularly at the start . . ."[43] Students boarded in nearby homes where a representative of the college would check each evening at curfew. The first female students arrived in 1950, but the first dormitory, Ashe Hall, was not built until 1958.

The Augustinian College of the Merrimack Valley, as it was called, offered Arts and Science courses, but half the student body chose business. Postwar enterprises desperate for trained workers were willing to help with funding and guarantee jobs upon graduation. While the first class was 99 percent Catholic, the school was always conscientiously open to all. This was not solely a matter of philosophy, but of practicality, since the new school would be applying for government grants. In 1968 the name was changed to Merrimack College to de-emphasize the visibility of the religious affiliation. Today, with an enrollment of

two thousand, Merrimack has come a long way. Father Wynne observes:

The fact that the college was in Massachusetts, and in Andover/North Andover in particular, helped us from the start. Phillips Academy was gracious from the beginning. We were able to use their facilities, and they welcomed us as another all-male school.[45]

Andover even has its own law school. Massachusetts School of Law opened in 1988 at Dundee Park, moving to River Road in 1991. By 1993 the school had eight hundred students, but accreditation was denied by the American Bar Association although it had received permission in 1990 to grant degrees. It is accredited with the Board of Regents and graduates are qualified to sit for the bar exam in Massachusetts and ten other jurisdictions. It is presently engaged in a lawsuit with the American Bar Association. As of June 1994 the school had produced 395 graduates.[46]

In summary, former Phillips Academy headmaster Theodore Sizer says:

This is a town that values education. People work toward this in both the public and private sectors. A good example is the library trustees where representatives from Phillips have been involved. The town has a remarkable library and its circulation figures are off the charts. The two school systems reinforce and support each other. This common commitment lifts the level of all schooling in town.[47]

Merrimack College purchased the seventy-acre Richardson farm in 1947.[44] Architect William B. Colleary designed the first building on campus, Cushing Hall, in 1949. Joseph McGann designed Sullivan in 1951, Austin in 1952, and the Chapel in 1954.

The little stone building on Shawsheen's green only showed the tops of its chimneys in the 1936 Flood, the worst in Andover's history. An early spring thaw and torrential rains caused the Merrimack to back up into the Shawsheen, flooding Marland and Shawsheen Villages. Rowboats plied up and down Haverhill Street. A garage on North Main Street floated into a neighbor's yard and 109 homes were evacuated. As the flood receded, two hundred youths from the CCC descended on the Shawsheen Village with shovels to clean up.[1]

Chapter Eleven

Plagues and Disasters

Plagues

In 1918 the nation was swept by the Spanish Influenza epidemic. On September 27 Andover's Board of Health closed public schools, Colonial Theatre, and Memorial Hall Library as a precautionary measure to slow the spread of infection. The public was advised to wear masks when caring for the sick and to use paper plates and cups, burning them immediately after use. Cardinal William O'Connell, archbishop of Boston, suspended Mass, but advised Catholic families to offer "such prayers to Almighty God the Eternal Father as might have Him appease this terrible scourge that now affects so many of our people."[2] The *Townsman* gave weekly updates. On October 11 the total was up to 634 cases in town. The average was twenty new cases per day.

It was wartime. Andover Company H was dispatched to Lawrence, where an open-air hospital had been set up in tents on Emery Hill. Many Andover citizens volunteered there, where they had to observe scrupulous sanitation procedures, wearing sterilized masks at all times. The *Townsman* reported:

The mask is thrown from the outside of the house through a slit in the wall. It lands in a large kettle of boiling water, then it travels through two or more boiling processes until it reaches an electrically heated oven in which it dries in a short time and is then ready for use again . . . bedding and all other articles used in the sick-room have their special houses in which they are sterilized and cared for.[3]

Andover suffered 1,503 cases in 1918, resulting in twenty-five deaths. The Board of Health reported, "Compared with the death rate throughout the state from influenza, our percentage has been remarkably low."

Everett Penney, Andover's director of public health today, says immunizations and antibiotics have done away with most infectious diseases. Smallpox vaccination began to be strictly enforced in 1898, followed by diphtheria immunization in the 1920s, tetanus about 1950, polio in 1955, measles in 1963, mumps in 1967, and rubella (German measles) in 1978. Emphasis gradually shifted to the study of environmental factors in disease. But Penney cautions:

Now bacteria are developing resistance to antibiotics and we are seeing the return of diseases like tuberculosis that are antibiotic-resistant. This is also true of some venereal diseases like syphilis and gonorrhea.[4]

The following diseases were listed as cause of death in the 1910 Annual Report:[5]

Consumption (tuberculosis)	7
Whooping cough	1
Typhoid	1
Erysipelas*	1
Infant cholera	3
Cholera	3
Pneumonia	6
Bronchitis	1
Heart disease	14
Diseases of the brain and spinal cord	10
Kidney disease and Bright's disease	9
Cancer	6
Suicide	1
Accident	5
Other	28

*a bacterial disease resulting in fever and severe inflammation of the skin

These diseases were combatted by milk inspection and pleas to clean up garbage. The Board of Health disinfected houses with formaldehyde after illness. It reported the quarantine policy in 1915:

We have had occasion to quarantine several persons who are wage earners, and in such cases they are entitled to an amount equal to three-quarters of their pay, provided it shall not amount to more than $2 per day.[6]

In 1918, 154 babies were born in Andover. Of these, thirteen died before age one, and five between ages one and five, an infant mortality rate of eighty-six per thousand live births.[7] Andover's infant mortality rate was zero per thousand in 1988, one in 1989, three in 1990, and one in 1992.[8]

In 1916 the first two cases of infantile paralysis (polio) appeared, one at Phillips Academy and the other a child in the public schools who played among the other children for some time before being diagnosed. The Board concluded: "It would seem that the danger of contagion from personal contact and association must be very slight." Nevertheless, school openings were delayed. That same year, Grace Woodburn was hired as the first school nurse. There were eight cases of Polio in 1927, seven cases in 1935, then none from 1936 to 1940. Many residents growing up in the 1940s and 1950s remember they were not allowed to go to public swimming areas because of the polio scare. While traveling, the family would take a picnic to avoid public restaurants. Ice cream was off limits. In 1955 the annual playground trip to Canobie Lake Park was cancelled. Andover had nine cases of polio, the highest ever. But that year the Salk vaccine came in, starting with first and second graders. In 1956 three thousand residents were vaccinated, and in 1957 five thousand residents, first with painful shots, but later with a drink from a little paper cup.

Bruce and Lee Dodd moved to Andover in April 1954, one week before the birth of their fourth child. They loved Argyle Street, where the children could run up and down the sidewalk with their friends. On August 7, 1955, they went out for dinner with their friends the Robertsons. Lee remembers:

The next morning, Bruce did not feel well. He went to work and came home again, and lay down on the sofa. I thought he had the flu. By the next day, he was

Lee Dodd was thirty-one when her husband, Bruce, thirty-four, contracted polio. EMR photo

Lee Dodd was thirty-one when her husband, Bruce, thirty-four, contracted polio. EMR photo

unable to get up to go to the bathroom. I called the doctor Sunday who sent him to Lawrence General and then Boston for tests. Monday, the hospital phoned and said he was in a respirator. I didn't know what it was. When I got to the hospital, he was in an iron lung. Bruce had Bulba polio and encephalitis. He was very sick and delirious for quite a while. When he recovered, he was completely paralyzed, except that he could turn his head and one hand. I saw Bud Lewis at Mass General. His wife had polio and she died that October.

All the kids vanished off the street, understandably. Pomp's Pond, where we had swum a lot that summer, cleared out. Only one of my friends, Bernice Warshaw, would come into the yard, although many called to offer support. Thayer Warshaw organized a group to raise money and the Andona Club brought us supper for a month. Bruce was in the hospital for a year and when he came home he spent all his time on a rocking bed with a respirator. We decided to make our house a place of welcome. My kids would bring in their friends to show off Bruce. There were so many, he had to make a rule they could only have a ride on the rocking bed if it was their birthday. Polio vaccine had already come in. Our oldest daughter had been given the Salk vaccine before Bruce got sick. Then of course we all were vaccinated.

Bruce got half his income for half a year. One day, Beverly Darling called and asked if I'd like to try Real Estate. After working for Beverly and several other people, I opened my own office in 1959. Bruce lived for twenty years, dying in 1976 just after seeing his first grandchild.9

Bruce Dodd's children remember that he was always there for them, as his son Douglas said, "He was a person who couldn't stand on his own two feet and yet he showed everyone around him how to stand on theirs."10

Throughout the century, the leading cause of death has been heart disease. According to a recent study, the death rate per hundred thousand people in Andover is 160.5 from heart disease and 117.5 from cancer (both lower than the state average), and 35.8 from breast cancer (considerably higher than average).11 Skin cancer and malignant melanoma death rates are also high among Andover men in their fifties, according to a Boston University and American Cancer Society study in 1992. Town Meeting voted in 1994 to ban smoking in all municipal buildings, restaurants, and public areas of retail stores.

The successor to the epidemics of old is AIDS (Acquired Immune Deficiency Syndrome). First identified in 1981, AIDS has no survivors. Originally appearing in male homosexual populations, AIDS soon spread to heterosexual populations, children born of AIDS-infected mothers, intravenous drug users, and those receiving contaminated blood transfusions. Since 1981, eleven cases of AIDS have been reported in Andover.12

Disasters

The Blizzard of 1898 was a storm to remember. Gale force winds drove two feet of snow into twelve-foot drifts. Trolleys and trains stalled, stranding passengers. Phone service broke down. Cost of cleanup was an unprecedented $3,000. The next day, temperatures dropped to 25 below zero and a lamplighter making his rounds suffered frostbite.13 There would be other blizzards, always measured against 1898. The "epochal" storms of February and March 1920 paralyzed trolleys for six weeks. In 1935 the *Townsman* reported the "worst snowstorm since 1898" and dual blizzards in March 1956 caused $10,000 damage. Back-to-back snowstorms in February 1969 dumped 34 inches in one week. A freak snowstorm on May 9, 1977, embarrassed residents who were leaving Town Meeting after a vote to cut funding for snow removal and the forestry department. The heavy, wet snow landing on fully leafed-out branches caused broken limbs everywhere.14

But the new record came in 1978, when the largest storm in memory brought Eastern Massachusetts to a halt. Thirty inches of snow were whipped by hurricane force winds in a storm that came on suddenly Monday, February 5, and verged on whiteout for most of Tuesday. It blew out a large window at Barcelos Market. Snow mounds in the business district ranged from 8 to 20 feet high. Governor Dukakis declared a state of emergency and banned road travel. Schools and businesses, including Raytheon and Western Electric, closed for a week.15 Tom Koravos at Ford's Coffee Shop recalls:

The snow was so high I had to dig a tunnel to the front door. People came downtown on skis, toboggans, showshoes, and sleds. It was just like a winter holiday. Men, women, and children parked their skis outside and came in for

Two children benefit from the Blizzard of 1898.

Residents traveled in sleighs as town rollers drawn by four horses cleared the snow in 1898, aided by men with shovels.

An ice storm in December 1921 ravaged trees at 18–20 Summer Street.

hot chocolate. "What a nice little shop," they said. Some had never been here.[16]

Phillips Headmaster Ted Sizer got a call from the Andover police. "Do you have any kids with shovels?" they asked. Protestant Chaplain Philip Zaeder mobilized 150 students. First they cleared out the Town House, then helped senior citizens at Frye Circle, Chestnut Court, and in private residences. "They dug out some people who hadn't eaten in a day," says Sizer.[17]

Until recently, the winter of 1947-1948 held the record for snowfall at 89.3 inches in Boston and 118.9 inches in Andover. The Boston record was broken in 1993-1994 with sixteen snowstorms totaling 96.3 inches, "the snowiest winter ever."[18] But Andover actually had more snow in 1992-1993, with 109.5 inches, compared to 90 inches in 1993-1994. Ironically the summer of 1994 had the hottest June–July stretch since records began in 1872. Average daily maximum temperature was 85.4 degrees with heavy humidity.[19]

Unseasonable rains landing on frozen ground caused a winter flood in 1979. River Road and Woburn Street were closed and Elm Street was a waterway according to the January 27 *Eagle-Tribune*. Ballardvale mills were flooded, and DASA Electronics in the Marland Mill suffered $250,000 damage when water rose to the first floor windows. Fifty residents were evacuated on North Main Street, including twenty-four units at Washington Park. Binney Street residents had to be evacuated by boat.

Flames engulf the former Hood barn on Franciscan Seminary property. Look photo, 1940s

The coming of spring did not always mean Andover was out of the woods. In April 1927 West Andover suffered a four-day forest fire. Starting Sunday on Wood Hill Road, it "roared and thundered through the pines and birches," swept across High Plain Road and crept down both sides of Cross Street. The *Townsman* reported:

Less than half a mile from Reuben Webb's on Cross Street the fire-fighters stopped the advancing flames by skillful backfiring. It was arduous work and if anyone wants to work for 50 cents per hour it can be earned three times over with a shovel controlling a back-fire. A facetious spirit, resting for a moment, suggested that if three of the Town's most prominent objectors to a new fire pump could be reached by telephone there was a shovel for each of them along the fire line.[20]

Tuesday, the fire broke out again and raced over a small cabin without scorching

Head washman Tom Neil helps bookkeeper Maude Drosos out of Shawsheen Laundry in the 1936 Flood.

it. Firefighters were surrounded, barely making it out alive. Wednesday, the fire swept southeast from High Plain Road toward three farms. Andover's aging fire apparatus broke down and an emergency call was made to Reading. Firefighters protected Bliss Stock Farm with backfiring and the other two with soaking from the Reading pump. Finally, it was stopped by a spectacular backfire in the Fish Brook swamp.[21]

Summers brought heat which sometimes caused mills and stores to close in the days before air conditioning. Autumns brought hurricane season. One of the great hurricanes of the century struck Wednesday, September 21, 1938. There was no warning and it had been more than one hundred years since New England had experienced a hurricane. Power went out quickly and the fire alarm was sounded by hand, summoning emergency workers. The *Townsman* reported:

An official estimate of the number of trees blown down was 350, which could only have been a guess since the trees came down so fast that no count was really possible. Officer Winthrop White, stationed at the desk, received almost continuous telephone calls for several hours during the night . . .[22]

In 1898 a summer cyclone on Holt Hill tore the roof off Miss Annie Sawyer's barn. Twenty-seven cattle were buried in the debris and a summer's worth of hay ruined by violent rain. A henhouse containing forty hens was blown 100 feet.

A huge tree fell across the Abbot homestead. Central Street near Hartwell Abbot bridge was the worst hit, and a cluster of giant trees fell together at Maple and Summer. Many fine old trees were lost at the academies.[23] With two-man hand saws, workers cut away sections just wide enough for a car to pass through. Trees were dragged off the road with trucks. The most spectacular damage was at Tyer Rubber on North Main Street, where the roof blew off, scattering bricks and girders onto Lewis Street.[24]

Hurricane Carol hit August 31, 1954. Chain saws were just coming into use. The *Townsman* reported, "At the beginning of the storm the town hired all of the power saws it could get, but since then has bought four units at a cost of $1250." Bulldozers pushed hundreds of tree trunks to the side of the road. 25 Pictured is 25 Central Street. Look photo

Sam Rogers remembers the Marland Mill during Hurricane Carol in 1954:

*Weather reports weren't very good in those days, so we didn't have much warning. When the water started to rise, Joe Higginson, the superintendent, and I had the men move all electric motors to the second floor. Then we realized that would not be enough. We had to move them all up to the third floor. We were moving machines night and day. All the electrical wiring was wrecked, and the dam got busted. It was months before we were in business again. I remember going through the mill with Joe in a rowboat to assess the damage. There's a plaque on one of the buildings marking the high water mark.*26

Barbara Nichols, daughter of the president of the Andover Companies, and Bill Kurth were married September 18, 1954, a week after Hurricane Edna. They had invited four hundred guests. Barbara's mother, Arita, remembered that people drew together to help out:

*Two trees had fallen across our front door, so we had to ask the town to come cut them away so the bride could leave for the church. Power was out everywhere. But St. Augustine's School had emergency lights which they shone across the street so our guests could find their way into Christ Church. Once inside, we could light the service with candles.*27

Such storms test the mettle of town employees. Smaller hurricanes have come and gone, while town staff struggled to maintain life as usual. During Hurricane Bob in 1991 intrepid traffic control officer David Cantone rode around in an open jeep pulling branches off the roads.

The most eerie disaster in recent memory came November 9, 1965. Televisions began to flicker, then streetlights faded. At 5:22 p.m., the town lost power completely. When residents turned on transistor radios, they learned that lights were out from Toronto to New York City. An uneasy feeling crept in. Had the Russians invaded? Was it aliens from Mars? The Andover Selectmen's meeting proceeded, lit by one bulb from the emergency generating system at the Town House. Only Paul Cronin was missing. Flying in from Washington, his plane was forced to land in Portland, since Logan was dark. Five planes circled at Lawrence airport until emergency power could light the runway.[29] Heat began to dissipate in the 30-degree night. Dinner plans went from hot food to sandwiches. Only at the Andover Inn, powered by the Academy's generator, did guests dine in full light. Power was out for three and one-half hours. The explanation was that a backup relay had given out on a main transmission line near Toronto. Power was then transferred to four other lines, which became overloaded and tripped the relay switches. The system shifted the load to other plants, which became overloaded and shut down. The chain reaction affected thirty million people over eighty thousand square miles from Canada to New York City, where the blackout lasted about thirteen hours.[30]

Twelve days after Carol, Hurricane Edna dumped six inches of rain. Roger's Brook rose so fast that many families did not realize they were surrounded until too late, and boats were dispatched to rescue them. Pictured is lower Bartlet Street. Weary crews set to work redoing their repairs of the previous week.[27] Look photo

Clifford Wrigley determined that Leonard Sherman helped Architect Perley Gilbert design the town seal mosaic in the Town House in 1900 and revised the town seal design for the *1906 Town Report*. Earlier, when the state decreed every town should have a seal in 1899, William Harnden Foster won the design competition while only twelve or thirteen. The *Townsman* stated, "the new town seal, similar to that used for the 250th Anniversary, was adopted."[1] Jeweler John Edward Whiting had designed the 250th Anniversary seal for a souvenir cloisonne pin. An 1896 photograph shows it in Whiting's shop window, and Andover Historical Society has a few samples (pictured). Whiting's advertisement in an 1895 *Townsman* says he drew Cutshamache standing on Indian Ridge pointing to the town below.[2]

Chapter Twelve

The Evolution of Town Government

For a long time, the source of Andover's Town Seal was a mystery. It pictures the Sachem Cutshamache selling "Cochichawicke" for six pounds and a coat. In "The Townswoman's Andover," Bessie Goldsmith said the general consensus was that local artist Leonard Sherman was the designer. Later, Caroline Underhill and Margaret Dodge at the Andover Historical Society traced it to artist William Harnden Foster. Finally in 1986 and 1987, retired art professor Clifford Wrigley researched the seal's design back to jeweler J. E. Whiting.

The seal may be relatively new, but the design of the town government goes back to earliest times. It was based upon the congregational system of church government, a reaction to the English authoritarian model. While the earliest records are lost, a Town Meeting record survives from 1656. Only male landowners were members of the Meeting. In listing the earliest town officers, Sarah Loring Bailey first mentions four selectmen in 1671.[3]

At sixty square miles, Andover was much larger than the average Massachusetts town. Since 1711 South Church had served as a second community center, and West Parish became a third in 1826. Punchard Free School was to be built in South Parish, leaving North Parish a little resentful. On March 6, 1854, Town Meeting voted it "expedient to divide the town according to the boundary line between the North and South Parishes, or thereabouts."[4] The legislature postponed it for a year. At Town Meeting in 1855, the issue was defeated but by then the Senate committee on towns had decided division was a good idea and despite opposition from the North Parish, the vote was in favor at a special Town Meeting on June 11, 1855. North Parish became North Andover and the South and West Parishes kept the name of Andover.

Andover paid North Andover $6,500 for losses, providing a complete copy of the town records (before the days of photocopies, this must have been no small task). Andover got the Almshouse and North Andover students had the right to attend Punchard School. The form of government stayed the same in both towns.

Three outstanding public servants were Roy Hardy and Sidney P. White, each of whom served as selectman for eighteen years, and J. Everett Collins, who served for twenty-one years. (A full list follows in the Appendix.) Barbara Loomer, retired executive director of the Andover Red Cross, describes their style of government as follows:

They ran the town as they ran their own businesses, building on the present with a look to the future. One reason our town is so well-planned is because of

Day-to-day operations were in the hands of three selectmen and numerous other officials, usually involved in full-time businesses of their own. Although they worked hard, town government was basically a part-time affair. Pictured at Shattuck's Country Store, from left, are: Selectman Sidney White, Barbara Loomer, and Edward Shattuck.

Thaxter Eaton served as town treasurer from 1929 to 1956. Eaton was so careful with town funds that he hand-delivered checks to save three cents' postage. George Winslow served a contemporaneous term to Eaton's as town clerk from 1931 to 1960.

the foresight of its selectmen in the 1930s and 1940s. People today have no idea of what went into the building of this town. These men never counted the hours they spent, basically as volunteers with little compensation. The town had a personal touch then. You called Roy or Sid or Everett with a question or a complaint and you got a personal answer.[5]

Women served on the School Committee in the 1890s, but the first female selectman was Janet Lake in 1974. Mary Collins was the first town accountant in 1930 and Anna Greeley succeeded Thaxter Eaton as town treasurer from 1956 to 1972. Greeley was a graduate of Punchard, Boston University, and Portia Law School. She served on the School Committee from 1950 to 1956, and on the Andover School Building Needs Committee. She practiced law sixteen years, and was treasurer of her father's grocery firm, the James E. Greeley Company, before taking the town treasurer job.

A hundred years after towns divided, some residents began to feel that local government needed reorganizing to accommodate the rapid growth. The League of Women Voters played a major part in changing the Town Charter in the 1950s to establish a system with a town manager and five selectmen. Barbara Moody remembers, "Some League members had come to the area with Western Electric in North Andover and AVCO in Wilmington. They had come from growth communities in places like New Jersey and brought new ideas."[6] The Andover Government Study Committee, headed by Howell Stillman, favored the town manager system. It would provide "a single trained official who would devote full time to the administration of the Town's affairs."[7] The manager would be more accessible than the present selectmen. Under the new charter, no selectman, School Committee member or Finance Committee member could hold another office. (Sid White had served simultaneously as selectman, assessor, welfare board member, and chairman of the Board of Public Works.) Voters were currently electing fifty individuals; the new charter would reduce this to twenty-six. Central purchasing would save money.8

Opponents believed the plan was "aided and abetted by a large number of new people who moved into town over the war years."9 It was breaking a long-time New England tradition. It was undemocratic. Retired Selectman Everett Collins asserted that only a "sick town" needed a town manager. He also argued cost: "Now, what is the initial expense of this town manager experiment? First a manger at at least $10,000 per annum, an executive secretary of no less than $5,000 per annum, and one or more purchasing clerks at from $60 to $70 per week or more. What then I ask you is to be saved?"10 The League of Women Voters, led by Wendy Forbes and Marion Laaf, formed study groups, visited other towns, studied their charters, and sent out flyers. The Andover Taxpayers' Association was another major supporter, led by Henry Wolfson. Town Meeting voted to study the change in 1955. The first year the issue was on the ballot, 1957, it was defeated (2,791 against—1,745 in favor). The League redoubled its efforts, sponsoring neighborhood coffees and hiring babysitters for Town Meeting. The second year, it passed (3,138 for—2,792 against). Town Meeting retained ultimate power and the Finance Committee would continue to review expenditures.

All incumbent selectmen were defeated in the 1959 election. William Stewart defeated Sidney White by five votes. Victor J. Mill Jr. served as volunteer town manager while a professional manager could be hired. He remembers:

I had friends in both groups, so I guess they thought both sides could trust me. Dave Nicoll, an excellent man, was police chief and Henry Hilton was fire chief. Anna Greeley was town treasurer and Stanley Chlebowski was in charge of highways, parks, and recreation. Edward Erickson was superintendent of schools. So I was really an "honorary town manager" with that group. We brought the town office over to my company, Lawrence Pumps Incorporated in Lawrence, and designated one gal to take the calls. All the layers of town government we have now were nonexistent.11

In June 1959 Thomas Duff was sworn in as the first professional town manager. He was succeeded by Richard Bowen (1965–1968), J. Maynard Austin (1969–1977), Sheldon S. Cohen (acting 1977), Jared S. A. Clark (1978–1981), Kenneth A. Mahony (1982–1990), and Reginald "Buzz" S. Stapczynski (1990–present). Richard Bowen and his wife Lucy stayed in town after his term was completed, raising six children here. He was elected selectman in 1976. He observes:

It wasn't a case of "throw the rascals out." The town was not disenchanted with its existing government. It had simply outgrown the old system. The first town manager was amiable, and had a difficult time saying no. I was hired to be a strong administrator and found it difficult to say yes. I worked to strengthen the internal system in town.12

Each town manager has made his unique contribution, coordinating the efforts of elected officials, paid staff, and an army of volunteers who throughout our history have served hundreds of hours on boards, commissions, and committees, empowering town government by the people and for the people. The Police and Fire Departments are now appointed by the town manager with the selectmen's approval. From the earliest days, the town had a "constable." The colonial period was not necessarily a time of model behavior. Bailey cites a 1678 case where one man, angered by damage done by his neighbor's horse, threatened to shoot the animal. The disagreement resulted in a knife fight where one man's face was slashed.14 Nevertheless, the Bylaws of 1895 do appear to come from a kinder,

Present Town Manager Buzz Stapczynski says, "I think the town manager system worked out better than they envisioned. I'm not God or the mayor. The policymakers are still the selectmen. I administer the policies they establish. I try to stay with the Board in their thinking, to work in partnership with their opinions and ideas. The Boards will stay. I won't."13

gentler age. If moving a house will cause damage to trees and shrubs, the house mover must pay damages to the trees' owner. "No person shall pasture any cattle, goats, or other animals, either with or without a keeper, upon any street or way in the town." "No person shall coast or slide on any sled . . . upon any public street or way in the town . . . But the Selectmen . . . may by public notice designate any streets where coasting may be permitted . . ."[15]

The police force in 1896 consisted of one full-time chief, George Mears, at $600 per year, and eight part-time men, dividing $460 between them. The chief reported sixty arrests, with drunkenness the chief cause (ten of the sixty). Seven incidents of larceny totaled $250 in value, while value of property recovered was $150. Five people were arrested for insanity. Officers patrolled on foot, and even the chief took the streetcar to work. As late as 1920, they hired a car from W. J. Morrissey when needed.[16]

Photographer Donald Look captured the 1940s Andover police force, led by Chief George Dane. At far left are Raymond Hickey and Jack Deyermond.

A century later, the 1993 expenditure for Police and Fire Department salaries was $6,499,951.50. The police force numbered forty-six officers, ten volunteer auxiliary officers, nine dispatchers, six matrons, three and a half clerical staff, an animal control officer, and a traffic control officer. The first female police officer, Sgt. Barbara Connolly, was hired in 1980. Today, the force owns nine police cars, two motorcycles, a three-wheeled parking enforcement vehicle, and eight other vehicles. The figures suggest a diminishing crime rate. Arrests for larceny decreased from 691 in 1989 to 386 in 1993. However, domestic violence is on the rise with thirty-three arrests in 1993. Chief James Johnson reports, "We are empowered to protect life and property, but, with the changing times of increasing social problems, our agency has become more service-oriented to the community."[17]

Certain families have had a long tradition of service. Lt. John K. Lynch has served twenty-seven years. His father John M. Lynch was an auxiliary policeman, his older brother, Laurence, was also a policeman, and two of his cousins, David and Raymond Lynch, are firefighters. His father's cousin, Sgt. James Lynch, served thirty years on the police force. James' son, Jim, is now deputy fire chief, and Jim's daughter, Jacqueline, is a firefighter. Lt. Hector Patullo has three sons; Brian and Don are policemen and Cliff is a fireman. Brothers Philip and Frank Froburg are presently both police officers. Lieutenant Lynch has seen significant changes over the years. In the 1940s and 1950s, the force was dominated by

Officer Roy Russell patrols Main Street on a motorcycle in 1953. Look photo

Scottish Protestants. In 1967 no officers had college degrees, while today, there are few who do not. Portable radios for every officer have dramatically increased coverage. Police revolvers have been upgraded to nine millimeter automatics. Lynch remembers just two shootouts in Andover. One was a drugstore robbery in the 1960s where his own brother on duty. The robber came at him with a knife, and Laurence Lynch shot the man in the knee. The second was a robbery at Lawrence Savings Bank in Shawsheen, July 18, 1980. Lynch recalls:

A couple of gentlemen rushed into the bank and one jumped over the counter. They didn't see Sgt. William MacKenzie standing by a large pillar. It was an inopportune time to make a challenge, as there were civilians nearby. When the man jumped back over the counter and headed for the door, MacKenzie shouted, "Stop, police!" He and the individual were shooting at each other at close range around the column. MacKenzie hit him, but had to pause to reload his revolver. The individual hobbled away, got in a car, and sped off down 495. He was apprehended in a Boston hospital. Sergeant MacKenzie received Police Officer of the Year awards from both the Commonwealth and the Massachusetts Police Association.[18]

The only death in the line of duty was Officer Robert Black, aged twenty-eight, who was standing on Main Street one evening in 1925, when he received a call in a nearby phone booth about a robbery in Lawrence. Shortly afterward, he stopped a car coming down Main Street because its left front brake was smoking. He recognized the license number. The car stopped in front of Andover Savings Bank and the man jumped out. Black could not find him until he reappeared from an alley. Black followed him down the sidewalk and the man turned and shot him point blank. The murderer escaped.[19]

During the last century, Andover's police force has been led by chiefs William L. Frye (1900–1907), Llewellyn P. Pomeroy (1907–1909), George Mears (second term: 1909–1914), Frank M. Smith (1914–1932), George A. Dane (1932–1952), David L. Nicoll (1952–1979), and James F. Johnson (1979–present).

Today's Fire Department chief, Harold Hayes, who is writing a history of the Fire Department which dates from 1829 with the "Friendly Fire Society," relates that when the towns divided, North Andover got two fire engines and Andover got one. In 1862 the Friendly Fire Society was renamed "Shawsheen Steam Fire Engine Company." Gradually, hand-pumpers were replaced by horse-drawn steam engines. One was installed at the 1864 Ballardvale Station which was relocated on Andover Street at the corner of Clark Road in 1895. A new fire station was built behind the Town House in 1882. An alarm system was linked to the telegraph in 1887, and electrical alarm boxes installed around town in 1897.

Andover's Fire Department was established by Town Meeting in 1924, with Charles F. Emerson, chief. C. Edward Buchan succeeded Emerson in 1941, and the work week was reduced from eighty-four hours to seventy-two. Henry L.

Lt. Albert Cole remembered one truck and a pair of horses at the Fire Department in 1919. Four men worked five twenty-four-hour days, then got a full day off. Pay was $18 a week. Brush fires were fought with small tanks. Cole said, "The men would keep on the run spraying the chemicals on the fire, scuttling back to the wagon to get more soda and acid, then to the water hole or well . . . to fill up with water."[20] Two of Cole's sons, Albert Jr. and John, followed their father as firefighters.

Hilton replaced Buchan in 1956, and the West Andover fire station was built on Chandler Road in 1966. The work week shrank to forty-two hours. When the department moved to the public safety building in 1970, Harold Hayes saved the old firebell. He worked all winter in his spare time to clean and polish it, displaying it on the lawn on North Main Street. In its layers of polish, he found names and dates of firefighters in days gone by.[21]

William Downs was the first chief appointed by the town manager in 1977, followed by Harold F. Hayes in 1986. Today firefighters must complete training at the Massachusetts Firefighting Academy and become emergency medical technicians. The first female firefighter, Maryann Frechette, was employed in 1988. The department includes forty-eight firefighters, thirteen lieutenants, five deputy chiefs, and one chief.

The first motorized fire truck was purchased in 1912, and the first ladder truck in 1923. Look photo, circa 1940s

When the town manager charter came in, the Board of Public Works was abolished and individual departments reported directly to the manager. This became cumbersome, so in 1970 Maynard Austin hired Robert E. McQuade as Public Works director. "When I came," says McQuade, "Andover was still openly burning trash at the Town Dump, it was still pouring raw sewage into the Merrimack River, and the town had a chronic water shortage problem."[22] Over the past twenty-five years, the dump was closed, trash shipped to a waste-to energy plant, and recycling initiated. But it is in water that McQuade has his special interest, and he has written a history of Andover's water system.

The first water pipes were laid from Rabbit Pond to thirteen hydrants in 1886. Town Meeting voted to construct a water system in 1890 and $188,263.82 [23] was appropriated for the Andover Waterworks. By 1893 water commissioners provided water for one hotel, one public stable, five manufacturing buildings, twelve public buildings, twenty-four stores or offices, three churches, two depots, three laundries, seven greenhouses, one racetrack, five clubhouses, and 662 families.[23] The system was extended to Ballardvale in 1902.

In 1941 the town developed a master plan for water and sewage. New mains were run to Bancroft Reservoir and West Andover. In 1958 the safe yield of Haggett's Pond was 1.5 million gallons per day (MGD) but water consumption averaged 1.9 MGD. Residents had to live with repeated water bans. Upon the

HAGGETT'S POND FROM THE PUMPING, STATION
ANDOVER, MASS.

Top: "The introduction of water has been a boon to many of our citizens, but its disposal has become a veritable nightmare," wrote the water commissioners in 1896. The Sewer Board was created in 1893, but construction did not begin until 1898. The *Andover Townsman* reported that Italians working on the new sewer were paid 12 1/2 cents per hour. By 1903 they had made 367 sewer connections. Here, workers rest on Bartlet Street.

A pumping station was built on the Haggett's Pond in 1889, and a reservoir off Bancroft Road.

advice of consultants, a dam was built in 1967 at the mouth of Fish Brook to pump water back into Haggett's and a chlorination facility and pumping station were constructed.[24] In 1974 a twelve MGD treatment plant was built on Haggett's Pond, designed by Camp, Dresser & McKee of Boston with considerable input from McQuade. In 1991 it was expanded to twenty-four MGD, and ozone treatment was added, reducing the need for chemicals. The plant was designed to meet an ever-increasing number of federal and state standards. The building was named the Robert E. McQuade Water Treatment Plant.

McQuade is also responsible for highways. In the early days, roads were everybody's job. It was ordered in 1661:

. . . that every male person of sixteen years shall upon three or four days warning attend the mending of the highways upon forfeit of double damage for every day's neglect by any person and soe likewise everie teame, that is, every man fower shillings a day so neglecting.[25]

196

In 1896 the state road (Route 28) was rebuilt from the Lawrence line south toward Andover center and the first streets were paved. Snow was rolled, not plowed. In 1905 two snowrollers were purchased, weighing 4,380 pounds each and requiring four horses to pull them. Police regulations of 1895 specify:

No person shall sprinkle, scatter, or put upon any sidewalk, crossing, or street, or upon the rails, switches, or other appliances of a street railway . . . , any salt or mixture of salt, except in accordance with a permit from the Selectmen.[26]

Streets were sanded by truck for the first time in 1920. By 1950 the town used eighty tons of salt, and by 1972, it was two thousand. An article in 1972 tried to prohibit the use of salt, but failed. In 1993-1994 the town used six thousand tons, not counting salt used by the state.[27] To the irritation of townspeople and merchants, parking meters were installed along Main Street in 1948. In 1967

In 1922 constant traffic had worn Main Street so badly that granite paving blocks were laid from Elm Square to School Street. The cobblestones were paved over with hot top in 1949–1950 (pictured). Phillips Academy, concerned for the safety of students crossing Main Street, contributed more than four hundred acres toward the Route 125 Bypass in 1930, a transaction involving fifty-six separate deeds. Phillips also contributed the cost of one mile's construction.[28] The State Police barracks was built in 1934.

they were removed. They remain in municipal parking lots on Main and Park Streets, however, and in the lot behind the library.

Memorial Hall Library is a model for surrounding communities, a headquarters for thirty-seven municipalities and a computer center for twenty-six public libraries. Andover is the only library in Massachusetts to provide both functions. "The first director, Ballard Holt 2nd, served as librarian and janitor from 1873 to 1900, when he resigned as librarian but continued as janitor," recalls Nancy Jacobson, director from 1974 to 1993. "Holt was succeeded by Edna Brown from 1900 to 1939, followed by Miriam Putnam."[29] Miriam Putnam remembers:

When I came in 1939, Andover was a small town. The library had a remarkable collection and a community tremendously interested in education. As new people began to arrive, they brought new interests. We felt the library should begin to represent the town as it is, not just as it was. We were fighting the image of the library being run by little old ladies in gum shoes, only interested in buying the most innocuous love stories and westerns.[30]

Miriam Putnam had mixed feelings about computers in the library at first. But when she saw the staff time they saved and how that translated into more money for books, she was won over. In 1967 the library became one of seven subregional centers in Eastern Massachusetts. In 1981 the library began

Privately funded from a bequest by John Smith of Smith & Dove and funds raised from townspeople in 1873, Memorial Hall Library was originally quite independent. Today, trustees are appointed by the town manager and approved by the selectmen.

computerizing all records and in 1982 Nancy Jacobson and Assistant Director Evelyn Kuo set up the structure for other towns to join the Andover computer system. Jacobson observes:

Computers revolutionized libraries. Most materials and holdings in the Commonwealth now could be searched, which facilitated interlibrary loan, reference, cataloguing, and circulation. We joined the Online Computer Library Center which provides access to more than twenty million items worldwide.[31]

The first library renovation in 1926 added a children's room, changed the

Ballardvale's Branch Library operated from 1913 to 1992, when drastic cutbacks forced its closing. Longtime librarian Ruth Sharpe knew everyone by name and reading interest. Courtesy of Bernice Haggerty

roofline from mansard to gable, and added a mezzanine. In 1961 the children's room was extended and in 1966 the reading room was enlarged. A $7.5 million addition in 1988 doubled the square footage.[32] A volunteer citizens' group, Friends of the Library, was formed in 1972. The library of 1896 had 14,000 volumes, 60 periodicals, and 5,949 cardholders in a town of sixty-five hundred. Circulation was 20,000 books per year. The library was preparing its first published card catalogue, supported by Mary Byers Smith. Director James Sutton reports that today's collection numbers 235,122 books; 420 subscriptions to periodicals; 4,000 rolls of microfilm; 6,143 long playing records; 1,694 audiocassettes; 2,657 videocassettes; 1,967 compact discs; and 200 art prints. Circulation for 1994 was 484,623, averaging 16 per capita, one of the highest in the state for towns this size.

Support for the library came more readily than support for low-cost housing. Andover's Housing Authority was formed in 1948 to help returning veterans. Francis "Frank" P. Markey, veterans' affairs agent, was instrumental in developing lots at High Street and Burnham Road, and erecting fifty units on Memorial Circle. William Dalton, selectman from 1982 to 1988, remarks:

I guess the biggest issue that occurred when I was selectman was affordable housing. Memorial Circle was the first and only project in thirty years. The number one item of my 1986 agenda as chairman was the creation of affordable housing. Ken Mahony picked up the ball, as did the Housing Committee. It became a case of "not in my neighborhood," the hottest series of hearings in years, but a number of complexes were built with 20 percent low-income units: one at Andover Street and Argilla Road and a big one on North Street, Brookside Estates. We were one of the few communities that met state guidelines.[33]

The Housing Authority manages 218 units of state-aided elderly housing: Chestnut Court, Grandview Terrace, Frye Circle, and Stowe Court, eight units of handicapped housing, and federally-funded subsidized housing for low income residents. Impetus from the state started the Council on Aging in 1966. The council opened a senior center, "The Haven," in a storefront on Barnard Street. The project was so successful that it moved to the theater building on Essex Street and in 1984 to the School Administration Building. The center offers elderly social day care, instructional classes, lectures and seminars, lunch programs, Meals on Wheels, social events, weekly bingo, health clinics, outreach services, and transportation.

The Department of Community Development and Planning was created in 1978 to govern land use. Four town departments combined—Planning, Conservation, Health, and Building—tying in with volunteer boards: the Zoning Board of Appeals, Planning Board, Fair Housing Committee, Design Advisory Group, Conservation Commission, Historical Commission, and Board of Health. This offered "one-stop shopping" for everything from electrical inspections to sewer permits, and fostered better communication and control of building projects.[34]

As early as 1992, the town began planning its 350th Anniversary celebration. The Historical Commission submitted an article for the 1993 Warrant, recommending a budget of $20,000. It passed without discussion. The selectmen appointed a committee, which first met June 15, 1993. Norma A. Gammon was elected chair; James D. Doherty, vice chair; Frederic A. Stott, treasurer and fund raiser; M. Louise Ordman, secretary; and Robert W. Phinney and Robert J. Macartney, executive board. The committee is coordinating a year of events:

Toni Harris submitted this winning entry in the 350th Anniversary logo design contest.

October 1995
Publication of 350th Anniversary history book by Andover Historical Society

January 21, 1996
Kickoff—an afternoon of American song, reception, and fireworks

February 17, 1996
"Andover at 400"—What kind of community should/will Andover be in 2046?
Led by Selectman Larry Larson

March 23, 1996
Celebration Ball—Phillips Academy

April 22–28, 1996
Festival of the Arts—drama, art displays, and an evening of music and dance

May 3–5, 1996
Anniversary Weekend—encampment of 28th Massachusetts Volunteer Infantry
Civil War unit, pancake breakfast, mini plays, entertainment, and games

May 11, 1996
The Anniversary Banquet—Merrimack College

Spring 1996
Brochure describing historic places and bus tours throughout Andover, North
Andover, and Lawrence

June 15, 1996
House and Garden Tour

June 23, 1996
Bicycle Race

July 4, 1996
Firemen's Muster

August 30–September 1
Soccer Tournament—Andover, England, Andover High School boys and girls,
and all Andovers in New England

September 15, 1996
Anniversary Parade

September 21, 1996
Boston Pops Concert at Merrimack College

Looking toward the future, Gerald Silverman, chairman of the Board of
Selectmen, says:

*Andover is more than just a place to live. It's a feeling. We're always working
for improvement. I think more people will begin to get involved, both people who
grew up here and new people, with less recycling of people who have put in their
time. I have a dream of opening up the town for the kids to come back, but I'm
afraid that's not going to happen.*[35]

Marching on Memorial Day 1994, from left are: Town Manager Reginald Stapczynski; Selectmen Gerald Silverman, chair, Charles Wesson Jr., and Larry Larson; State Senator John O'Brien; State Representative Gary Coon; and Selectmen James Barenboim, and William Downs. EMR photo

William Wood Jr. and Rosalind Wood walk "Keough."

Chapter Thirteen

What We Did For Fun

It is hard to imagine that formerly people came to Andover for only the summer. For William Wood's family, "Arden" was a country retreat and working farm. They returned to Boston for the winter. Cornelius Wood Jr. tells of a family dog named "Keough" who, when city life got to be too much, would amble down to the North Station, pick out the Andover train among twenty-three tracks, and ride out to Shawsheen, where he would disembark and trot over to Arden for some rest and recuperation. All the trainmen knew him and would see that he got off at the right stop.[1]

The Charles Ward family abandoned Ward (Holt) Hill for Brookline in the fall, and Phillips Brooks left North Andover for Boston. Foster's Pond supported a cluster of more modest summer cottages, as did River Street in Ballardvale. The

Daytrippers came by train from Lawrence to Bailey's Grove dance hall on the shores of Haggett's Pond.

Boston and Maine Railroad promoted day trips from Boston to Pole Hill in Ballardvale at the turn of the century. Ruth Sharpe's grandfather, William Trautmann, remembered carloads of visitors disembarking for the day. They bought souvenirs from Shattuck's Drug Store, then crossed the tracks to The Grove of pines. They could buy lunch at Maynard Clemens' Camp run by Charles Ormsby. They would swim in the Shawsheen River, and in the evening they would dance on Pole Hill. The police were kept busy, says Sharpe, there was so much fighting. One night a man was killed, so police put a stop to the excursion trains about 1906.[2]

But Ballardvale continued to be a recreation spot for townspeople. The German Club took picnics down the river, and school classes came to The Grove. One could take an excursion boat from Abbot Bridge down to Ballardvale wharf. The Andover Canoe Club was particularly popular with the young. Bud Lewis remembers:

My mother lived on Elm Street and my father lived on Lowell Street. He would walk with his little sister down Reservation Road (a path then) to the Canoe Club in the corner of Central Street and Lupine Road next to the river. My mother would

People would rent canoes at Parker's on the Shawsheen in Ballardvale, or dance upstairs in the ballroom. Courtesy of Bernice Haggerty

Bernice Haggerty remembers, "The Balmoral Spa had black marble pillars and a marble soda fountain. Then there were two or three steps down through a doorway to the outdoor dance area. It was decorated with shrubbery and beautiful lights, and a shell for the band. Roland Russell's orchestra provided big band music. The floor was red slate, and there was a ticket taker at its edge—three dances for twenty-five cents." Courtesy of Bernice Haggerty

walk from Elm Street with her little sister. I guess those little sisters were, in effect, chaperones. This was probably 1917, because they were married in January 1918.[3]

In the 1920s people danced outdoors at the Balmoral Spa in Shawsheen during the summer, or at the Crystal Ballroom in winter. Bernice Haggerty remembers the late 1930s:

The Balmoral Spa was open every Wednesday and Saturday evening. It was a happy time. If it rained, my family couldn't live with me. Boys had to wear suits and ties. Sometimes they'd wait outside until they saw a girl they wanted to dance with, then borrow a coat and tie from a friend. It was a dancing era and Benny Goodman had people dancing in the aisles at Carnegie Hall. We would Jitterbug, and dance the Shag, the Big Apple, and the Stomp.

The Crystal Ballroom was very beautiful with a marble floor and a many-faceted crystal ball hanging from the ceiling that sent sparkling lights all over the room. We didn't jitterbug there—it was bad for the floor. If you did, a policeman would tap you on the shoulder and say, "No breaking." We were mostly local people. I don't remember one minute's trouble. It was a nice place to be. We also had school dances in the gym. There was a folding wall at the back of the stage in Memorial Auditorium that opened into the gym, so our parents could sit in the audience and watch the grand march. We hired a decorator for our prom who transformed the gym with trees and stars in the sky.[4]

The Balmoral Spa was sold to Hardy and Ross in 1930, and to the Andover Companies in 1951. But Benjamin Babb ran the Crystal Ballroom for thirty-five years. He sold it in 1957 and it was used as an employment office for Raytheon. Sacred Heart School bought it in 1966.

Before disc jockeys, Harold Phinney, owner of Temple's Radio Shop, started running dances at the high school with recordings and a sound system. From the left are: Mary McNulty, orchestra leader Vaughn Munroe, Harold Phinney, and Mrs. Phinney. Look photo

As early as 1897 Andover set up a Park Commission, perhaps inspired by the Andover Village Improvement Society. Commissioners Albert Poor, William Goldsmith, and Frank Mills reported that they built a carriage trail circling Carmel Woods, the town forest of twenty-nine acres, pounded "state nails" into the trees they wished to protect from cutting, planted shrubs, and built benches. But in 1908 they complained of vandalism. "Unless it is patrolled, it is of little use," they concluded. In 1933 "the hardwood trees in Carmel Woods were cut down and given to the needy."[5] Depression era work parties from the ERA and WPA planted twenty-five hundred hemlocks and cut brush.

The Park Commission's second concern was a large tract in the town center known as Richardson Field. The town voted to purchase it in 1899, along with an adjoining parcel owned by J. W. Berry, bringing the total to just under four acres. The Common or Central Park eventually became simply known as The Park. Roger's Brook ran through the center of it, causing problems from the start. In 1901 gravel removed from Main Street was used as fill. The next year, a 16-inch drainage pipe was installed.

Meanwhile, the first of the Park's stately trees were planted in 1904. Ornamental shrubs were added and elegant gravel walks laid out. The commissioners proposed a combined bandstand and tool shed, built in 1913 at a cost of $1,000. Two band concerts were held the first year, and band concerts became a popular summer evening pastime.

In 1905 a stone bridge was built and in 1906 Roger's Brook was dammed to create a pond. Park commissioners promised, "An attractive resting place will be provided for summer saunterers."[6] But their frustration is evident in 1912: "There is either too much water or too little." In 1968 the brook was confined to an underground pipe but the bridge remains.

As early as 1904 a group of private citizens was working to purchase a larger plot nearby for a playground. Finally in 1910 Town Meeting voted to purchase 6 1/2 acres east of the schoolhouse at a cost of $976.70. It was named The Playstead. In 1911 it was reported that "the Park Commissioners have done a good job on the Playstead and very few ball teams will have a better diamond to play on than our boys." Bleachers were built in 1924 and moved seasonally from baseball diamond to football field.

Until 1968 high school games were at the Playstead. Shown here is a Baseball team from 1930.

In 1939 the Punchard Football team was undefeated. In the thirty years that Eugene "Pop" Lovely was coach, his teams won 158 games, while they only lost 59. In 1948 a group of men who had gathered to watch the football team warm up were dismayed to learn there was no money for uniforms. Many were members of the Andover Sportsman's Club. Hastily they called together a few friends in Everett Collins' office that evening to form the Andover Boosters Club. The founding members were Collins, Hal Wennik, "Stretch" Pearson, Jim Christie, Charlie McCullom, Hervey Guertin, and Charlie Dalton. Over the years, they outfitted the football team, the All-Girls' Band, put on the annual sports banquet, and raised a flagpole at the Playstead. They rented bleachers, later purchased by the town. They funded the first Little League team in 1951 and prepared the first Little League diamond at the Playstead. They assisted the Church Basketball League (1946), the Junior League (1953), Junior Football (1960), and Pee Wee Hockey (1960).[7]

Little League added a Ballardvale team in 1954 and a West Center team in 1955. By 1961 five hundred boys aged ten to thirteen were enrolled. There were a hundred in the Junior League aged thirteen to fifteen. The Twilight Baseball League was founded in 1945 partly for returning war veterans. It was still going

strong in 1959 with sixty boys and men playing twenty-five well-attended games. Pony League baseball and football were organized in 1960, the Girls' Softball League in 1961 and the Andover Soccer Program in 1980.

Many mills supported athletic teams. Bill Dalton remembers that his uncle was paid to play baseball for various companies. American Woolen Company's Soccer Team was National Champion in 1925. Today Hewlett-Packard has laid out a baseball diamond, basketball courts, and volleyball courts on its grounds, boasting

Bill Dalton says, "In the 1940s there were huge crowds at the high school football games. The town and the school were one. We knew every athlete's name. Later attendance was lower. Now there is a variety of sports and there are women's sports. But there is a loss of community spirit."[8] Look photo, 1948

Smith & Dove owned a cricket field off Lupine Road for workers from the British Isles. Here, soccer goalie John Monro defends his turf. Courtesy of Dorothy Piercy, circa 1915

an in-house league of twelve softball teams. Gillette has softball, volleyball, basketball, and bowling leagues, while Genetics Institute has indoor soccer and hockey leagues, as well as on-site aerobics.

A swimming hole off the Smith & Dove cricket field, known as The Ten Footer, was popular early in the century. Phillips students were fond of sneaking off to Pomp's Pond, even though the 1895 bylaw forbade "any swimming in any public or exposed place in town." By 1923 however, a citizen group arranged for supervised swimming at Pomp's. The pond was named for Pompey Lovejoy, who came to Andover in 1733 at age nine, a slave of Captain William Lovejoy. In 1762 shortly before the Captain's death, he freed Pompey, then aged thirty-eight. Pompey enjoyed his freedom a long time, living to age 102. He served in the Revolution, and swam almost daily in the pond near his house. He and his wife, Rose Coburn, are buried in South Church Cemetery. His gravestone reads: "Pomp Lovejoy, born in Boston, a slave; died in Andover, a free man, Feb. 23, 1826; much respected as a sensible, amiable and upright man."[9]

The town took over Pomp's Pond in March 1924. That summer, they built a

In 1927 a second bathhouse was constructed at Pomp's, "Sanitaries" were installed, and People's Ice Company donated ice to cool the drinking water. Pictured is an ice house on the Pond.

bathhouse and hired lifeguards Rolland Estabrook and William Atwood. The next year, Frank McBride began as lifeguard. Woodrow Crowley was lifeguard at Hussey's Pond in Shawsheen. A parking lot was built for automobiles, but many families did not own cars. Eve Cross Glendenning remembers one day in 1928 when her family was sitting on their porch at Central and School Streets:

A family came walking down the street with several small children. The mother carried a baby and the father carried a toddler, while three or four other little ones trudged along beside them. It was a very hot day and it was obvious they were headed for Pomp's Pond. They had a long way to go. I think all four of us had the idea at the same time. "What about the coal trucks?" A truck was cleaned out and benches installed, and my father gave one of his men a job driving it during the slack summer period.[10]

The Cross Coal truck made the rounds of the town, picking up children. Thus began a tradition which continued for more than twenty years through the generosity of the Crosses.

Pomp's Pond, 1941

Betty Bodwell Stevens remembers she was the youngest child to swim around Pomp's Pond. The *Andover Townsman* reported on August 12, 1927, that the youngest boy to complete the swim was nine-year-old Garrett Burke, but that the Bodwell girl had done it at eight. The children were closely followed by a rowboat. Stevens remembers that Frank McBride "was wonderful with us kids and helped us learn to swim."[11]

Water safety classes began in 1953. Six years later, enrollment had swelled to 617. In 1957 the town began issuing beach stickers. The largest attendance in one day was 4,675 on a June Sunday in 1959. Total attendance that year was 134,107. But by 1967 it was down to 34,000 and in 1983, just 12,000. People began to leave for the summer, build pools, or enroll their children in other activities. The present bathhouse and concession stand were built in 1975.

In 1930 the new Playground Committee purchased equipment for the Playstead and the Ballardvale playground. The equipment was set up in the spring and taken down in the fall. In 1936 the Committee, headed by Henry G. Tyer, opened three summer playground programs. Total registration was 1,997. Playgrounds were opened at Indian Ridge School in 1945, West Center in 1946, and North School in 1954. Penguin Park, geared to toddlers, was built by a group of parents on Iceland Road in May 1990, but moved in August to Burnham Road, for better parking.

At first the town occupied Pomp's Pond beach courtesy of the Boston Missionary Society, sponsors of Camp Andover, which leased the land from Homer Foster. In 1935 Foster asked the town for rent of $100 per summer. In 1947 the town purchased eight acres of Foster land for $1,000, and in 1963 bought the former Camp Manning Boy Scout Camp (pictured) to create Recreation Park. The main building was designated Recreation Lodge. Heat and sanitary facilities were installed and the Andover Garden Club landscaped the grounds. Four lighted tennis courts were built in 1976. In 1978 the Rec Lodge burned. A shelter and rest rooms were erected in 1982.

Stafford A. Lindsay became chairman of the Playground Committee in 1938, serving fifteen years. The first playground supervisor, Margaret Davis, designed a program that set a pattern for years to come. Tournaments were held in sand-building, jackstones, checkers, heel toss, midget bowling, box hockey, and paddle tennis. There were soap bubble contests, Professor Quiz contests, a doll show, a pet show, boxing night, couple races, and a field day. A highlight was the picnic at Canobie Lake Park. Parents held carnivals to raise money for equipment, and all ages attended evening events.

The Board of Public Works took over the parks in 1913. In 1930 they flooded

North School's playground opened in 1954.

Selectmen could designate streets for coasting after big storms. Margaret Roberts remembers coasting down Chestnut and Morton Streets. Jerry Cross remembers climbing on his sled at the top of School Street, flying down to South Church, past the depot, down Essex Street, and across the river, where the momentum would take him nearly up to Cuba Street.[12] Phillips students rode bobsleds down Phillips and Central Streets to Abbot Bridge. Donald Mulvey skied on the sixth hole at Andover Country Club. Here, circa 1950, children coast on School Street. Look photo

the Playstead for skating. By 1939 they were also using Rabbit Pond, Hussey's Pond, and the Ballardvale flats of the Shawsheen River. After several drownings in 1947, skating on natural ponds was discouraged, and the Brothers of the Sacred Heart offered their rink in Shawsheen. When Phillips Academy built its artificial rink in 1950, the first such facility in the history of prep schools in America,[13] the town was also granted ice time. Phillips hosted the first Peewee hockey in 1960.

Phillips Academy was also a leader in adult education. At the suggestion of Alan Blackmer, a few professors decided to open their regular discussion group to the public in 1935. Especially welcome were those whose formal education had been limited. Between 1935 and 1963, eight thousand individuals enrolled for eighteen thousand courses in the Evening Study Program, everything from Drownproofing to The Classical Inheritance of the Middle Ages. Ultimately the program grew too big for the academy. In 1964 the Community Council for Recreation offered its first adult programs. In 1975, academy and town programs combined, offering 101 courses. Three hundred people had to be turned away. Today town and academy still work together under the Department of Community Services, instituted in 1978 to oversee all recreation and enrichment programs.

The academies sponsored a string of speakers and performers. Helen Keller spoke at Abbot in 1898 and T. S. Eliot visited three times, invited by teacher Emily Hale. Phillips sponsored concerts by organist Louis Vierne (1927), Sergei Rachmaninoff (1928), Percy Grainger (1942), and the Indianapolis Symphony (1946). Booker T. Washington (1899), Barry Goldwater (1963), and Roy Wilkins of the NAACP (1968) spoke at Phillips, and Dustin Hoffman campaigned there for Senator Eugene McCarthy (1968). In 1965 the Boston Patriots trained at the Academy.

Nor was Andover short on presidential visits. President George Bush came to Phillips in 1989 to commemorate George Washington's 1789 visit. Theodore Roosevelt came to see his son graduate in 1913, and President Coolidge attended the school's sesquicentennial in 1928.

A wholesome environment for youth has been an ongoing need. Ovid Chapman's Chappie's at 127 Main Street was an early hangout. Later it became "Doc" Davidson's, and after that the Coffee Mill. There were Dalton's Drug Store and Ford's Coffee Shop in the center, and The Den on High Street. Some went south to Howard Johnson's near Reading.

Beyond academies and athletics, an alternative for youth was the Andover Guild, run for many years by Donald Dunn. The Guild opened a Boys' Club in 1895 and a Girls' Club in 1901 on Brook Street. The latter was a drop-in center, staffed with a full-time housemother. Membership was ten cents per month. Among other attractions was a large workbench area for "Sloyd" work, a popular Swedish woodworking program. A second building added in 1908, housed a bowling alley and the first community gymnasium.

The Teen Center was organized in 1961, spearheaded by Dorothy Birdsall who ran the Coffee Mill. It was located in the Grange next to West Parish Church. Teenagers dusted, scrubbed, and painted the old building, but within two years, moved to Recreation Park. There they raised $500 to install lavatories in the lodge, while the town installed heat. But delays in getting an occupancy permit meant the teens who raised the money never got to use the center.[15] They moved to the Guild

A favorite teen hangout was the Brown Jug on Lowell Street, formerly the Duck Inn. Opened by sisters Peggy Wood and Cleo Trott in 1952, the Jug was a rustic cabin with a large fireplace and a jukebox in the corner. Hot dogs, hamburgers, and ice cream were sold. Teens could stay as long as they liked. Once when the Jug closed for cleanup, kids came to help so it would reopen sooner. Peggy and Cleo never made much money off the Jug, but they performed a great public service. It closed in 1956.[14] Photo courtesy of Cleo Trott

until it was taken over by the YMCA in 1968. Then a Student Activity Center opened at the new high school. Briefly in 1970 teens used the old fire station behind the Town House, before the wrecker's ball leveled it. Today the most popular place appears to be the back steps of the library. But plans are in the works for a new center at Recreation Park.

All ages are brought together by holidays, and the Recreation Department has spared no effort in making them enjoyable. James Doherty, playground director in 1950, wrote of the Easter Egg hunt at the Park: "After a blast of the fire whistle, 1,000 children picked up more than 11,000 candy packages in three minutes."[16] In the Halloween Parade seventeen hundred men, women, and children marched through the center to a party in Memorial Auditorium. Many local groups contributed work and money to make these events memorable.

A number of oganizations host annual events. Andover Sportsman's Club held its first Annual Fishing Derby in 1950. The Board of Trade and Boosters Club started a Thanksgiving parade in 1951. St. Francis Seminary and Brickstone Square

Ballardvale's Fourth of July included a road race in 1909. Courtesy of Bernice Haggerty

The Fourth of July Horribles Parade, pictured on Essex Street about 1900, fizzled during World War II. From 1943 until the 1950s, Andover Service Men's Fund Association put on a five-day Fourth of July Carnival. For a number of years there was little or no observance. Then in 1970 Andover Service Club revived it, and the Horribles were resurrected in 1982. Today fleets of small children decorate their bicycles and neighborhood groups march together. It is preceded by an outdoor pancake breakfast and followed by a band concert. In the evening, high school fields are littered with bodies gazing at fireworks.

have put on magnificent displays of Christmas lights. Andover Center Association's Sidewalk Bazaar Days (1961) close Main Street to traffic. Andover Artists' Guild's Art-in-the-Park (1975), a huge outdoor gallery, raises scholarships for promising young art students. Crafts-in-the-Park, benefiting AFS (American Field Service) began in 1976.

Veterans Day and Memorial Day were fraught with conflict during the Vietnam era, ripping the generations asunder. Today we can once again honor those who served their country. Memorial Day in particular, with its brilliant May sunshine,

Town firefighters initiated the Santa Claus Parade in 1956. Look photo

lends itself to a stirring march down Main Street. History passes before our eyes. Townspeople line the street in front of the Town House. First come the selectmen and the town manager. Vietnam veterans, flanked by those from Korea and the Persian Gulf, wear jungle camouflage. World War II veterans are next, the eldest riding in a convertible, while others march, still trim in their uniforms at age seventy-five. The survivors of the Bataan Death March and Corregidor carry their banner proudly. Minutemen fire their muskets, frightening small children. The Andover High School Golden Warriors Band surges by in blue and gold with blazing trumpets and pounding drums, followed by the St. Matthew's Lodge of Masons, wearing their 1822 regalia. The Boy Scouts, Girl Scouts, Brownies, and Cub Scouts, our hope for the future, complete the procession.

The Andona Society started Clown Town in
The Park in 1956, raising money for Andover
youth activities. *Andover Townsman* photo

Clan MacPherson sweeps by, blasting on
bagpipes and beating drums to remind us of
its Scottish heritage. EMR photo, Memorial
Day 1994

The divisions gather on the steps of Memorial Auditorium under a giant American
flag. Spectators fan out on the green grass around the bandstand or seek the shade
of old trees in the Park. A bagpiper plays "Amazing Grace" and a trumpeter plays
taps in the distance—a baby cries and an old man weeps. For one brief moment,
all together in one place, we can feel the pulsing life which is Andover.

Andover's 250th Anniversary, 1896. Courtesy of the North Andover Historical Society

Chapter Fourteen

Profiles
Business and Family

The Andover Historical Society is grateful to the *Eagle-Tribune* and the *Andover Townsman* for their generous sponsorship. A special thank you also to our local businesses and families whose profiles contributed to and supported the publication of this book.

—Barbara Thibault, Director
Andover Historical Society
Andover's Historical Museum and Research Center

Railroad crossing at the intersection of Haggett's Pond Road and Lowell Street, West Andover.

Illustration courtesy of Andover Bank

⧄B AndoverBank

1834	Thirty citizens of Andover petitioned the Massachusetts legislature seeking to establish a "mutual" savings institution. On December 17, the first recorded meeting of the bank held was at Locke Tavern.
1835	Deacon Amos Abbott was chosen as the Bank's first president. On Saturday May 16, the Andover Institution for Savings opened for business in a second floor office of the Valpey Block. Banking hours were 2 to 5 p.m. every Saturday. First depositor, Abigail Anderson of Andover, opened with $90.
1849	Bank moves to railroad station on Essex Street. 1851 Bank moves to the Swift block on Essex Street.
1853	Name shortened to Andover Savings Bank; bank moves to Andover National Bank building, 23 Main Street.
1855	In addition to its usual 5 percent annual dividend, Bank paid an extra dividend of 40 percent.
1870	Hours expanded to 2 to 5 p.m. weekdays, March to October; 2 to 4 p.m. all other seasons.
1873	Deposits pass the $1,000,000 mark.
1877	Bank installs gas and electrical utilities.
1900	Bank installs first telephone.
1919	Assets exceed $5,000,000.
1924	Bank moves to present building at 61 Main Street, October 1.
1944	First branch office opened at 108 Main Street, North Andover.
1952	Second branch opened at 5 Hampshire Street, Methuen.
1964	First automated data processing equipment installed.
1968	Methuen office relocates to 547 Broadway.
1973	Construction completed on a contemporary addition to Main Street office. Assets $96,882,000.
1977	Two additonal branch offices opened, 91 Pleasant Valley Street, Methuen, and 995 Main Street, Tewksbury, in historic Brown's Tavern.
1980	Added to main office—retail space on Main Street; first automated teller machine.
1983	Merger with Valley Co-operative Bank in Lawrence.
1984	150th Anniversary of Andover Savings Bank.
1985	Corporators and Board of Trustees voted to convert "The Bank" from a mutual to a stock institution. North Andover branches consolidated to Main Street location.
1986	Bank officially converted to a stockholder owned corporation.
1987	Andover Bancorp Incorporated organized with Andover Bank as its wholly owned subsidiary; River Road branch opened.
1991	Name changed to Andover Bank.
1994	Andover Bank acquired Community Savings Bank of Lawrence, bringing the total to ten offices. 160th Anniversary of Andover Bank.
1996	350th Anniversary of Andover.

Andover Country Club. EMR photo

Andover Country Club

William M. Wood bought 175 acres on William Street Extension in 1923, with high hopes of developing the best possible executive golf course for employees of the American Woolen Company. He appointed a committee to organize the club and planned a spacious clubhouse in the Mediterranean stucco style. The course was designed by Boston architect W. H. Follett and construction began that summer, but Follett died before it was complete. The course was not finished until autumn 1925 and was later reworked by Donald Ross, designer of the Pebble Beach golf course. The club's first organizational meeting was held in July 1923, but due to difficulties within the company, did not officially open until May 3, 1926. Members from both American Woolen and the community were welcome.

The club was purchased from American Woolen on December 19, 1925, by the Andover Company, a holding company owned by local stockholders who were mostly club members. During the Depression, the mortgage was taken over by Ellsworth and Hilda Lewis and Foster and Elizabeth Barnard who foreclosed in 1940, gaining ownership, and leasing the property back to the Country Club. The Lewises and Barnards enjoyed minimum success with the venture, deciding to sell out to Edward and Ruth Donohue and Agnes and Leon Davidson (owner of the Andover Shop and "Doc" Davidson's restaurant at 125 Main Street) in 1949. President Eisenhower's affection for the game helped to give golf a surge of popularity during the 1950s. The two couples renovated the deteriorating clubhouse and Doc ran the kitchen at the club most successfully for about fifteen years. They continued to buy up adjacent land. After Davidson died, Donohue continued to operate the club until selling to Yvon Cormier in 1979. By then the property comprised 353 acres.

Yvon Cormier, the present owner, revitalized the interior of the club and while preserving the golf course, built houses on the adjacent land. Today the clubhouse has three ballrooms, twenty-six overnight guest accommodations, a dining room, and a lounge for members. A Pro Shop is located in a separate building near the clubhouse. Membership stands at four hundred. In addition, Andover Country Club hosts more than two hundred weddings and fifty corporate golf outings each year in addition to many smaller functions and meetings.

Asoian, Tully and Gilman
P.C., Attorney at Law

Congratulations to the Town of Andover on its 350th birthday and best wishes for the community's continued prosperity and success.

Union Building, first home of Andover National bank, now BayBank

BayBank

BayBank's early roots in Andover began on July 1, 1826, when the Andover Bank opened in a brick building on the Essex Turnpike, now 23 Main Street. The stockholders elected Mark Newman as moderator and Amos Blanchard as secretary and cashier at their first meeting, held at the home of James Locke (The Locke Tavern). Interestingly, the Andover Historical Society is now located in what was Amos Blanchard's house. Elected to serve as directors were several leading local citizens: Samuel Farrar, Esq. (first president); Mark Newman, Esq.; Joseph Kittredge, Esq.; Hon. Hobart Clark, Esq.; Hon. Amos Spaulding, Esq.; Mr. Amos Abbot; Captain Stephen Abbot; Captain Nathaniel Stevens; and Mr. Francis Kidder. Between 1888 and 1890, the bank had a new building designed and built. Ninety years later, in 1981-1982, the bank completely renovated the building, incorporating a large new addition.

The Andover National Bank and the Merrimack National Bank, the two oldest national banks in the Merrimack Valley, merged in 1956 to form the Andover and Merrimack National Bank. Abbot Stevens (great-grandson of Captain Nathaniel Stevens) was chosen chairman of the Board and Charles W. Arnold, president. In 1957 the Methuen National Bank was acquired, and in 1964 the resultant Merrimack Valley National Bank became one of ten Massachusetts banks under the umbrella of the holding company BayBanks, Incorporated (then the BayState Corporation). Merrimack Valley National Bank changed its name to BayBank Merrimack Valley in 1976. All of the individual BayBanks merged in 1991 into one BayBank, which today has over two hundred offices across Massachusetts.

Andover has seen sweeping changes over the past 350 years, and many more changes lie ahead. Institutions such as BayBank will be helping the residents and businesses of Andover meet the challenges of the coming years, as they have helped since 1826. From handwritten ledgers in the horse-and-buggy age to the availability of more than one thousand BayBank X-Press 24® banking machines in 1994, BayBank continually looks ahead, offering the best in banking to help its customers meet life's challenges, now and into the twenty-first century.

Congratulations

on your

350ᵗʰ

Anniversary

from your friends at

MARKET BASKET

Doherty Insurance Agency, Incorporated

With a gift of $25 from his Uncle Martin, William A. Doherty began the Doherty Insurance Agency, Incorporated on June 6, 1934. A back room in the Musgrove building was his office and with his never-failing determination (some would say stubbornness) he built the business so that in July 1937, his brother, James D. Doherty, joined him.

The team was formed and soon space became a problem. They moved from the Musgrove building to 4 Main Street in 1953, where their Insurance and Real Estate business remained until they moved to their own building at 21 Elm Street in 1964. They purchased seven agencies throughout the Valley, which led to a branch in North Andover in 1971.

Jim and Bill never forgot who really built their business—the people in the community. So they tried to give something back every chance they had. Bill served on the School Committee for thirty-nine consecutive years, for which he was given the honor of having a school named for him. Jim has served as the town moderator for seventeen years. Few in town have any doubt as to who "Uncle Bill" and "Mr. Moderator" are. Bill continued to be a champion for the schools and "the kids" till his death in 1987.

The business is currently owned and operated by Jim's children, Jay, Sheila, and Mary, and a staff of twenty-five. They purchased the Agency in July 1985, and are very proud of the legacy left by Jim and Bill. They are committed to the same high standards and community involvement as "Uncle Bill" and "Mr. Moderator."

As we celebrate our 60th Anniversary, we look forward to Andover's 350th and to our continued commitment to the people of Andover.

4 Main Street office, courtesy of Dohertys

21 Elm Street, courtesy of Dohertys

Andover's 1931 U.S. Post Office will be Andover Essex Bancorp's new Andover office.

First Essex Bancorp

$\mathbf{F}$rom its founding in 1847, the history of the First Essex Bank has been an integral part of the history of the towns it still serves. In 1947 before the final stone was laid in the Great Stone Dam that made Lawrence's textile industry possible, the First Essex Bank was established by men like Charles Storrow, who created the city as well. The bank soon became a vital factor in the area's economic life, offering services to both depositors and borrowers in the rapidly growing Merrimack Valley.

By 1863 the First Essex Bank was successful enough to support the Union cause by purchasing $40,000 in U.S. bonds. The bank continued to grow through the years with the textile industry. Even during the Depression, the bank remained able to meet the demands of its depositors. World War II witnessed significant economic growth and the First Essex Bank responded with more than $22,000,000 in U.S. bonds. The bank's primary mission, however, has always been local, and it has supported the purchase of thousands of area homes and businesses.

The years since the war have seen many changes. In 1951 the bank began to post entries by machine rather than by hand, and the 1960s brought computers into the process. Today First Essex offers a wide range of banking services for individuals and businesses, undreamed of a century ago. The bank has expanded its branches to include towns from Andover, Massachusetts, to Londonderry, New Hampshire, and its directors work and volunteer throughout the Merrimack Valley. The bank continues to fund local economic growth and is growing itself with its new headquarters at Andover's newly restored former U.S. Post Office, 71 Main Street, a National Register historic building.

Hewlett-Packard Company Medical Products Group

In 1917 Tufts University professor Frank Sanborn began manufacturing a water level recorder and a blood pressure gauge in a one-room office in Boston. In 1939 Bill Hewlett and Dave Packard founded the Hewlett-Packard Company in a garage in Palo Alto, California, to produce audio oscillators. By 1954 Sanborn Company was cramped for space. It leased a pig farm off the new Route 128 in Waltham to build a modern manufacturing facility. In 1961 the Sanborn Company became a wholly-owned subsidiary of Hewlett-Packard, and the Medical Products Group was born.

By 1972 the demand for medical technology caused the Medical Products Group to search for larger quarters. It chose the former Lewis and Shattuck properties along the Merrimack River in Andover. After a vote by the town in 1973 to extend services to the River Road site, Hewlett-Packard leased the property and built its first building, which opened October 14, 1976. It purchased the land in 1980. In the course of negotiations, the realtor, Arkwright-Boston, donated eight acres of conservation land along the Merrimack River to the town, a critical link in the shoreline path.

Hewlett-Packard added manufacturing and cafeteria/training buildings in 1982. It completed a fourth building in 1993, bringing the total floor space to 745,000 square feet. Today the Medical Products Group is a leader in cardiac ultra-sound imaging systems, patient monitoring and clinical information systems.

Dominic Mannarino and pilot Walter Porter, employees of Hewlett-Packard, took to the air to photograph the company's beautiful site in the bend of the Merrimack River. Courtesy of Hewlett-Packard Company

LAWRENCE PUMPS INC...

Three Generations of Leadership from the Mill Family

In the spring of 1935, a time marked by widespread financial uncertainty, a highly acclaimed and ambitious engineer named Victor J. Mill, Sr. purchased Lawrence Machine and Pump Company. After settling his family in Andover, Mr. Mill quickly engaged his four person company in the task of engineering high performance centrifugal pumps for industry's most demanding applications. As an early indication of future success, the company supplied all primary pumping equipment to the dredging company that was moving fill from the bottom of Boston Harbor for the construction of Logan Airport.

Leveraging the successes of specialty pumps for irrigation and chemical and process industry applications, Lawrence Pumps Inc. emerged as a dynamic company committed to investing in the resources of its community for continued growth.

Over the last 60 years, Lawrence Pumps has been piloted by three generations of the Mill family. Pictured from left to right are V.J. Mill, Jr., V.J. Mill, Sr. (1887-1972), V.J. Mill III.

Currently in its third generation design, Lawrence Pumps Reactor Circulator Propeller pump is an industry standard for critical chemical processing applications.

Pioneering the Development of the Engineered Centrifugal Pump

From the day he graduated from Yale with a degree in mechanical engineering, Victor J. Mill, Sr. embraced a vision to create a pump company unique in its endeavor to do the toughest jobs–the kinds of jobs nobody else wanted, or could do. True to this vision, Mr. Mill applied his vast experience and education in hydraulic theory to redesign each of several centrifugal pump lines. These advanced designs marked the beginning of a legacy of industry leadership in the design and manufacture of engineered centrifugal pumps.

A New Generation. A World of Opportunities.

In 1941 Victor J. Mill, Jr., a Yale graduate with a degree in industrial administration, joined his father at Lawrence Pumps and quickly encouraged a focus on research and development and quality control. As Victor J. Mill, Jr. became increasingly more involved in the business during the 50's and 60's, the company expanded its facilities and grew to 70 employees to support the design and manufacture of a wide range of pump technologies.

With continued success and the growth of key industries worldwide, Mr. Mill Jr. began exploring opportunities for selling specialized pumps outside the U.S. This forward thinking by the Mill family's second generation of leadership has had a profound impact on Lawrence Pumps evolution as a leading worldwide supplier of engineered pump solutions.

Lawrence Pumps has built its reputation on engineering large, heavy duty, customized pumps for industrial applications involving abrasive solids in suspension, corrosive liquids, and extreme temperatures and pressures.

Embracing Technology in a Continuing Commitment to Engineered Pump Leadership Worldwide

Today Lawrence Pumps employs more than 150 people from the Merrimack Valley area in its worldwide headquarters that has expanded to comprise the city block bounded by Market, Parker, and Foster streets and the B&M railroad track. Instrumental to the company's continued development is V.J. Mill III, President and CEO.

Representing the third generation of Mill family leadership, VJ joined his father at Lawrence Pumps in 1965 after graduating from Villanova with a degree in industrial administration. Since 1973, when he and his father introduced computer-programmed, numerically controlled machinery into the plant, VJ has continued to embrace emerging technologies to streamline manufacturing and communications capabilities.

To ensure continued leadership in today's global marketplace, Lawrence Pumps was one of the first pump companies to gain ISO9001 certification–a quality standard recognized throughout the world. Through his commitment to global expansion, VJ has established several joint ventures and service centers strategically located worldwide.

To support its customers, who represent global companies from a wide range of critical process industries, Lawrence Pumps will be opening a new Technology Center in 1995. The new facility will have state-of-the-art electronic data acquisition capabilities and will be able to test pumps that are 70 feet in length.

The Mill family continues its commitment to supporting the community by creating opportunities for its people and services.

V.J. Mill III, President and CEO

Worldwide Strategic Alliances

Joint Ventures

Servicing Latin and South America	Servicing the Pacific Rim	Servicing Europe

Service Centers

North America - Houston, Baton Rouge, Cleveland   **Europe** - Rotterdam, Holland   **Pacific Rim** - Singapore

South America - Maracaibo, Venezuela   **Latin America** - Mexico City, Mexico

▲ **Joint Ventures**
■ **Service Centers**

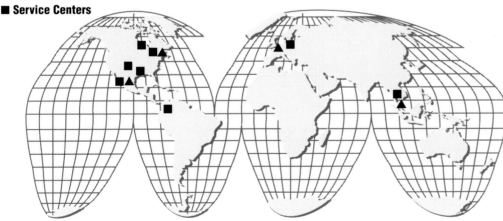

Global Markets Served

Hydrocarbon Processing

Chemical Processing

Power Generation

Metals Processing

Nuclear Remediation

Polyolefins Production

ISO 9001
QUALITY SYSTEM CERTIFIED

Lawrence Savings Bank in the Shawsheen Village

The building that once housed the Shawsheen Village Post Office and Community Market is home today to the Lawrence Savings Bank in Andover. Lawrence Savings Bank opened this office in 1979. The inside was remodeled, but the historical features of the building were preserved.

A pamphlet published by the American Woolen Company in 1924 proclaims "Conveniently reached from all parts of the village, at the crossing of the main highway and Haverhill Street, is the Post Office, surmounted by a handsome colonial tower and clock . . ." Shawsheen Village was designed as a model community for the employees of the American Woolen Company.

The original intent of this building was to house more than one business concern and it will do so once again. The building was acquired by new owners in 1995 and will contain the Lawrence Savings Bank office on the first floor and law offices on the second floor. Lawrence Savings Bank opened its doors in a small second floor office in downtown Lawrence on May 14, 1868. On the first day of business there were thirteen depositors for a total of $537.00. By 1930 Lawrence Savings Bank had relocated and unveiled a premier banking facility that boasted room for twenty-eight tellers! Almost a hundred years after that first day of business, the Bank opened its first branch office on Jackson Street in Methuen. Lawrence Savings Bank celebrated its 125th Anniversary in 1993 and currently has deposits of more than $252 million.

Lawrence Savings Bank has six full service banking offices, twenty-four-hour banking machines and offers a wide variety of savings and loan services to both individuals and businesses.

Lawrence Savings Bank in Shawsheen Village. Courtesy of the bank

Mahony Family

Ken and Gratia Mahony congratulate the Town of Andover on its 350th Anniversary. Ken served as town manager from 1982 to 1990 while Gratia, a professional genealogist, served as president of the Andover Historical Society. Ken recalls his years as Town manager, the eighties, as a time of change for Andover. The demographic growth created a tension that was magnified by economic dislocation. Proposition 2 1/2, a law capping real estate tax increases, caused more uncertainty as the decade began. Andover elected a strong, decisive Board of Selectmen that remained largely intact through that period. While of diverse backgrounds and political views, they steered a steady course.

Local economic strength meant not only balanced budgets but also diversification of the industrial base. Andover was second only to Boston in its use of Industrial Revenue Bonds throughout the eighties. To preserve the Central Business District, parking was expanded downtown and the town invested in the Memorial Hall Library and the Town House. The construction of the Collins Center, improvement of the parks, the Dragon's Lair, and tot lot playgrounds all received attention and support.

The quality of life was addressed through the acquisition of more than five hundred acres of conservation land. The new water treatment facility, watershed protection, closing a filling station on Haggett's Pond, tree planting, recycling, the expansion of Greater Lawrence Sanitary District's role in treatment of industrial waste, New England Solid Waste Commission (NESWC), chemical response teams, and Superfund Amendments and Reauthorization Act (SARA), all were achieved within Proposition 2 1/2.

Perhaps of greatest pride to the governmental community was the fact that Andover was the only suburban Massachusetts community to meet its affordable housing goals. This was a tremendous accomplishment that has received less attention than it deserved.

The eighties will be remembered as a time of change, a time of unrest, but a time where the future of the community was enhanced by strong, decisive action, not only by the elected officials but also by the residents and the municipal staff.

Ken and Gratia Mahony enjoy the park area in front of the Town House. Ken's leadership was pivotal in renovating the town's first public buiding, erected in 1858. EMR photo

Phillips Academy in the Twentieth Century

A time-traveling Phillips Academy alumnus from the turn of the century would have little trouble recognizing Andover Hill as his alma mater. True, the elms would be taller, and the campus dotted with "new" construction and ringed by a stone wall. But not even such a dramatic addition as the Memorial Tower could disguise the tranquil, rolling green lawns of Phillips, and many of its colonial buildings stand virtually unchanged. Still, despite its nearly pastoral setting, PA is not the same independent college preparatory school it was in 1900 when the faculty numbered eighteen and the student population was 427.

The single most conspicuous change over the past century was the school's merger in 1973 with nearby Abbot Academy, which brought women into its classrooms. Other transformations include an increasingly cosmopolitan population, the evolution of a more comprehensive curriculum, and an enhanced interrelationship with the Town of Andover.

Though the school's original 1778 constitution called for the education of "youth from every quarter," this mission tended to be more narrowly defined in the eighteenth and nineteenth centuries. Until twenty years ago young women were educated well but separately at Abbot, founded in 1828. According to historian Frederick S. Allis Jr., Phillips Academy's Class of 1899 included only four blacks. Foreign student representation included three boys from Turkey, two from Canada, and one each from Africa, England, and Greece. The student roster listed fewer than twenty Andover residents.

By contrast, about half today's students are girls. Minority enrollment tops 25 percent. Forty percent of the student body receives financial aid, which genuinely opens doors to youth from "every quarter." Over 12 percent come from other lands, while 25 percent are day students from Andover and surrounding towns.

The faculty, too, is more diverse. More than 15 percent are people of color, and a full complement of female teachers and administrators includes PA's fourteenth head of school, Barbara Landis Chase, installed in September 1994.

Despite campus modernization and growth, the academy has retained its original ambiance, meeting new needs without overcrowding or ruining the vista with jarringly contemporary or out-of-scale structures. PA's physical development is inseparable from programmatic and cultural changes—for example, the decision early in this century to move all residential students out of off-campus boardinghouses and into dormitories required a flurry of construction. The 1908 removal of the Andover Theological Seminary to Cambridge enabled PA to site

Merrill Gate, Abbot Circle, and Draper Hall, Abbot Academy. Courtesy of Phillips Academy

its campus primarily on the east side of Main Street. Campus construction was particularly marked during Headmaster Alfred Stearns' administration, from 1903 to 1933. According to academy archivist Ruth Quattlebaum, Phillips owes much of its present appearance to visionary Trustee Thomas Cochran, a 1890 graduate. "While his affluent contemporaries were busy supporting their colleges and universities," she writes, "Cochran turned to Andover with a plan to make his high school an academic and visual showplace. Along with landscape architect Frederick Law Olmsted and architect Charles Platt, Cochran expanded and transformed the campus of 1920 into the campus we see today."

Besides dorms and a library, additions included academic and dining facilities. Some enhancements would also capture the public eye and bring new cultural resources to the broader community. Among them were the Cochran Chapel, which hosts musical events; Memorial Tower, built to honor PA graduates lost in World War I, which provided the academy and the town with a visual symbol; and the Addison Gallery of American Art, housing the work of such artists as Copley, Homer, Hopper, O'Keeffe, Pollock, Wyeth, and PA alumnus Frank Stella. Like PA's Robert S. Peabody Museum of Archaeology, which contains an exceptional collection of Native American artifacts, the Addison welcomes the public free of charge and is a resource for scholars from around the world.

The aims of the academy's founders are still embedded in a sound basic education that includes classical learning and athletics, but today's students enjoy a more varied program than their forebears, supported by computer centers, eight science laboratories, a licensed radio station, two theaters, twenty art and music studios, and extensive sports facilities.

Quattlebaum credits Headmaster John Kemper (1948–1971) with increasing the academy's endowment, adding facilities to the campus and "re-making Andover into a national high school for young men." Abbot Academy, under the leadership of Marguerite C. Hearsey and Mary H. Crane, also gained a national reputation for excellence in the post-World War II years. It was after Theodore Sizer took the headmaster's reins following Kemper's death that a strengthening movement toward merging Phillips and Abbot into a single, top-notch school came to a head. The marriage took place on June 20, 1973, and in 1978 the institution celebrated its 200th birthday. The bicentennial momentum enabled the school to raise $52 million in support, mostly for endowment. Donald McNemar's administration (1981–1994) was distinguished by an increasingly international perspective, enhanced diversity and tolerance, and further advances in the endowment.

Today the school serves twelve hundred students, with a faculty of 234 and a $235 million endowment. PA's current curriculum reflects breadth, depth, balance, and rigor. Off-campus and exchange programs offer in-depth experiences in nine foreign countries, a chance to study environmental science on the Maine coast, and government internship opportunities in Washington, D.C.

Many of Andover's academic riches are available to public high school students through an intensive summer session founded in the 1940s. Annually, it attracts about seven hundred highly motivated youth from around the globe. In addition, there are summer programs designed to meet particular needs, among them (MS)^2 (mathematics and science for minority students) and the Institute for Recruitment of Teachers (which helps minority college students explore an interest in teaching and gain admission to graduate schools). Other resources PA shares with the public encompass guest lectures and athletics facilities, plus cultural events that include performances by the school's hundred-member orchestra. Perhaps the academy's most intensive interactions with the outside community today occur through its active voluntarism program. In 1993-1994, over seven hundred PA students participated in community service projects regionally and locally. In October 1994, PA distinguished itself at "Serv-a-thon" day, sponsored by the youth service corps City Year, by sending 180 volunteers to Boston to clean, paint, and clear away debris at inner city sites.

That the quality of the school's academic experience is undiminished by all these changes is evident in the continued success of PA graduates. Not only do they consistently earn a disproportionate number of National Merit honors and go on to gain admission to such institutions as the Ivy League schools, MIT, and Stanford, but they also boast important achievements in the wider world. Some become household names.

Famous alumni of this century include photographer Walker Evans; movie star Jack Lemmon; computer pioneer Marvin Minsky; actress Dana Delany; four-star General Barry R. McCaffrey; Time, Incorporated, President Nicholas J. Nicholas Jr.; Bristol-Myers Squibb President Richard L. Gelb; and best-selling author Elizabeth Marshall Thomas. Other noteworthies include John Fitzgerald Kennedy Jr., TV actor Matt Salinger (Picket Fences), author Tracy Kidder, past baseball commissioner and Yale University president A. Bartlet Giamatti, and cartoonist Jeff MacNelly. Without question, Phillips Academy is at this very moment educating twenty-first-century world leaders in the arts, in business, in industry, and in government.

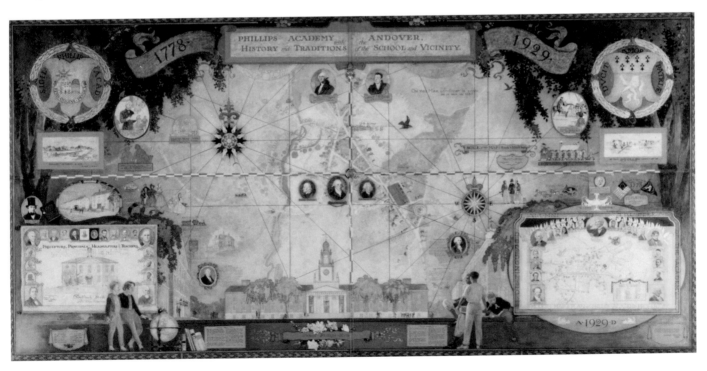

Artistic illustration and map of Phillips Academy, 1778–1929. George Adams photo

The Andover Bookstore— Then and Now

The Andover Bookstore traces its beginnings to a wooden building on the campus of Andover Theological Seminary. In 1809 Mark Newman resigned as principal of Phillips Academy to become bookseller to the Academy and the Seminary. The bookstore was on the first floor of this building. In 1813 Dr. Eliphalet Pearson moved an existing printing press to the second floor of Newman's building. From that time on, the two businesses evolved along parallel paths into the Andover Press and the Andover Bookstore.

Timothy Flagg and Abraham J. Gould operated the press from 1813 to 1832. They developed a valued reputation as printers and possessed the first fonts of Greek and Hebrew type in America. The press and bookstore moved across the street and further north to the Brick House in 1831, where the Memorial Gateway to the West Quadrant now stands. With the death of Timothy Flagg that year, Mark H. Newman, son of the original owner, took over.

Warren F. Draper became the sole proprietor in 1854 and the business prospered under his leadership. He continued the role of bookseller and provider of stationery to Phillips and Abbot Academies and the Seminary. In the late 1860s, Draper moved the press and bookstore downtown to 37 Main Street in what became known as the Draper Block. A group of prominent businessmen purchased the press and the bookstore from Draper in 1887, and John N. Cole was appointed treasurer and business manager. Here Cole started publication of the *Andover Townsman*. In an 1895 advertising pamphlet, John N. Cole notes the merits of his bookstore business: "The Andover Bookstore was founded in 1809. Which means almost a century of successful service for the people of Andover in stationery and book lines."

The press moved to the corner of Main and Chestnut Streets in 1906, where the bookstore was housed in the front part of the first floor. John N. Cole died in 1922 and was succeeded by his son, Philip P. Cole. Cole's ownership continued until 1960, when Jerome Cross purchased the Andover Bookstore and the Andover Press ceased operation. Cross used this vacated space to expand his line of paperback and hardcover books. The Crosses moved the bookstore to its present location in Olde Andover Village in the spring of 1964, renovating an old barn to include a balcony and a working fireplace. The store continued to be the sole provider of textbooks to Phillips Academy students.

William and Carolyn Dalton purchased the bookstore in 1990, adding a lower level. They sold it in 1992 to Robert Hugo, a Marblehead bookseller with more than thirty years' experience. The Andover Bookstore continues its tradition of being bookseller to the Academy as well as a unique and personal bookstore for Andover and the North Shore.

Newman's store where the press was between 1812 and 1832.

Andover Bookstore interior, 1994. Karen Harris photo

The Andover Castles
Since 1861

The Castles had their origins in Andover when Abby Locke moved with her family to the Abbot Tavern at 70 Elm Street in 1861. In her diaries, now part of the Andover Historical Society collection, Abby described Andover as a strict, conservative town: "... no cards, no dancing, or any other sport. To go to a horse race was to lose one's reputation of good character." It was said that the town became more liberal after the Lockes came.

Four of the five Locke sisters attended Abbot Academy, but Abby had to leave early to care for her mother. Later Abby Locke married T. Dennie Thomson, son of the Christ Church rector, and they built a house at 54 Abbot Street. Their daughter, Eleanor, attended Abbot Academy, where she met Alfred Castle, brother of classmates who came all the way from Illinois to Abbot. Another daughter, Rosamond, married Dr. Joesph H. Pratt and the Pratts' daughter, Sylvia, married Phillips Academy Headmaster John Kemper, living for fourteen years in Phelps House until her untimely death in 1961. Sylvia Pratt Kemper Chapel was named for her.

After their marriage, Eleanor and Alfred Castle maintained their Andover connection while raising four children in Quincy, Illinois. Their eldest daughter, Lorna, spent summers visiting her grandmother, Abby Thomson, at 54 Abbot Street and her aunt, Florence Locke, who still owned 70 Elm Street. Marian, the youngest of four Locke sisters, was born at 70 Elm Street in 1862. She married Henry Morrison and after he died in 1945, she returned to Andover, living at 54 Abbot Street, where she died in 1948. Lorna, after her marriage to Ernest Young in 1935, resided in the old Locke house at 70 Elm Street for fifty-five years until it was sold out of the family.

Lorna's sister, Rosamond "Posy," married Dino Olivetti, an internationally known industrialist, and they acquired 54 Abbot Street. Their sister, Abby, also found Andover her home after she married the widower, John Kemper, headmaster at Phillips Academy. Alfred Castle, their only brother, married Frances Golick, and remained in Illinois. But his son, Frank, frequently visited Andover and after his marriage, he and his wife, Hanne Henriksen, came to live at 14 Orchard Street. Although present day life takes them all over the world, Andover remains home base for Frank and Hanne Castle.

70 Elm Street

54 Abbot Street

237

THE ANDOVER TOWNSMAN

"Andover, everywhere and always, first, last, she has been the manly, straight-forward, sober, patriotic, New England Town." Phillips Brooks, The Andover Townsman, October 14, 1887.

All news in the *Townsman* is local, all of it. A weekly newspaper, read by most of the community's twenty-nine thousand residents and many outside of town, it runs an average of eighty pages a week.

Behold, Andover, from the pages of various issues of the *Townsman:*

100 years ago:

A horse belonging to William Tucker caused a little excitement Tuesday morning. He was left untied in front of the Bank Building, being harnessed to a wagon full of empty milk cans. Becoming frightened at some passing vehicle, he ran up Main, through Chestnut and Bartlet Streets back to Main, distributing the milk cans as he went.

50 years ago:

Jeremiah Twomey served his country in World War I and has been serving the interests of his fellow veterans ever since. Thursday afternoon he and Mrs. Twomey learned that they still had to give more for their country—a telegram from Washington told them that their son, Pfc. Gerard N. Twomey, one of the finest of Andover's fine boys, had given his life on the battlefields of France. The young man, a Phillips Academy graduate, was killed in action on Nov. 28.

25 years ago:

For nearly a century and a half, Abbot Academy has lived up on the hill, ever since Miss Sarah Abbot asked her friend Squire Farrar, "What shall I do with my surplus funds?" to which he promptly replied, "Found an academy in Andover for the education of young women!" And she did. Never in those 142 years of steady growth through early hardship and later success has there been more activity, change and new directions for Abbot than in the past three, under male headmaster Donald Gordon. To cap it off, she is now considering marriage. The betrothal of Abbot and next door neighbor Phillips Academy was announced.

10 years ago:

The Andover Village Improvement Society has just received a substantial gift of land for another major reservation to be preserved for the townspeople.

2 years ago:

A swan that apparently was frozen in the ice of Fosters Pond Tuesday morning gave Andover firefighters an opportunity to practice ice-rescue procedures, but managed to free itself and evade capture.

The *Townsman* is Andover's hometown weekly newspaper, published continuously since 1887. The *Townsman* is Andover, which is why its readers tend to be as loyal to it as they are to the town in which they reside. Owned and operated since 1949 by the Rogers family of Andover, the *Townsman* has labored for all of its 100-plus years to live up to the aspirations of founding publisher John N. Cole to "be of service to the entire community."

Irving E. Rogers Jr. is the publisher. The *Townsman* is located in its own building at 33 Chestnut Street.

Courtesy of Bernice Haggerty

The Eagle-Tribune.

From the left are: Irving E. Rogers Jr., Irving E. Rogers Sr., Allan B. Rogers, and Business Manager William L. Lucy Sr. in 1959.

For ninety-seven years the Rogers family has owned the *Eagle-Tribune* and been committed to the stability and growth of the Merrimack Valley. Today, when more than a quarter of daily newspapers in the country are owned by twenty conglomerates, the fifth generation of Rogers are involved with managing the *Eagle-Tribune*. On August 20, 1982, Publisher Irving E. Rogers stepped aside on his eightieth birthday, handing leadership of the paper over to his eldest son, Irving E. Rogers Jr. The day he chose was the fortieth anniversary of the day in 1942 when he became the publisher because of the sudden death of his father, Alexander H. Rogers.

The family newspaper tradition started with Alexander, a twelve-dollar-a-week reporter/printer with the rival *Lawrence American* before he moved to the *Lawrence Daily Eagle* in the early 1890s. In 1898 Alexander was invited by *Evening Tribune* Manager H. Frank Hildreth to form a partnership to buy the *Eagle* and *Tribune* from the heirs of Publisher H. A. Wadsworth. Alexander's father Barnett, who brought his family to Andover from Arbroath, Scotland, in 1870 when Alexander was two, backed the venture.

Irving Sr. joined the company in 1922 after graduating from Phillips Academy and attending Dartmouth College and the University of Wisconsin School of Journalism. He, too, started as a reporter. After a stint in advertising and as a photographer, he became assistant business manager. He managed radio station WLAW from its inception in 1937 until its sale in 1953.

His sons Irving Jr. and Allan B. followed their father into the business, Irving Jr. as businessmanager and Allan in the editorial department. Allan became the managing editor in 1956 and editor two years later, a job he held until his untimely death on June 11, 1962, two days after his thirty-first birthday. Today Irving Jr. is president of the Eagle-Tribune Publishing Company, Andover Publishing Company (*Andover Townsman*), Consolidated Press Incorporated (Eagle Offset Printing), and Derry Publishing Company (*Derry News*). Irving Jr.'s oldest son, Irving E. Rogers III, is general manager of the *Eagle Tribune*. Allan's oldest son, Allan B. Rogers Jr., is general manager of the *Derry News*, a twice-weekly paper which is an *Eagle-Tribune* affiliate. His younger brother Walter is associated with the promotions department at the *Eagle-Tribune*.

Alexander H. Rogers began the family newspaper publishing tradition in 1898. Here he is at apple harvesting time as a young man.

The Pike School

Residents of Andover are justifiably proud of the excellent educational institutions which are located in their community. One of these is The Pike School, an independent day school for children in pre-kindergarten through grade nine. Since its founding in 1926, Pike has played an important role in educating Andover's children as well as those from scores of other towns throughout the Merrimack Valley.

At Pike, learning is viewed as an exciting process, approached with a seriousness of purpose and respect for the creativity and individual learning style of each child. At the center of the academic program is a commitment to the basic disciplines: reading, writing, mathematics, science, history. Integration of technology into the fabric of the school and frequent, unique opportunities for enrichment create a vibrant atmosphere.

All children participate in the school's strong arts program. Fine arts teachers coach students as they experiment with a variety of media, ranging from sculpture to photography. Each spring, the school-wide art show affords the opportunity to appreciate the creativity of children at all age levels. The performing arts are pursued with equal intensity; presentations, both musical and theatrical, are offered at frequent intervals throughout the year. The availability of afterschool instrumental music instruction brings an added dimension to the arts program.

The school's physical education course provides developmentally appropriate activities for children. In addition, Pike offers Project Adventure, an approach to physical activity which encourages children to move beyond previously set limits and helps them learn to solve problems together. Older children also participate in an outdoor education program and may join in team interscholastic sports.

Pike's educational philosophy emphasizes the partnership of family and faculty in creating a learning environment which fosters success. Moreover, parents often help in classrooms, assist with field trips, and help to organize special events. The Pike School Parents Association is responsible for numerous projects, among them the spring Pike School Fair which has become a popular Andover event.

Pike's long history parallels the growth of Andover. A handful of students comprised the entire enrollment of "Mrs. Pike's" in 1926. Today, under the leadership of its sixth head of school, John M. Waters, Pike continues to thrive and looks forward to many more years of offering an extraordinary educational experience to children of Andover and surrounding communities.

This profile was made possible through the generosity of The Board of Trustees of The Pike School.

Pike School students. Stanley Rowin photo, 1992

Shawmut Bank

Shawmut Bank has been a Massachusetts institution since 1836. Its involvement in the Andover community reaches back to its presence there as part of the Arlington Trust Company. Shawmut, today a $31 billion financial institution, remains proud of its roots in the communities it serves and of its history as a family of smaller, community-based banking institutions.

In the fall of 1991 Shawmut expanded its presence in the town of Andover with the opening of its Andover Center branch office, located in the heart of town. Valuing the uniqueness of Andover's character, Shawmut worked in concert with the Andover Historical Society to design the bank's new facilities at 68 Main Street. The Andover Center branch joined the longtime Shawsheen branch office in the delivery of banking services to local residents and businesses. In addition, Shawmut expanded its service in Andover with augmented trust and private banking services.

Shawmut professionals provide Andover residents and businesses with the kind of quality service they have come to expect. Most importantly, Shawmut employees continue a rich tradition of community and civic involvement, participating in a number of activities designed to enhance the quality of the community, economically, socially, and civically. Shawmut looks forward to its continuing role in Andover's rich history.

Shawmut Bank in the recently rehabilitated K&D Block (also called the Merchants' Building). Ray Sprague photo, 1995

Batchelder Farm

"Rolling Acres" 1927–1951

"The Jamison Farm on Argilla Road owned by Dr. Emma Batchelder, recently of Exeter, is being managed by her nephew, Sidney S. Batchelder who has stocked the farm with some good cattle and established a milk route. Mr. Batchelder engages to supply customers with high quality, pure, raw milk showing better than four percent butterfat and also with cream. Vegetables in season will also be sold to customers on the milk route."—*Andover Townsman*, May 18, 1928

Thus began "Rolling Acres Farm" and the Batchelders' move to West Parish. Emma purchased the farm at 97 Argilla Road (once part of William Wood's "Arden Trust") on June 15, 1927. Other parcels of land were added to create the 109-acre farm. Sidney S. was living at 134 Summer Street (then number 98) in the house he built in 1913 for his new bride, Isabella Hamilton Gamble. He established a small milk route near the center of town in 1919 but with a growing business and family, he struck a deal with his aunt and swapped properties in October 1930. Sidney, Belle, and their five children—Sidney Abbott, Isabella Ellen, Albert Longfellow, Gertrude Currier, and Loring Eugene—took up residence at "Rolling Acres." They would have two more childlren, David Hamilton and Priscilla Anne, both born at the farm.

An Essex automobile was first used to deliver milk but was replaced by a series of pickup trucks. The first tractor, a 1920s Fordson with iron wheels, later replaced with a 1939 Allis Chalmers, pulled the harrow, manure spreader, wooden hay wagon, stake wagon, and dump cart. The hay tedder and hay rake were both drawn by "Gabriel," a workhorse. Twelve Holstein milkers provided the daily supply of milk. The rest of the herd, a bull, chickens, ducks, pigs, a cat, and two Border collies named "Pat" and "Mike" completed the barnyard inventory.

Albert continued the management of the farm after Sidney S. died in 1948. Isabella H. Batchelder sold the farm on December 21, 1951 and Albert moved the entire dairy operation to Bacon Hill, New York. With the sale of "Rolling Acres" went the last remaining dairy farm on Argilla Road. S. Abbott and Helen (Ferrier) Batchelder continue to live at 93 Argilla Road in the house they built fifty-five years ago in the cow yard next to the farm.

Summer Street house. Courtesy of the Batchelder family

West Andover, A Community Unto Itself

A century ago in West Andover, no doors were locked, differences were put aside, and neighboring farms watched out for each other. Winters were hard and made things all the more remote. Teams of horses and hand shovels were the only method of clearing snow off the roads. It was during this time that third-generation Kearn descendants Charles Albert, Mildred Arline, and Frederick James Kearn became residents of the West Andover community.

Charles operated a spring water company on Webster Street and owned another parcel on the south side of Bailey Road at the intersection of Pleasant Street. The granite foundation remains there today. Charles was killed by a bus while delivering water on Essex Street, August 28, 1943. Mildred Kearn married William M. Flint and went to live and work on the Flint farm at 13 (now 11) Bailey Road. One parcel of this farm was later sold to build St. Robert Bellarmine Church. William Flint's sister, Cynthia, who was born and raised at 13 Bailey Road, married Walter Pike. She later founded the Pike School. Her husband, Walter, built the magnificent archway that marks the entrance to West Parish Cemetery. The youngest brother, Frederick, bought a small farm with two parcels, one at 44 (now 236) Haggetts Pond Road and the other at 394 High Plain Road, where his son, Warren, now resides. Frederick was employed by the Boston & Albany Railroad. He walked daily to the depot, now 48 Haggett's Pond Road, for transportation to his job in Boston. When the Great Depression forced an early retirement, he spent the remainder of his life as a farmer and carpenter, building many barns and new additions in Andover and Lawrence.

Frederick's grandson, Stephen, married Gwen Batchelder, an Andover native, whose grandparents, the Anderson family, had owned and operated Pine Grove Hatchery at 100 Ballardvale Road since the early 1900s. Stephen and Gwen have two children, Erin Elizabeth and Christopher Stephen. Stephen owns S. W. Kearn Equipment, a small machinery distribution and brokerage business in Andover.

Flint family members gather for a portrait in front of the farmhouse at 13 Bailey Road. From the left are: unknown, George E. Flint, Cynthia Flint Pike (foreground in black), George M. Flint, Mrs. George E. Flint, and William M. Flint, holding the horse.

Frederick and Mary Kearn pose in front of their house and Model T Ford with their daughters, Ruth and Lillian, center, and cousins, Mildred and Gladys O'Connor of Biddeford, Maine, to the left and right of the Kearn girls.

Topham, Fardy & Co.

Topham, Fardy & Co., a firm of certified public accountants, has helped small businesses and individuals succeed in changing financial climates. Professional services are rendered primarily to clients in Merrimack Valley and Southern New Hampshire. The demand from satisfied clients has extended the practice as far as Maine, Florida, and California. The firm's partners are Walter W. Topham, a graduate of Dartmouth College, and Thomas E. Fardy, a graduate of Bentley College. Both hold master of science degrees in taxation from Bentley. The two spent ten years through the management levels in the international public accounting firm of Deloitte and Touche before deciding to create a smaller firm specializing in small business and individual financial needs. "We brought the training and expertise of an international accounting firm to our hometown clients." In 1984 the partners moved from 15 Central Street to 26 Essex Street, where they restored a 1917 building which once housed the town's post office. They purchased the building from Town Printing and renovated its row of outdated multi-level storefronts into a single-level office building appropriate to modern business needs. At present the firm totals nine: two principals, a professional staff of four and an administrative staff of three. This team offers stability, personal service, and technical skills with the most up-to-date tax and other information available. Walter and Tom have represented their clients, as advocates, before the Internal Revenue Service and state tax authorities on numerous occasions. Services also include audits; reviews or compilation of financial statements; consulting; management advisory services; income and estate tax return preparation and planning; mergers and acquisitions; regulatory reporting; accounting assistance; and other business and financial consultation. The firm has recently received an unqualified report on its quality control system from a peer firm.

Walter and Tom's concern for the community has gone far beyond their own business, however. They have held leadership positions in statewide professional accounting associations as well as in numerous nonprofit community service organizations in the Merrimack Valley, including the Vesper Country Club, the Merrimack Valley Chapter of the American Red Cross, the Lawrence Rotary Club and Kiwanis Club, the Finance Committee of the Town of Andover, and the Methuen Board of Trade. In addition, Topham and Fardy serve on the executive committees of First Essex Savings Bank and Northmark Bank, respectively.

Partners Thomas Fardy and Walter Topham consult on a case. Courtesy of Topham, Fardy & Co.

The Howe Agency

Forty years ago, Douglas N. Howe Sr. established his real estate and insurance business in Andover. Today the company has grown into multi-office corporations serving the Merrimack Valley. Doug Sr. began his career in Andover in 1951 with the W. Shirley Barnard Agency. Sensing the growth in Andover, he opened his own business four years later just a few doors up Main Street above Elander and Swanton's Clothing Store (now Royal Jewelers). Both sons, Doug Jr. and Cliff, joined their father's business in 1972.

By 1977 the Howe Agency bought 4 Punchard Avenue, occupied by the Red Cross and the one-time Andover Home for the Aged. Howe Real Estate, with Doug Jr. as president, is an independently owned and operated member of the Prudential Real Estate Affliates, Incorporated. They celebrate a proud tradition of consistently serving the buying and selling needs of individuals and families. A fine reputation for integrity, innovation, and exemplary service reflects their commitment to excellence.

4 Punchard Avenue

The Howe Insurance Agency, with a staff of seventeen full-time, experienced, insurance people under the leadership of Cliff, provides quality service to townspeople as well as to individuals and business clients in Eastern Massachusetts and Southern New Hampshire. Contributing both as a professional, independent agency and as a responsible member of the local business community, they continually grow with referrals from satisfied clients.

The Howe family has been active in the Merrimack Valley, as leading members of the Greater Lawrence Insurance Agents Association, the Greater Lawrence Board of Realtors, the Chamber of Commerce, and Andover's Finance Committee.

Left to right, are the Howe men: Cliff, Doug Sr., and Doug Jr., 1994

Headquarters of
Watts Industries, Inc.,
North Andover, MA

T imothy P. Horne of Andover is the third generation of the Horne family to lead this company founded in Lawrence in 1874 by Joseph E. Watts. Horne is Chairman of the Board and Chief Executive Officer. Horne's grandfather, Burchard Everett Horne, bought the company in 1918. Burchard's son, George, joined the firm in the 1930's, and his grandson in 1959.

Watts Regulator, as it was originally called, made its reputation on valves to regulate steam and on safety valves for water heaters and boilers. In the rapidly expanding water quality markets of the 1970's, the company began a period of growth which contributed to rapidly increasing sales from $19 million in 1970 to $103 million in 1984.

From 1984 through 1994, the company has grown to $519 million through additional new product development and also by a series of 28 acquisitions of valve companies and valve product lines complementing its core products.

From plumbing and heating, the company has expanded into valves for municipal waterworks, chemical processing industries, oil and gas, and steam markets.

The broad array of valve products offered by Watts Industries enables many of its customers to purchase all of its valve requirements in one package, thus giving Watts a competitive edge in the marketplace.

Headquarters today are on Chestnut Street in North Andover, Massachusetts. The company has 17 manufacturing plants in the United States, 3 in Canada, 8 in Europe, and a majority controlled joint venture manufacturing plant in Tianjin, People's Republic of China. Plans are also underway for expansion into the emerging growth markets of eastern Europe. With the growth opportunities inherent in a truly global economy, Watts has established an objective of having $1 billion in sales by the end of the decade.

Timothy P. Horne

George B. Horne

Burchard E. Horne

Watts Industries: Committed to the achievement of sustained long-term growth. (Fifteen year history)

Net Sales (millions)
Compounded Annual Growth Rate 17%

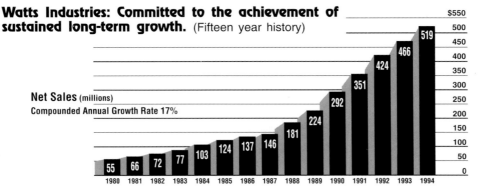

Year	Net Sales
1980	55
1981	66
1982	72
1983	77
1984	103
1985	124
1986	137
1987	146
1988	181
1989	224
1990	292
1991	351
1992	424
1993	466
1994	519

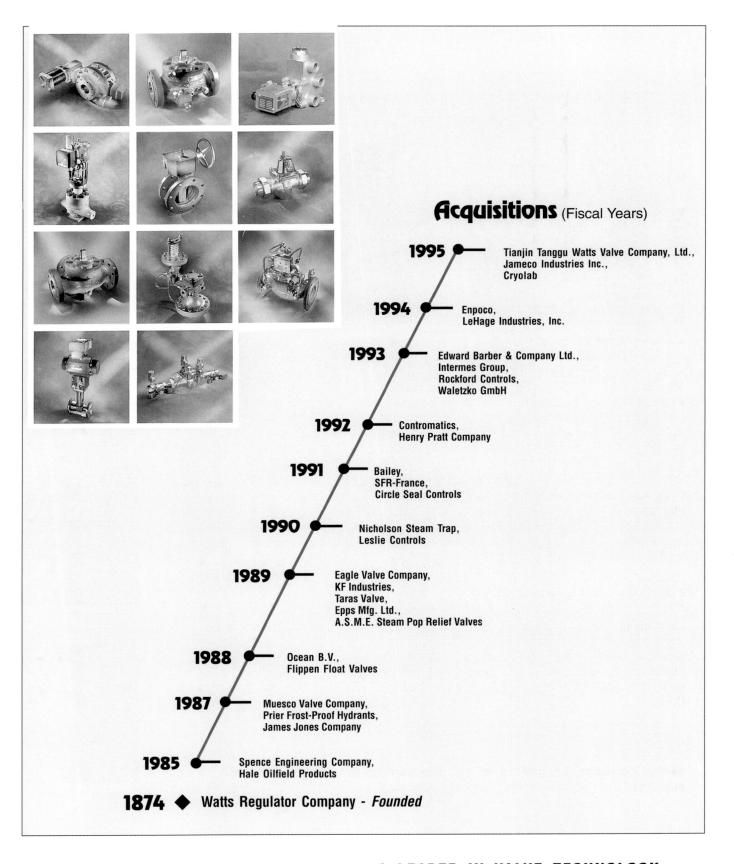

Acquisitions (Fiscal Years)

1995 — Tianjin Tanggu Watts Valve Company, Ltd.,
Jameco Industries Inc.,
Cryolab

1994 — Enpoco,
LeHage Industries, Inc.

1993 — Edward Barber & Company Ltd.,
Intermes Group,
Rockford Controls,
Waletzko GmbH

1992 — Contromatics,
Henry Pratt Company

1991 — Bailey,
SFR-France,
Circle Seal Controls

1990 — Nicholson Steam Trap,
Leslie Controls

1989 — Eagle Valve Company,
KF Industries,
Taras Valve,
Epps Mfg. Ltd.,
A.S.M.E. Steam Pop Relief Valves

1988 — Ocean B.V.,
Flippen Float Valves

1987 — Muesco Valve Company,
Prier Frost-Proof Hydrants,
James Jones Company

1985 — Spence Engineering Company,
Hale Oilfield Products

1874 ◆ Watts Regulator Company - *Founded*

A LEADER IN VALVE TECHNOLOGY
WATTS®
INDUSTRIES, INC.
SINCE 1874

Main Street, circa 1920. The Andover Historical Society building, number 97, is on the left.

Appendix

Andover Clergy since 1880

(Sarah Loring Bailey's book, *Historical Sketches of Andover*, lists clergy prior to 1880)

1711   South Church, 41 Central Street. Ministers:

James H. Laird	1877–1883
John J. Blair	1884–18930
Frank P. Shipman	1893–1913
E. Victor Bigelow	1914–1928
Frederick B. Noss	1931–1966
J. Everett Bodge	1968–1977
Westy A. Egmont	1978–1986
Calvin F. Mutti	1989–present

1816   Cochran Chapel, Phillips Academy. Chaplains:

(Andover Theological Seminary ministers until 1908.)

Alfred E. Stearns, headmaster	1908–1933
Rev. Markham W. Stackpole	1907–1917; 1919
Rev. A. Graham Baldwin	1934–1966
Rev. James Rae Whyte	1966–1976
Rabbi Everett Gendler	1976–present
Rev. Philip Zaeder (Protestant)	1977–present
Rev. Thomas Hennigan (Catholic)	1977–1981
Rev. Richard Gross, S.J. (Catholic)	1982–1992
Rev. Michael Hall, O.S.B.(Catholic)	1992–present

1826   West Parish Church, 129 Reservation Road. Ministers:

Rev. Austin Hannahs Burr	1880–1885
Rev. Frederick W. Greene	1885–1894
Rev. Robert Andrew Macfadden	1896–1989
Rev. George Arthur Andrews	1899–1904
Rev. John Edgar Park	1904–1907
Rev. Dean Augustus Walker Ph.D.	1908–1914
Rev. Newman Matthews	1914–1937
minister emeritus	1937–1951
Rev. Donald H. Savage	1937–1944
Rev. Leslie John Adkins	1945–1946
Rev. John Gilbert Gaskill	1946–1953
Rev. Hugh Burill Penney	1954–1959
Rev. Howard A. Andrews	1960–1963
Rev. Bruce Van Blair	1963–1967
Rev. Norman E. Dubie Sr.	1967–1972
Rev. Dr. Otis Maxfield	1973–1983

Rev. Graham Ward   1983–1986
Rev. Joseph LaDu   1988–present

1832   **First Baptist Church, 7 Central Street. Pastors:**

Dr. Benjamin F. Bronson	1881–1887
Rev. Joel V. Stratton	1888–1889
Rev. George W. Clough	1891–1893
Rev. Frederick W. Klein	1895–1900
Rev. Arthur T. Belknap	1900–1905
Rev. William E. Lombard	1906–1917
Rev. Edwin H. Prescott	1917–1920
Rev. C. Norman Bartlett	1922–1930
Rev. Lorentz I. Hansen	1931–1937
Rev. Samuel Overstreet	1937–1940
Rev. Elton E. Smith	1940–1945
Rev. Roy E. Nelson Jr.	1950–1956
Rev. Donald J. Ryder	1955–1960
Rev. W. Carter Johnson	1961–1964
Rev. Earl B. Robinson	1964–1977
Rev. Reginald Angus MacDonald	1978-1985
Rev. Phillips Brooks Henderson (interim)	1985–1987
Rev. Thomas Goldthwaite	1988–present

1835   **The Parish of Christ Church, Episcopal, 25 Central Street. Rectors:**

The Rev. Malcolm Douglass	1875–1884
The Rev. Leverett Bradley	1884–1888
The Rev. Frederick Palmer	1888–1913
The Rev. Charles W. Henry	1913–1937
The Rev. Albert C. Morris	1937–1941
The Rev. John S. Moses	1941–1959
The Rev. J. Edison Pike	1959–1980
The Rev. James A. Diamond	1981–present

1846   **Free Christian Church; first building, Railroad Avenue; second building, 31 Elm Street. Ministers:**

Rev. G. Frederick Wright	1872–1881
Rev. F. Barrows Make Peace	1881–1889
Rev. Frederick A. Wilson	1889–1919
pastor emeritus	1919–1936
Rev. Arthur S. Wheelock	1920–1924
Rev. Alfred C. Church	1925–1937
Rev. Herman C. Johnson	1937–1943
Rev. Frank Dunn	1943–1945
Rev. Levering Reynolds	1945–1957
Rev. Horace Seldon	1957–1959
Rev. J. Allyn Bradford	1959–1971
Rev. Richard B. Balmforth	1971–1976
Rev. Jack L. Daniel Jr.	1977–present

1850   **Methodist Episcopal Church in Ballardvale, corner of Tewksbury and Marland Streets. Ministers 1880–1955: (merged in 1955 to form United Church in BV)**

Rev. Walter Wilkie	1878–1880
Rev. A. H. Hoyt	1881
Rev. R. W. Harlow	1882
Rev. J. A. Day	1883–1888
Rev. N. H. Martin	1883–1888
Rev. Edward E. Small	1889
Rev. W. F. Stewart	1891
Rev. E. H. Fuller	1892

Rev. T. A. Hodgdon	1893–1895
Rev. V. E. Hills	1896–1897
Rev. LeVerne Roberts	1897–1899
Rev. Thomas Livingston	1898–1900
Rev. L. G. March	1900
Rev. C. K. Hudson	1901
Rev. H. S. Cramton	1902
Rev. William Ferguson	1905–1907
Rev. Alvin E. Worman	1907–1909
Rev. Elwin D. Lane	1910
Rev. William S. Handy	1911
Rev. Connart J. Mekelson	1912
Rev. Perry S. Neldon	1912–1914
Rev. James King	1915
Rev. Ralph Scott	1915–1916
Rev. Frank A. Everett	1916–1918
Rev. J. P. Cordero	1918–1920
Rev. C. E. Wintringham	1920–1922
Rev. C. M. Schaub	1922–1923
Rev. Thomas Adams	1923–1924
Rev. Clifford Reynolds	1925
Rev. J. R. Wonder	1926–1927
Rev. Elwyn Scheyer	1928–1930
Rev. Everett R. Barrows	1930–1933
Rev. Elwyn Ewing	1934–1935
Rev. Carl L. Craine	1935–1937
Rev. Wilbert W. Marzahn	1938–1940
Rev. Carl W. Wilson	1941–1942
Rev. William Crawford	1943–1948
Rev. Earl D. Haywood	1949–1950
Rev. Allen F. Kerns	1950–1952
Rev. Robert McCune	1952–1953
Rev. Anthony Perino	1953–1955

1850   **Ballard Vale Union Society; 1854—name changed to Union Congregational Church, corner of Andover and Church Streets Ministers 1880–1955 (Merged in 1955 to form United Church of Ballardvale)**

Rev. Henry S. Greene	1855–1880
Rev. J. W. Savage	1881–1882
Rev. Samuel Bowker	1884–1888
Rev. G. S. Butler	1888–1891
Rev. Emil Bary	1891–1892
Rev. J. C. C. Evans	1893–1896
Rev. Arthur Golden	1896–1898
Rev. Edwin Smith	1899–1903
Rev. Augustus H. Fuller	1904–1926
Rev. Wesley G. Nicholson	1926–1927
Rev. Herman Van Lunen	1927–1930
Rev. Marion Phelps	1930–1937
Rev. Claude A. Butterfield	1938–1939
Rev. David I. Segerstrom	1939–1943
Rev. Arnold M. Kenseth	1943–1947
Rev. Phillip M. Kelsey	1947–1949
Rev. Paul E. Callahan	1949–1952
Rev. Raymond B. Wilbur	1952–1954
Rev. Roland D. Seger	1954–1955

1852	**St. Augustine's Parish; first building, Central Street; and second building, 43 Essex Street. Pastors:**	
	Rev. Michael F. Gallagher, O.S.A.	1866–1869
	Rev. Ambrose A. Mullen, O.S.A.	1869–1883
	Rev. Maurice J. Murphy, O.S.A.	1883–1887
	Rev. Jeremiah J. Ryan, O.S.A.	1887–1894
	Rev. Thomas A. Field, O.S.A.	1894–1898
	Rev. Daniel J. O'Mahoney, O.S.A.	1898–1902
	Very Rev. Charles M. Driscoll, O.S.A.	1902–1903
	Rev. James A. McGowan, O.S.A.	1903–1907
	Rev. Frederick S. Riordan, O.S.A.	1907–1918
	Rev. John A. Nugent, O.S.A.	1918–1926
	Rev. Charles A. Branton, O.S.A.	1926–1935
	Rev. John A. McErlain, O.S.A.	1935–1935
	Rev. Thomas B. Austin, O.S.A.	1935–1944
	Rev. Thomas P. Fogarty, O.S.A.	1944–1950
	Rev. Patrick J. Campbell, O.S.A.	1950–1956
	Rev. Henry B. Smith, O.S.A.	1956–1963
	Rev. Francis X. N. McGuire, O.S.A.	1963–1965
	Rev. Kenneth J. Kennedy, O.S.A.	1965–1971
	Rev. Jerome Holland, O.S.A.	1972–1974
	Rev. Edward Robinson, O.S.A.	1975–1978
	Rev. Joseph Keffer, O.S.A.	1978–1981
	Rev. Richard O'Leary, O.S.A.	1981–1986
	Rev. Arthur Johnson, O.S.A.	1986–1994
	Rev. Alfred Ellis, O.S.A.	1994–present

1955	**Ballardvale United Church, Clark Road. Ministers:**	
	Rev. Ralph Rosenblad	1955–1960
	Rev. Haldean Lindsey	1960–1961
	Rev. Wendell E. Minnigh	1961–1964
	Rev. Robert Bossdorf	1964–1968
	Rev. Charles Fowlie	1968–1974
	Rev. David Hollenbeck	1974–1981
	Rev. Gary Cornell	1982–1988
	Rev. Susan Morrison	1988–present

1961	**St. Robert Bellarmine Parish, Haggett's Pond Road. Pastors:**	
	Rev. Francis Sullivan	1961–1967
	Rev. William Fitzgerald	1967–1977
	Rev. Frederick Collins	1977–1989
	Rev. Arthur Driscoll	1989–present

1962	**Faith Lutheran Church, 360 South Main Street. Pastors:**	
	Rev. Hartland H. Gifford	1962–1970
	Rev. Donald B. Myrom	1971–1977
	Rev. Dennis P. Kohl	1977–1988
	Rev. Richard E. Lindgren	1989–1992
	Rev. Jonathan T. Heydenreich	1993–present

1964	**Unitarian Universalist Congregation in Andover; founded in 1847 in Lawrence; first building, 244 Lowell Street; second building, 6 Locke Street. Ministers (in Andover):**	
	Rev. Keith C. Munson	1960–1968
	Rev. Richard M. Woodman	1969–1974
	Rev. Randolph Lehman–Becker	1975–1980
	Rev. Gail K. Lehman–Becker	1978–1980
	Rev. Rosemarie C. Smurzynski	1981–1989
	Rev. Peter T. Richardson	1992–present

1977   **Siddha Yoga Meditation Center of Andover, 6 Locke Street.**
            Leaders:
            Joanne and Al Dahlgren, founders   1977–1990
            Bonnie Doyle   1990–1992
            Susan Lenoe   1992–present

1979   **Temple Emanuel (Founded in 1920 in Lawrence), 7 Haggett's Pond**
            Road. Rabbis (in Andover):
            Rabbi Harry A. Roth   1962–1990
            Rabbi Robert S. Goldstein   1990–present

            First Invested Cantor:
            Cantor Donn Rosensweig   1986–present

1981   **North Boston Korean United Methodist Church; March 1977,**
            Lawrence; September 1977, Methuen; 1981, Andover, 244 Lowell Street.
            Pastors:
            Dr. Young Bok Rha   1977–1981
            Rev. Hongsuk Choi   1981–1986
            Rev. Sung Kim   1986–present

1982   **New England Bible Church, 60 Chandler Road. Pastor:**
            Rev. Chip Thompson   1982–present

1988   **Saints Constantine and Helen Church Greek Orthodox Church, founded**
            in1917 in Lawrence; 71 Chandler Road. Pastors:
            Rev. Dr. George Karahalios   1971–1993
            Rev. Paul Pantelis   1993–present

1988   **BrookRidge Community Church, 16 Haverhill Street.**
            Pastor:
            Rev. Bill Watson   1988–present

1990   **Congregation Tifereth Israel, founded 1889 in Lawrence; 501 South**
            Main Street. Rabbis:
            Rabbi Barbara Penzner   1991–1993
            Rabbi Howard Kosovske   1993–present

1992   **Chabad Jewish Center of the Merrimack Valley. Rabbi:**
            Rabbi Osher Bronstein   1992–present

1993   **Victory Free Methodist Church, meets at Andover Baptist Church, 7**
            Central Street; formerly Spanish Free Methodist Church. Pastors:
            Rev. Rafael Reyes   1992–1993
            Rev. Juan D. Grullon   1993–present

School Administrators

Superintendents of Andover Public Schools

Heman Allen Halstead	1890–1892
W. A. Baldwin	1892–1895
George E. Johnson	1895–1901
Corwin Ford Palmer	1901–1908
Sherburn C. Hutchinson	1908–1911
George M. Bemis	1911–1914
J. Francis Allison	1914–1916
Henry C. Sanborn	1916–1939
Kenneth L. Sherman*	1939–1942; 1945–1953

Edward I. Erickson	1942–1945; 1953–1969
Kenneth R. Seifert	1969–1990
Mark K. McQuillan	1991–1994
Richard Neal**	1994–present

*Military leave   **acting

Principals of Punchard/Andover High School since 1896

Frank Otis Baldwin	1888–1894; 1895–1902
Allen Latham	1894–1895
S. Hale Baker	1902–1903
Alton W. Pierce	1903–1904
Charles L. Curtis	1904–1910
Nathan Chipman Hamblin	1910–1941
Eugene V. Lovely	1941–1950
Charles A. Gregory*	1949–1950
Harold Howe II	1950–1953
Lindsey Jackson March	1953–1962
Philip F. Wormwood	1962–1981
Mary Athley Jennings**	1981–1987
Stephen C. Richardson*	1984–1985; 1987–1987
Wilbur Hixon	1987–1991
Timothy Thomas	1991–present

* acting **leave of absence

Superintendents of Greater Lawrence Technical School

James A. Booth	1965–1975
Louis E. Gleason	1976–1991
Marsha A. McDonough	1991–present

Principals of St. Augustine's School

Sister Helen Bernardine	1914–1921; 1927–1931
Sister Marie Catherine	1921–1924
Sister Berchmans of the Blessed Sacrament	1924–1927
Sister Paula	1931–1935
Sister Mary Wilfred	1935–1944
Sister Regina Marie	1944–1950
Sister Ellen Saint John	1950–1958
Sister Marie Saint James	1958–1962
Sister Owen Marie	1962–1965
Sister Catherine Carmelita	1965–1966
Sister Marie Rosalie	1966–1978
Sister Rita Heywood	1978–1981
Sister Madeline Carrabino	1981–1982
Brother Tom Shady	1982–1986
Dr. Marie Galinski, Ph.D.	1986–present

Principals and Headmasters of the Pike School

Cynthia E. Pike	1926–1951
Margaret J. Little	1951–1956
William J. Harding	1956–1971
Raymond A. Nelson	1971–1977
E. Standish Bradford*	1977–1978
David A. Frothingham	1978–1994
John M. Waters	1994–present

*interim

Principals of Abbot Academy since 1859

Philena McKeen	1859–1892
Laura Sophia Watson	1892–1898
Emily Adams Means	1898–1911
Bertha Bailey	1912–1935
Marguerite Capen Hearsey	1936–1955
Mary Hinckley Crane	1955–1966
Eleanor Tucker*	1966–1968
Donald Gordon	1967–1973

*Acting Principal

Principals, Headmasters, and Heads of Phillips Academy since 1873

Cecil F. P. Bancroft	1873–1901
Alfred Ernest Stearns	1903–1933
Claude M. Fuess	1934–1948
John Mason Kemper	1948–1971
Theodore R. Sizer	1972–1981
Donald W. McNemar	1981–1994
Barbara Landis Chase	1994–present

Presidents of Merrimack College

Reverend Vincent A. McQuade, O.S.A.	1947–1968
Reverend John R. Aherne, O.S.A.	1968–1976
Rev. John A. Coughlan, O.S.A.	1976–1981
Rev. John E. Deegan, O.S.A.	1981–1994
Richard J. Santagati*	1994–present

*interim

St. Francis Seraphic Seminary

Rev. Aloysius M. Costa, O.F.M.	1930–1931
Rev. Romano Simoni, O.F.M.	1931–1934
Rev. Aloysius M. Costa, O.F.M.	1934–1943
Rev. Bernardine Mazzarella, O.F.M.	1943–1945
Rev. Leonard Bacigalupo, O.F.M.	1945–1946
Rev. Bernardine Mazzarella, O.F.M.	1946–1949
Rev. Gregory Palma, O.F.M.	1949–1952
Rev. Matthew De Benedictis, O.F.M.	1952–1959
Rev. Matthias Pastore, O.F.M.	1959–1968
Rev. Columban Leonard, O.F.M.	1968–1970
Rev. Luke Ciampi, O.F.M.	1970–1973
Rev. Roland Petinge, O.F.M.	1973–1976
Rev. Luke Ciampi, O.F.M.	1976–1977

Selectmen and Town Managers

Selectmen from 1896

Samuel H. Boutwell	1882–91; 1891–1905;
B. Frank Smith	1888–89; 1902–07
John S. Stark	1889–1902
Arthur Bliss	1893–98
William G. Goldsmith	1898–1903
Samuel H. Bailey	1902–1912
Walter S. Donald	1905–1923
Harry M. Eames	1907–1918
Charles Bowman	1912–1930
Andrew McTernen	1922–1928; 1931–1934

Frank H. Hardy	1923–1935
Jeremiah J. Daly	1928–1936
Howell F. Shepard	1934–1942; 1946–1949
J. Everett Collins	1954
Edward P. Hall	1942–1946, 1959–1960
Sidney P. White	1949–1961; 1966–1972
Stafford A. Lindsay	1954–1960
William L. McDonald	1955–1958
William V. Emmons	1956–1959
Eugene A. Bernardin Jr.	1959–1962
William Stewart	1959–1971
Philip K. Allen	1959–1970
James D. Wilson	1959–1964
Russell G. Doyle	1960–1963
B. Allen Rowland	1962–1964
Paul W. Cronin	1963–1966
Robert A. Watters	1964–1973
Roger W. Collins	1964–1965, 1965–1974
George E. Heseltine	1970–1976
Milton Greenberg	1971–1977
Alan F. French	1972–1977
Edmund E. Sullivan Jr.	1973–1976
Janet D. Lake	1974–1977
Richard J. Bowen	1976–1978
Susan T. Poore	1976–1982
Phillip J. Salamone	1977–1978
Virginia H. Cole	1978–1979
Albert Cole Jr.	1977–1979
Edward M. Harris	1977–1983
James Abramson	1978–1981
Lawrence J. Sullivan	1979–1980
Norma A. Gammon	1979–1985
Gerald H. Silverman	1980–
Donn B. Byrne	1981–1986
William J. Dalton	1982–1988
Charles H. Wesson Jr.,	1983–
John I. Scileppi	1985–1987
William T. Downs	1987–
Gail L. Ralston	1987–1991
James M. Barenboim	1988–
Larry L. Larsen	1991–

Town Managers

Victor J. Mill Jr.	interim 1959
Thomas Duff	1959–1965
Richard Bowen	1965–1968
J. Maynard Austin	1969–1977
Sheldon S. Cohen	acting 1977
Jared S.A. Clark	1978–1981
Kenneth A. Mahony	1982–1990
Reginald S. ("Buzz") Stapczynski	1990–

Endnotes

Chapter One—No Notes

Chapter Two Notes

1. Telephone interview with Jay Leno, February 14, 1994.

2. Interview with Morris Krinsky, Nov. 23, 1993, H. Krinsky and Son Junkyard, Park Street.

3. Fuess, Claude M., *Andover: The Evolution of a Town*, Andover Historical Society Collection and North Andover Historical Society, 1959.

4. *Boston Sunday Transcript*, July 12, 1896.

5. Information on Cole's life from *The Andover Townsman, Centennial Issue*, July 21, 1988, story by Melissa M. DeMeo, and from Andover Historical Society archives.

6. Jim Doherty says Goldsmith was not the town's first policewoman, as is commonly claimed. The first was Esther Smith, a descendant of Peter Smith of the Smith & Dove Mills. (*Andover As I Remember It*, p. 80.)

7. Interview with Richard Graber, Dec. 3, 1993, 212 Salem Street. (Source of quote is actually from Tacitus' history, "They create a desert and call it peace," said by Calgicus, a british Celt, describing the Romans.)

8. Mofford, Juliet Haines, *AVIS—A History in Conservation*, Andover Village Improvement Society, 1980, pp. 22-33.

9. Ibid., p. 26.

10. Oral history interview of Thayer Warshaw, Jan. 8, 1992, on tape in Andover Historical Society Collection.

11. Dalton, Bill, *Local Touch*, published by Bill Dalton, 1985, "The Old Town Hall."

12. Material on William Wood from *Mills, Mansions and Mergers*, published by Merrimack Valley Textile Museum, North Andover, Mass., 1982, from interviews and manuscript assistance by Cornelius A. Wood Jr., grandson of William M. Wood, on October 28, 1994, and from a walking tour of Shawsheen Village by Andover native Warren ("Bud") Lewis.

13. The Academy's Constitution still states, "Protestants only shall ever be concerned in the Trust or Instruction of this Seminary." This stipulation is now ignored. From an interview with James Doherty, Jan. 6, 1994, 21 Elm St. For more information on the Doherty family, see Doherty, James, *Andover As I Remember It*, privately published, 1992.

14. Interview with James D. Doherty, January 6, 1994, 21 Elm Street.

15. Interview with William Dalton, December 9 and 13, 1993, at 199 Chestnut St., and manuscript by his aunt, Frances Dalton, in 1980, courtesy of William Dalton.

16. Interview with Beverly Darling, Nov. 29, 1993, 18 Alden St.

17. Interview with Tom and Stella Koravos, Dec. 30, 1993, Ford's Coffee Shop, 14 Main St.

18. Interview with Phil Allen by Virginia Cole and Barbara Thibault, Feb. 7, 1990, tape courtesy of Andover Historical Society.

19. Interview with Joshua L. Miner, November 15, 1994, 42 School Street.

20. Interview with Thayer Warshaw, January 8, 1992, 45 Clark Road, on file at Andover Historical Society.

21. Telephone interview with Paul Cronin, February 17, 1994.

22. Telephone interview with Jerry Cohen, January 15, 1994.

23. Telephone interview with Susan Tucker, January 11, 1994.

Chapter Three Notes

1. Bylaws—Andover Village Improvement Society, the Andover Press, Printers 1896

2. Minutes of Andover Village Improvement Society, May 7, 1894, Andover Historical Society Collection.

3. *Andover Townsman*, April 23, 1894.

4. Mofford, Juliet Hanes, *AVIS—A History in Conservation,* Andover, Mass., Andover Village Improvement Society, 1980, pp. 40-43 and 76-79.

5. The transaction was complicated—a detailed description is provided in the chapter on mills.

6. Minutes of Andover Natural History Society, Andover Historical Society Collection, June 4, 1904.

7. Minutes of the Andover Natural History Society, June 4, June 25, July 2, July 20, and Dec. 3, 1904.

8. John Kimball, telephone interview, Jan. 18. 1994

9. Minutes of the Andover Historical Society, p. 1, Andover Historical Society Collection.

10. Minutes of the Andover Historical Society, Dec. 12, 1913.

11. *Andover Historical Society Newsletter*, Summer 1981, Vol. 6, No. 2.

12. Domingue, Robert A., *Phillips Academy, Andover, Massachusetts,* RAD Publishing Company, 1990, pp. 63-65; and Barbara Thibault, Andover Historical Society.

13. Domingue, Robert A., op. cit. pp. 56-63.

14. Ibid., p. 59, 66-72.

15. Jim Batchelder, interview, November 18, 1993, Andover Historical Society.

16. Interview with Jane Griswold, January 11, 1994, Andover Historical Society.

17. Sarah Loring Bailey, *Historical Sketches of Andover*, Boston: Houghton, Mifflin and Company, 1880, p. 147; (seventeeth-century petition by residents of Andover to the Massachusetts General Court) from Mass. Archives, vol. cxii, page 202.

18. Pegg Keck, telephone interview, January 18, 1994.

19. Robert Pustell, interview, January 17, 1994, 85 Porter Road, Andover.

20. Telephone interview with Nat Smith, Jan. 20, 1994.

21. Mofford, op. cit., p. 175.

22. *Andover Historical Society Newsletter*, Vol. 19, No. 2, Summer 1994.

23. John Sullivan, interview, January 14, 1994, 50 Sunset Rock Road, Andover.

24. Karen Herman, interview, January 19, 1994, Andover Historical Society.

25. Scrapbooks of the Andover Committee, Appalachian Mountain Club, Volume 1, courtesy of Martin Wells.

26. Interview with John Sullivan, January 14, 1994, 50 Sunset Rock Road, Andover.

27. *The Bay Circuit and AVIS—Guide to Walks in Andover*, produced jointly by the Andover Trails Committee and the Andover Village Improvement Society, Andover, Mass., 1992. Printed, of course, on recycled paper.

28. Liz Tentarelli, telephone interview, January 18, 1994.

Chapter Four Notes

1. Jim Doherty interview, Jan. 6, 1994, 21 Elm St., Andover.

2. *Andover Townsman,* November 5, 1920.

3. *Andover Townsman*, article by Lisa Boudreau, May 21, 1992.

4. Excerpts printed courtesy of Donald Mulvey. Published in the *Andover Townsman*, Nov. 25, Dec. 3, 10, 17 and 31, 1993. The long-suffering Miss Bailey's first name was Evelyn.

5. Manuscript of Peatman lecture at Andover Historical Society, Nov. 15, 1988.

6. Thibault, Barbara, "Ballardvale Walking Tour," Andover Historical Society and Andover Arts Lottery, 1988.

7. Andover Historical Society Collection.

8. *Andover Townsman*, April 1, 1909.

9. Interview with Margot Bixby, Jan. 24, 1994, 25 Abbot St.

10. Interview with Philip Allen by Virginia Cole and Barbara Thibault, Feb. 7, 1990, tape at Andover Historical Society.

11. Telephone interview with Christie Cunningham, Feb. 11, 1994.

Chapter Five Notes

1. Interview with Louise Roberge, 100 1/2 Main St., Feb. 23, 1994.

2. Telephone interview with Louise Marshall, March 3, 1994.

3. Interview with Adeline Wright, Feb. 18, 1994, 41 Bancroft Road.

4. In 1938, this was changed to 8,500 SF.

5. Telephone interview with Virginia Hammond, January 19, 1994.

6. Arthur Peatman interview, 46 Cutler Road, Feb. 26, 1994.

7. Tape of interview of Roger Lewis by Virginia Cole and Karen Herman, June 1986, at Andover Historical Society.

8. Interview with Robert Colombosian, 55 Argilla Road, Feb. 28, 1994.

9. Domingue, Robert, op. cit., p. 166.

10. Bernice Haggerty interview with Andover Historical Society, October 17, 1994.

11. Interview with Phidias Dantos, October 24, 1994, Main Street.

12. *Andover Townsman Centennial Issue*, July 21, 1988, p. 119A.

13. Fuess, Claude, op. cit. p. 456.

14. Richard Graber interview, 212 Salem St., Dec. 3, 1993.

15. Interview with John Doherty, March 7, 1994, 12 Bartlet St.

16. Telephone interview with Ed Powers, Public Relations Office, Raytheon Company, March 3, 1994.

17. Dalton, William, op. cit., "Purchasing Food: The Way It Used To Be."

18. Telephone interview with Roy Williams, U.S. Census, Amherst, Mass., April 26, 1994.

19. Interview with Virginia Cole, February 24, 1994, 268 Highland Road.

Chapter Six Notes

1. *Business History of Andover—Anniversary Souvenir Number of the Andover Townsman*, May 20, 1896, p. 13.

2. *Andover Townsman*, July 6, 1934, courtesy of Bernice Haggerty.

3. Doherty, Paul, manuscript on file at Andover Historical Society, October 14, 1985.

4. Telephone interview with George Redman, April 14, 1994.

5. Thibault, Barbara, "Andover Village Industrial District Walking Tour," Andover Arts Lottery and Andover Historical Society Collection, 1991.

6. *Andover Townsman*, December 6, 1912.

7. Interview with Vera Daly, March 10, 1994, 15 Cuba Street.

8. Bailey, Sarah Loring, op. cit. p. 590.

9. Telephone interview with Samuel S. Rogers, March 21, 1994.

10. Leland, Lucile Conant, "An Introduction to the Wool Industry of New England," manuscript on file in Andover Historical Society Collection, 1951.

11. Interview with Mary and David Reynolds, March 10, 1994, 129 Summer St.

12. Telephone interview with Bertram R. Paley, March 22, 1994.

13. Interview with Mary and David Reynolds, Ibid.

14. "Shoe Industry Ills More than Imports," *Andover Townsman*, June 8, 1963, article by Michelle Farrington.

15. *Andover Townsman*, Feb. 7, 1946.

16. Fuess, Claude, Op. Cit. p. 314.

17. Material on William Wood from *Mills, Mansions and Mergers*, published by Merrimack Valley Textile Museum, North Andover, Mass., 1982; from interviews and manuscript assistance by Cornelius A. Wood Jr., grandson of William M. Wood, on October 28 and November 6, 1994; and from a walking tour of Shawsheen Village by Andover native Warren ("Bud") Lewis.

18. Telephone interview with Daniel Schevis, director of operations for Brickstone, March 22, 1994.

19. Interview with Lawrence S. Spiegel, April 20, 1994, 76 Holt Road.

20. Interview with Fred Stott, Dec. 8, 1993, 4 Robandy Road.

21. Interview with Richard Bowen, March 2, 1994, 12 Bannister Road.

22. Telephone interview with Dean Morton, March 15, 1994.

23. Interview with William Sousa, Hewlett-Packard, Minuteman Drive, March 16, 1994.

24. Telephone interview with Gina Brazier, Manager of Corporate Communications, March 22, 1994.

25. Andover Planning Division, "Summary of Industrial Developments in Andover," 1990.

26. Telephone interview with Samuel S. Rogers, Ibid.

Chapter Seven Notes

1. *Andover Historical Society Newsletter*, Spring 1992.

2. Harold Tyning, interview, April 1, 1994, Northeast Rehabilitation Hospital, Salem, N.H.

3. *Andover Bulletin*, May 1972, p. 2. "One Year After Required Chapel."

4. Warshaw, Thayer, interview, March 28, 1994, 45 Clark Road.

5. Belknap, Rev. Arthur T., "The Andover Baptist Church, Seventieth Anniversary, September 21, 1902."

6. This church was what we would call Methodist today; the "Episcopal" refers to its government by bishops.

7. "The Parish of Christ Church," Christ Church Historical Commission, 1987, p. 9. For the above historical facts about Christ Church, we are heavily indebted to this little volume.

8. Allis, Frederick S. Jr., *Youth From Every Quarter: A Bicentennial History of Phillips Academy, Andover*, Phillips Academy, Andover, 1979, p. 139.

9. Smith, Mary Byers, "The Founding of the Free Christian Church of Andover read at the 100th Anniversary of Its Founding," 1946.

10. Byington, Steven, "The Story of Union Congregational Church, Ballardvale, Massachusetts, 1854–1954," manuscript courtesy of Ruth Sharpe of Ballardvale, p. 2.

11. Ibid.

12. Sharpe, Ruth, "Two Ballard Vale Personalities: Steven T. Byington and William Shaw, '"*Andover Historical Society Newsletter*, Vol. 13, No. 1, Spring 1988 and interview with Ruth Sharpe, April 4, 1994, 197 Andover Street.

13. Lawrence *Eagle–Tribune,* October 25, 1965.

14. Kearn, Warren, "St. Robert Bellarmine Church—Before and After—as our family experienced It," manuscript courtesy of St. Robert's Church.

15. Interview with Sister Veronica Foley, May 17, 1994, Monastery of St. Clare, 460 River Road.

16. Thoren, Sally, in "Memories: Recalled by early members of Faith Lutheran Church, Andover, MA, (1963–1993)," booklet produced by the church.

17. Telephone interview with Rev. Chip Thompson, April 7, 1994.

18. Interview with Rabbi Bronstein, March 25, 1994, 44 Oriole Drive.

19. Faith Church's Rev. Hartland Gifford quoted in *Andover Townsman*, April 8, 1965. Gifford chaired the bylaws committee.

20. *Andover Townsman*, April 8, 1965. "Dilemma Disrupts Council of Churches."

21. Mulvey, Nancy, "Roots and Recollections," UU Church of Andover, September 1989.

22. Zahka, Joseph, talk given at the UU Church of Andover, Sunday, March 20, 1994.

23. Watters, Robert A., correspondent, "Brief History of the Andover Bible Chapel," January 30, 1981, at Andover Historical Society.

24. Telephone interview with Joel Labell, April 6, 1994.

25. Thayer Warshaw, interview, March 28, 1994, 45 Clark Road.

26. Telephone interview with Donald Lasser, April 7, 1994.

27. History issued by the Korean Methodist Church, October 21, 1986.

28. Telephone interview with Rev. Juan D. Grullon, April 8, 1994.

29. Telephone interview with Nancy Morehardt, April 6, 1994.

30. Telephone interview with Joanne Dahlgren, March 30, 1994.

31. Telephone interview with Jane Griswold, March 30, 1994.

32. Telephone interview with Marsha Cohen, April 7, 1994.

33. Telephone interview with Rev. Bill Watson, April 5, 1994.

Chapter Eight Notes:

1. Interview with Chau N. Dang, April 19, 1994, 219 High Plain Road.

2. Interview with Pete Loosigian, April 20, 1994, 245 Lowell St.

3. *Andover Townsman*, October 25, 1935, p. 1.

4. Interview with James Batchelder, May 18, 1994, Andover Historical Society.

5. Interview with Elizabeth May (Shorten) Bell, April 4, 1994, 40 Elm St.

6. Interview with Joan Patrakis, April 18, 1994, 35 Chandler Road.

7. Interview with Alice, Peter and Pete Loosigian, April 20, 1994, 254 Lowell St.

8. Ibid.

9. Interview with Cornelia Lawrence and Edith Latham, April 19, 1994, at the residence of Mrs. Lawrence, 23 Moraine Street.

10. Manuscript by Ruth Sharpe, Andover Historical Society Collection.

11. Telephone interview with Mary Furnari, April 25, 1994.

12. Interview with Herta Stern and Hildegarde Lebow, June 17, 1994, 3 Kensington St.

13. Interview with Elsie Wu, April 18, 1994, 4 Matthew Street.

14. Interview with Madhu Sridhar, April 26, 1994, 75 Rattlesnake Hill Road.

15. Bailey, Sarah Loring, Op. Cit., p. 27.

16. Telephone interview with Richard Meyers, August 1, 1994.

17. Interview with David and Louise Abbot, May 1, 1994, 72 Central Street.

Chapter Nine Notes

1. A vast majority of the information in this chapter is derived from Andover street directories published by A.B. Sparrow & Co. of Shirley, Mass., Henry M. Meek Directory Co. of Salem, Mass., *Andover Townsman*, and the Crosby Publishing Company of North Hampton, N.H., in the years 1897 to 1953.

2. Andover Historical Society, "Made in Andover" Exhibit Script, Oct. 1989-April 1990.

3. "Twas 1896," manuscript by Mrs. G. Richard (Florence) Abbott, Andover Historical Society.

4. "Andover Press—1798–1931," published by Andover Press, 1931, copy at Andover Historical Society.

5. Ibid.

6. *Andover Townsman*, Centennial Issue, July 21, 1988.

7. Interview with Richard Lally, June 8, 1994, 48 Central Street.

8. *Business History of Andover*, 1896, Op. Cit.

9. Interview with Richard Lally, Ibid.

10. Telephone interview with Beatrice Hall, August 2, 1994.

11. Bessie Goldsmith writes in *The Townswoman's Andover* that Bacigalupo at 42 Main Street was the first to sell coconuts.

12. Telephone interview with Phidias Dantos, June 15, 1994.

13. Interview with Helen Reilly, Dec. 6, 1994, 79 Haverhill Street.

14. *Andover Townsman Centennial* edition, July 21, 1988, "My Andover," by Bob Finneran, editor.

15. *Andover Townsman*, Nov. 8, 1924.

16. Conversation with Norma Gammon, June 29, 1994.

17. Interview with Richard Lally, Ibid.

18. Interview with John Freitas, June 9, 1994, 17 Main Street.

19. Manuscript by Cornelia Fitts, Andover Historical Society.

20. Interview with Richard Chapell, May 31, 1994.

21. Telephone interview with Alan Wilson, June 12, 1994.

22. "Andover Thrift Shop Celebrates Its Fiftieth Anniversary," *Andover Historical Society Newsletter*, Spring 1991.

23. Dalton, William, *Local Touch*, 1985, "Working Downtown."

24. *Eagle-Tribune*, Centennial Edition, Sept. 25, 1990.

25. Interview with Irving Rogers Jr. and Irving ("Chip") Rogers III, May 31, 1994, *Eagle-Tribune* offices, 100 Turnpike Street, North Andover.

26. Interview with Virgil Marson, May 23, 1994, 127 Main Street.

27. *Andover Townsman*, January 10, 1980, "Cole Hardware expands," by Robert Finneran, editor.

28. Telephone interview with Douglas Howe Jr., June 7, 1994.

29. Telephone interview with Russell Doyle, June 7, 1994.

30. *Andover Townsman*, July 8, 1993.

31. Telephone interview with Phidias Dantos, June 15, 1994.

32. Ibid.

33. Telephone interview with Geneva Killorin, June 9, 1994.

34. Interview with Ethel and Jerry Cross, May 31, 1994, 59 Central Street.

35. Ibid.

36. *Eagle-Tribune*, July 2, 1987, "Musgrove Building Sold for $2.9M," by Lewis C. Howe.

37. Interview with Carolyn ("Lynie") Bernardin (Mrs. Eugene) and her daughter, Lucy, June 9, 1994, 60 Main Street, and telephone interview June 9, 1994, with Amy Bernardin.

Chapter Ten Notes

1. Interview with Carol Znamierowski, May 10, 1994, 36 Bartlet St.

2. Interview with Isabelle Dobbie, May 9, 1994, 17 Beech Circle.

3. Interview with James Batchelder, May 2, 1994. Batchelder, art teacher at Andover High School, and former president of the Andover Historical Society, has conducted extensive research on Andover schools.

4. Interview with Rita and Margaret Cronin, Feb. 23, 1994, 18 Summer Street.

5. Report of Andover School Committee, 1918.

6. Article by Richard Graber in *Today*, an alternative newspaper, October 30, 1974, pp. 10-11.

7. *Seventy-fifth Anniversary of First Commencement of Punchard School*, 1934.

8. Telephone interview with Virginia Cole, May 16, 1994.

9. Interview with Richard Bowen, March 2, 1994, 12 Bannister Road.

10. Telephone interview with Adeline Wright May 17, 1994.

11. Interview with Mark McQuillan, May 12, 1994, 36 Bartlet St.

12. Interview with Frank Vacirca and Mary Beth Sullivan, May 17, 1994, Greater Lawrence Technical School

13. Interview with Helen Reilly, Dec. 6, 1994, 79 Haverhill St.

14. *Andover, What it Was, What it Is*, 300th Anniversary Publication, 1946.

15. Telephone interview with Robert Monette, August 9, 1994.

16. Information on Pike School from an interview with Tony Dyer, May 5, 1994, at Pike School.

17. Ibid.

18. Information on Abbot Academy is mostly derived from Susan McIntosh Lloyd's *A Singular School*, Phillips Academy, Andover, 1979.

19. Ibid. p. 170, quoting Kelsey's Sketches, p. 51.

20. Ibid., p. 203 from a letter by Bailey to M. Stackpole, Sept. 18, 1911.

21. Interview with Cathleen Elmer, Dec. 9, 1993, 2 Chestnut St.

22. Lloyd, Op. Cit., p. 316.

23. Ibid., p. 368.

24. Domingue, Robert, Op. Cit., various pages.

25. Allis, Frederick S. Jr., Op. Cit., p. 372.

26. Interview with Donald McNemar, May 4, 1994, Phillips Academy.

27. Allis, Frederick S. Jr., *Youth From Every Quarter,* Phillips Academy, Andover, 1979.

28. Monette, Paul, *Becoming a Man: Half a Life Story*, Harper San Francisco, 1992, pp. 92-93.

29. Interview with Theodore Sizer, June 10, 1994, Andover Inn.

30. Telephone interview with Mary McCabe, June 16, 1994.

31. Published by Phillips Academy, 1986.

32. Ibid., p. 11.

33. *Andover Bulletin*, Spring 1993.

34. Lloyd, Susan, Op. Cit., p. 129.

35. Williams, George H., editor, *The Harvard Divinity School—Its Place in Harvard University and in American Culture*, Beacon Press, Boston, 1954, p. 193.

36. Ibid., pp. 189-190.

37. Allis, Frederick S. Jr., Op. Cit. p. 147.

38. *The Harvard Divinity School*, p. 192.

39. Information on St. Francis Seminary from an interview with Rev. Claude Scrima, O.F.M., May 17, 1994, St. Francis Retreat Center, River Road.

40. *Andover 1946-1971* by Andover's 325th Anniversary Committee, essay on Private Education by John H. Fenton, p. 39.

41. Interview with Rev. Scrima cited above.

42. Roddy, Edward G. Jr., *Merrimack College: Genesis and Growth 1947-1972,* Merrimack College Press, Andover, Mass., 1972.

43. Ibid., p. 31.

44. Ibid., pp. 21, 22.

45. Interview with the Rev. William Wynne, O.S.A., May 6, 1994, Austin Hall, Merrimack College.

46. Telephone interview with Robert Ciampitti Jr., Student Bar Association President, Massachusetts School of Law, 500 Federal Street, August 10, 1994.

47. Interview with Theodore M. Sizer, June 10, 1994, Andover Inn.

Chapter Eleven Notes

1. Information on 1936 flood from the *Andover Townsman*, March 27, 1936.

2. *Andover Townsman*, October 4, 1918.

3. *Andover Townsman*, October 25, 1918.

4. Everett Penney interview, June 23, 1994.

5. Andover Board of Health Report 1910.

6. Town Report 1915, p. 53.

7. *Andover Townsman*, May 17, 1918.

8. Figures supplied by Massachusetts Department of Public Health, Statistics Division.

9. Interview with Lee Dodd, July 1, 1994, 199 Chestnut Street.

10. Memorial service tribute to Bruce Dodd by his son Douglas Van Everen Dodd, June 25, 1976.

11. Statistics compiled by the Massachusetts Department of Public Health and reported in the *Andover Townsman*, Nov. 15, 1993.

12. Figures supplied by Massachusetts Department of Public Health—AIDS Surveillance Program.

13. From a retrospective by Kay Noyes, *Andover Townsman*, January 26, 1956.

14. *Andover Townsman*, Centennial Edition, July 21, 1988.

15. *Andover Townsman*, February 9, 1978, story by Robert Finneran, editor.

16. Interview with Tom Koravos, December 30, 1993.

17. Interview with Theodore R. Sizer, June 10, 1994.

18. Figures supplied by the National Weather Service, Logan Airport.

19. Figures supplied by Robert E. Lautzenheimer, climatologist, from his Andover station.

20. April 22, 1927.

21. Ibid.

22. Sept. 22, 1938, p. 1.

23. Ibid.

24. Ibid.

25. *Andover Townsman*, September 9, 1954.

26. Telephone interview with Samuel S. Rogers, March 21, 1994.

27. Interview with Arita Nichols, December 23, 1993, 246 Highland Road.

28. *Andover Townsman*, September 16, 1954.

29. Information on the Blackout is from the *Eagle-Tribune,* Wednesday, Nov. 10, 1965.

30. *Encyclopedia Americana,* Vol. 22, p. 508, 1988 edition.

Chapter Twelve Notes

1. *Andover Townsman*, Centennial Issue, July 21, 1988.

2. Manuscript on the origin of the Andover Town Seal by Clifford Wrigley, loaned to the author.

3. In 1776, the town had voted 180 to 1 that "the Governor, Lieutenant-Governor, Counsellors, Senators, and Representatives ought to be of the Protestant Religion." Bailey, Sarah Loring, Op. Cit., p. 357.

4. Fuess, Op. Cit. p. 303.

5. Telephone interview with Barbara Loomer, Jan. 4, 1994.

6. Telephone interview with Barbara Moody, Feb. 17, 1994.

7. *Lawrence Eagle-Tribune*, Feb. 3, 1956.

8. *Andover Townsman*, January 19, 1956.

9. *Lawrence Eagle-Tribune*, March 2, 1956.

10. *Andover Townsman*, March 8, 1956.

11. Interview with Victor Mill Jr., July 5, 1994, Andover Inn.

12. Interview with Richard Bowen, March 2, 1994, 12 Bannister Road.

13. Interview with Reginald S. Stapczynski, July 1. 1994.

14. Bailey, Sarah Loring, Op. cit. p. 35.

15. Town of Andover, By-laws, Revised March 1895, pp. vii, viii, x; Andover Historical Society Collection.

16. Andover Town Report 1920.

17. Andover Town Report 1993, p. 33.

18. Interview with Lt. John K. Lynch, Sept. 22, 1994, Andover Public Safety Building.

19. *Andover Townsman*, Dec. 4, 1925.

20. *Andover Townsman,* June 19, 1958.

21. From "Fire Department History in Andover, Massachusetts, 1994," manuscript loaned by author Harold Hayes, and interview with Harold Hayes, July 6, 1994, Andover Public Safety Building.

22. Interview with Robert McQuade, July 1, 1994, Robert E. McQuade Water Treatment Plant.

23. Andover Town Report, 1890, p. 40.

24. McQuade, Robert, manuscript on history of town water system, 1976, loaned by Robert McQuade.

25. Bailey, Sarah Loring, Op. Cit. p. 64.

26. Town of Andover, By-laws, revisions March 1895, p. ix; in Andover Historical Society Collection.

27. Information compiled by Richard Graber.

28. Allis, Frederick S. Jr., Op. Cit., pp. 382-383.

29. Interview with Nancy Jacobson, July 6, 1994.

30. Interview with Miriam Putnam, January 5, 1994, 57 High Street.

31. Interview with Nancy Jacobson, Ibid.

32. Memorial Hall Library, brochure by Nancy Jacobson, 1993 edition.

33. Interview with William Dalton, Dec. 6, 1993, 199 Chestnut Street.

34. Telephone interview with Everett Penney, Director of Public Health, July 22, 1994.

35. Interview with Gerald H. Silverman, July 5, 1994, Andover Historical Society.

Chapter Thirteen Notes

1. Interview with Cornelius A. Wood Jr., November 6, 1994, 199 Chestnut St.

2. Interview with Ruth Sharpe, Andover Historical Society, August 17, 1994.

3. Telephone interview with Warren (Bud) Lewis, August 22, 1994.

4. Interview with Bernice Haggerty, November 17, 1993, Andover Historical Society.

5. Town Report, 1933, p. 17.

6. Town Report, Year ending January 15, 1907.

7. *Andover Townsman*, Sept. 19, 1963.

8. Interview with William Dalton, Dec. 6, 1993, 199 Chestnut St.

9. Story by Winthrop Newman in the *Andover Townsman*, March 28, 1963.

10. Interview with Eve Cross Glendenning in "The Park," September 17, 1994.

11. Telephone interview with Betty Bodwell Stevens, June 7, 1994.

12. Interview with Ethel and Jerry Cross, May 31, 1994.

13. Domingue, Robert, Op. Cit., p. 168.

14. "Old Brown Jug Restaurant Once a Teen-Age Favorite," *Lawrence Eagle-Tribune*, January 31, 1963.

15. Minutes of Andover Teen Center, 1961-1964, loaned by Adeline Wright, secretary.

16. Town Report 1950, p. 135.

Chapter Fourteen—No Notes

Bibliography

Abbot, Abiel, A.M. *History of Andover from its Settlement to 1829.* Andover: printed and published by Flagg & Gould, 1829.

Allis, Frederick S. Jr. *Youth From Every Quarter.* Andover: Phillips Academy, 1979.

"An Archaeological Survey and the Documentary History of the Shattuck Farm, Andover, Massachusetts." March 1981, supported by the Catherine G. Shattuck Memorial Trust and the Massachusetts Historical Commission.

Andover 1946–1971. Published by Andover's 325th Anniversary Committee, 1971.

Andover, Massachusetts—Proceedings at the Celebration of the Two Hundred and Fiftieth Anniversary of the Incorporation of the Town, May 20, 1896. Andover: The Andover Press, 1897.

Andover, Mass., Town Reports 1886–1993.

Andover, Mass., School Committee Reports 1896–1993.

Andover-Punchard High School Alumni Directory. Norfolk, Va.: Bernard C. Harris Publishing Company, Inc., 1993.

Andover Town Handbook. Andover: League of Women Voters, 1994.

Andover Townsman. Various issues, 1895–1994.

Andover: What It Was, What It Is. Andover: *Andover Townsman*, 1946.

Bailey, Sarah Loring. *Historical Sketches of Andover, Massachusetts (Comprising the Present Towns of North Andover and Andover).* Boston: Houghton, Mifflin and Company, The Riverside Press, Cambridge, 1880.

The Bay Circuit and AVIS: A Guide to Walks in Andover. Andover: produced by Andover Trails Committee and Andover Village Improvement Society, supported by National Park Service River & Trail Conservation Assistance Program, and Bay Circuit Alliance, 1992.

Campbell, Eleanor. *West of the Shawsheen—A Story of the People of West Parish Church in Andover, Massachusetts.* Andover: West Parish Church, 1975.

Campbell, Eleanor; Gorrie, Elizabeth; and Roberts, Margaret. "A Red Cloak for Mother. The History of the Smith Family of Andover, West Parish Church, Andover," 1992.

Cole, Donald B. *Immigrant City: Lawrence, Massachusetts 1845–1921.* Chapel Hill: The University of North Carolina Press, 1963.

Dalton, Bill. *Local Touch.* Andover: Bill Dalton, 1985.

Dalton, Kathleen M. *A Portrait of a School: Coeducation at Andover—A Report on Research of the Committee on Coeducation.* Andover: Phillips Academy, 1986.

Doherty, James D. *Andover As I Remember It.* Andover: James D. Doherty, 1992.

Domingue, Robert A. *Phillips Academy, Andover—An Illustrated History of the Property (Including Abbot Academy).* Andover: RAD Publishing Co., 1990.

Fuess, Claude M. *Andover: The Evolution of a Town.* Andover: Andover Historical Society and North Andover Historical Society, 1959.

Goldsmith, Bessie. *The Townswoman's Andover*. Andover: Andover Historical Society, 1964.

Historic Andover—325th Anniversary 1646–1971. Andover: compiled by a Committee of George Glennie, Arthur Kerwien, Donald Hayes Jr., and Vincent Foley, and published courtesy of Raytheon Company.

Lawrence Eagle-Tribune, various issues, 1896–1996.

Lloyd, Susan McIntosh. *A Singular School*. Andover: Phillips Academy, 1979.

Luedtke, Barbara E. "The Camp in the Bend in the River." University of Massachusetts at Boston, 1985, supported by the Catherine G. Shattuck Memorial Trust and the Massachusetts Historical Commission.

Mofford, Juliet Haines. *And Firm Thine Ancient Vow: The History of North Parish Church of North Andover 1645–1974*. North Andover: Juliet Haines Mofford, 1975.

Mofford, Juliet Haines. *AVIS: A History in Conservation*. Andover: Andover Village Improvement Society, 1980.

Mofford, Juliet Haines. *Greater Lawrence: A Bibliography—An Annotated Guide to the History of Andover, Methuen, Lawrence and North Andover*. North Andover: Merrimack Valley Textile Museum, 1978.

Monette, Paul. *Becoming A Man: Half a Life Story*. New York: Harcourt, Brace, Jovanovich, 1992.

Roddy, Edward G. *Merrimack College: Genesis and Growth*. North Andover: Merrimack College Press, 1972.

Roddy, Edward G. *Mills, Mansions and Mergers: The Life of William M. Wood*. North Andover: Merrimack Valley Textile Museum, 1982.

Index

A

A Better Chance (ABC), 57, 58
A&P, 138, 149
Abbot, Abel and Paschal, 81
Abbot Academy, 11, 18, 20, 21, 28, 144, 168, 169, 171, 172, 215, 234, 235, 236, 237, 238
Abbot Academy, Principals of, 255
Abbot, Amos, 225
Abbot, Stephen, Captain, 225
Abbot, Charles, 135
Abbot, Charlotte Helen, 35
Abbot Circle, 169
Abbot, David and Louise, 131
Abbot, Deacon Amos, 222
Abbot District School, 156
Abbot family, 21, 131
Abbot, Florence, 33, 135
Abbot Hall (building), Abbot Academy, 45
Abbot homestead, 65, 139, 185
Abbot, Marion, 138
Abbot Mill, 81
Abbot Street, 167
Abbot Tavern, 237
Abbot Village, 15, 48, 53, 56, 79, 81, 84, 104
Abbot Village Checkers Club, 82
Abbot Village Coal Society, 82
Abbot Village Hall, 82
Abbot Village schools, 83
Abbott, Charles E., Dr., 34
Abbott, George, 34
Abolitionists, 102
Abraham, Ron, 144
Acquired Immune Deficiency Syndrome (AIDS), 180
Adams, J. H., 133
Addison Gallery of American Art, Phillips Academy, 170, 234
Adult education, 215
Adventurers, 50
Africans, 129
Agricultural Restriction Law, 67
Alden, Priscilla, 42
Alden Street, 24
All-Girls' Band, 207
Allen, Bernard (Barney), 26
Allen Brothers' Drug Store, 134
Allen, Elizabeth Warner, 27, 28
Allen, Philip K., 25, 26, 42, 58, 169
Allied Chemicals, 96
Allis, Frederick "Fritz" S., Jr., 20, 170, 171, 172, 173, 234
Almshouse, 32, 33, 91, 141, 189
American Degreasing, 89
American Express Company, 134

American Field Service, 218
American Hellenic Progressive Association, 54
American Legion, 50
American Legion Post 8, 48
American Woolen Company, 23, 66, 75, 86, 90, 91, 101, 166, 208, 223, 232
Americans, Native, 11
Ames, S. K., 138
AMVETS Post 43, 48
Amy, Marietta, 20
Anderson & Bowman, 135
Anderson, Abigail, 222
Anderson family, 245
Anderson Santorium, 141
Andona Club, 179
Andona Society, The, 52, 219
Andonian, John P., 72
Andover Advertiser, 137
Andover Animal Hospital, 64, 67
Andover Art Studio, 142
Andover Artist's Guild, 218
Andover Bank, 36, 133, 134, 152, 153, 153, 222
Andover Baptist Church, 102, 115
Andover Barber Shop, 144
Andover Bible Chapel, 113
Andover Bookstore, 133, 150, 151, 236
Andover Boosters Club, 207
Andover Brass Band, 50
Andover Burns Club, 82
Andover Canoe Club, 204
Andover Center Association, 218
Andover Chinese Cultural Exchange, 54
Andover Choral Society, 50
Andover Clergy Association, 111
Andover Club, 51
Andover Commons, 88
Andover Community Orchestra, 50
Andover Companies, 49, 95, 186, 134, 205
Andover Company H (infantry), 177
Andover Consumer's Cooperative, 24, 142, 144, 145
Andover Controls, 91
Andover Council of Churches, 111
Andover Country Club, 58, 91, 214, 223
Andover Cricket Club, 82
Andover Electric Company, 136
Andover Elks, 145

Andover Endowment for the Arts, 134
Andover, England, 200
Andover Equal Suffrage League, 49
Andover Fish Market, 138
Andover Fraternal Building, 54
Andover Fund for Education, 56
Andover Garden Club, 18, 55, 213
Andover Guild, 25, 48, 126, 216
Andover Harvard Library, 173
Andover High School, 17, 18, 20, 28, 29, 31, 77, 130, 155, 159, 164, 165, 200, 216, 217, 218
Andover Historical Society, 6, 7, 9, 26, 34, 35, 37, 41, 42, 43, 96, 188, 189, 200, 225, 237, 241, 233
Andover Home for Aged People, 52, 243
Andover Industrial Park, 37
Andover Inn, 187
Andover Junior High, 161
Andover Lodge of Elks, 53
Andover Male Choir, 28, 50
Andover Manufacturing Company, 145
Andover Marriott, 44
Andover Mills Realty Limited Partnership, 91
Andover National Bank, 47, 132, 133, 144, 222, 225
Andover Natural History Society, 33
Andover Playhouse, 138, 147
Andover Preservation Award, 151
Andover Press, 133, 136, 136, 137, 150, 168, 236
Andover Public Schools, 155, 164
Andover Public Schools, superintendents of, 253
Andover Retirement Board, 26
Andover Savings Bank, 132, 134, 141, 142, 144, 194, 222
Andover School of Business, 149
Andover Service Club, 217
Andover Shop, 147, 149
Andover Silver Company, 146
Andover Spa, 126, 141, 149
Andover Sports Hall of Fame, 26
Andover Sportsman's Club, 58, 207, 216
Andover Steam Laundry, 136
Andover Street, 50, 53, 64, 65, 79, 106, 135, 146, 194, 199

Andover Taxpayers' Association, 49, 191
Andover Tech Center, 94
Andover Theatre Company, 43, 50
Andover Theological Seminary, 11, 18, 35-36, 99, 103, 105, 136, 140, 170, 171, 172, 173, 234, 236
,Andover Thrift Shop, 146
Andover Townsman, 19, 32, 51, 73, 88, 133, 136, 137, 146, 146, 177, 184, 185, 188, 196, 211, 236, 238
Andover Trails Committee, 43, 44, 45
Andover Video, 151
Andover Village, 151
Andover Village Improvement Society (AVIS), 18, 20, 30, 31, 32, 38, 39, 40, 41, 42, 63, 206, 238
Andover Weaving Company, 146
Andover Youth Football, 59
Andrews, F. M. and T. E., 91
Andrews house, 34
Angus, Mary, 47, 145
Ann Beha Associates, 43
Ann's Andover Cottage, 145
Appalachian Mountain Club (AMC), Andover Committee of, 43
Arabs, 129
Archibald, Dave, 44
Arco building, 137, 167
Arden, 23, 203
Arekalian family, 123
Argilla Road, 38, 50 66, 67, 68, 123, 199, 242
Argilla Road Neighborhood Association, 49
Argyle Street, 35, 178
Arkwright-Boston, 67, 94, 229
Armenians, 122
Arnold, Charles W., 225
Arrow Cleaners, 137
Artigianhi, Dino, 133
Art-in-the-Park, 218
Arundel Street, 128
Ascom-Timeplex Incorporated, 94
Ashe Hall, Merrimack College, 174
Asian Indians, 130
Asians, 129
Asoian, Tully and Gilman, 224
AT&T, 95
Athlete's Corner, 153
Atwood, William, 210
Auchterlonie, John, 141

Austin, J. Maynard, 39, 92, 191, 195
Austin Hall, Merrimack College, 175
AVCO, 190
Avery, Anne, 116
Axelrod, Harry, 25, 149
Ayer, Frederick, 22, 23
Ayer Mill, 38
Aznoian, Nicholas, 149

B

Babb, Benjamin, 205
Bailey, Bertha, 168, 169
Bailey Controls Company, 94
Bailey, Evelyn, 51
Bailey Farm, 66
Bailey, Mabel Roxie, 156
Bailey Road, 12, 245
Bailey, Sarah Loring, 19, 84, 130, 189, 191
Baker, Bella, 18
Baker, Harriet Woods, 137
Baker's Lane, 81
Ballard, Timothy, 78
Ballardvale, 13, 42, 53, 56, 58, 62, 64, 68, 77, 78, 79, 87, 95, 105, 105, 106, 108, 124, 135, 138,139, 141, 142, 146, 149, 183, 194, 195, 198, 203, 204, 207, 215
Ballardvale Chemical, 138
Ballardvale Improvement Society, 28, 49
Ballardvale Lithia Company, 95
Ballardvale Machine Company, 62, 80
Ballardvale playground, 211
Ballardvale PTA, 56
Ballardvale Road, 245
Ballardvale Stoneware Manufacturing Company, 80
Ballardvale United Church, 106, 167, 252
Ballardvale's Fourth of July, 217
Balmoral Condominiums, 92
Balmoral Spa, 90, 126, 134, 204, 205
Balmoral Street, 35
Balsama, Steve, 144
Bancroft Reservoir, 195
Bancroft Road, 21, 38, 103, 196
Bancroft School, 130, 160
Bandstand, 207
Bank of Boston, 153
Baptist Church, 75, 135
Barcelos Market, 145, 152, 180
Barenboim, James, 201
Barnard Block, 12, 135, 135, 139, 140, 147, 152

Barnard building, Jacob, 140,143
Barnard family, 133,139
Barnard, Jacob W., 133, 139
Barnard Street, 135, 140, 146, 199
Barnard, W. Shirley, 140, 142, 143, 144, 243
Barnard, Foster and Elizabeth, 223
Barnstormers, the, 50
Bartlet Chapel, 36, 172, 173
Bartlet Hall, 36, 172, 173
Bartlet Street, 29, 43, 138, 155, 187, 196, 238
Bartlett, Nathaniel E., 34
Basso's Fruit, 141
Batchelder, Abbott, 68
Batchelder family, 242
Batchelder, James S., 37, 42, 120
Battle of Bunker Hill, 11
Baxter, Charles, 144
Bay Circuit, 44, 45
Bay State York, 146
BayBank, 133, 153, 225
BayBank Merrimack Valley, 134
Beacon Street, 155
Beaver Manufacturing, 138
Beene, Irma, 138, 139, 140
Belanger, George H., 75
Belheumer, Tom, 152
Bell, May (Shorten), 42, 120
Bellevue Road, 114
Benedict, Grenville, 169
Benevie, 47
Bennie's Barbershop, 144
Bernardin, Amy, 152
Bernardin, Daniel, 152
Bernardin, Eugene A., III, 151
Bernardin family, 152
Berry, J. W., 206
Berthold, Wolf, 92
Bertucci/Menucci, 149
Bertucci's King's Pizza, 153
Bicentennial Park, 55
Bicycle club, 58
Billings, Walter, 133
Binney Street, 61, 183
Birdsall, Dorothy, 147, 216
Birdsall, John, 147
Bixby, George and Margot, 57
Black families, 125
Black, Officer Robert, 193, 194
Blackmer, Alan, 215
Blackout of 1965, 187
Blackshaw, John, 133
Blanchard, Amos, 35, 225
Blanchard House, Amos, 6
Bliss Stock Farm, 185
Bliss' drugstore, 132
Blizzard of 1898, 180, 181
Blizzard of 1978, 180
Blomerth, Carl and Priscilla, 35
Board of Assessors, 26
Board of Health, 177, 178, 199
Board of Public Works, 26, 190, 213
Board of Selectmen, 26
Board of Taxpayers Association, 28
Board of Trade, 152, 216
Board of Visitors, 172, 173
Bodwell, Sally, 145
Bogart, Humphrey, 18
Bok Rha, Pastor Dr. Young, 114
Bolian family, 123
Boosters Club, 216
Booth, James, 164
Bossdorf, Rev. Robert, 106
Boston and Maine Railroad, 203
Boston Missionary Society, 213
Boston Patriots, 215
Boston Road, 49
Boutwell Road, 66

Bowen, Richard, 20, 38, 39, 93, 160, 191
Boxford, 11
Boy Scout Troop 1, 56
Boy Scouts, 101, 218
Boynton, Donald, 168
Bradlee Hall, 79
Bradlee, Helen, 79
Bradlee, Josiah Putnam, 78, 79, 108
Bradlee Mill, 78
Bradlee School, 56
Bradley, R. M., 94
Bramley, Maude, 18
Bread and Roses, 107
Brechin Hall, Andover Theological Seminary, 36
Brechin Terrace, 83, 85
Brennan and Associates, John, 115
Brian, Ruth, 24
Brickstone Square, 91, 92, 216
Briggs, Amy, 167
Briggs and Allen School, 167
Brigham's Ice Cream, 149
Broadley, Fred, 141
Brockway Smith, 96
Bronstein, Rabbi Osher, 111
Brook Street, 48, 126
BrookRidge Community Church, 117, 253
Brooks, Phillips, 203, 238
Brooks, Rev., Phillips, 103
Brooks School, 168
Brookside Estates, 199
Brothers, Joyce, 51
Brothers of the Sacred Heart, 166, 215
Brown, Edna, 197
Brown, W. G., 135
Brownell, Mrs. C. H., 158
Brownies, 218
Brucksch, John P., 35
Bruegger's Bagels, 152
Buchan & McNally Plumbing, 136
Buchan, C. Edward, 194
Buchan Furniture, Charles, 140
Buck, Alice, 21, 30, 31
Burgess, Jordan, 84
Burke, Garrett, 211
Burnham Road, 199, 211
Burns, Marilyn, 41
Burns night, Robert, 120
Burns, W. J., 133, 136
Burtt farm, 38, 95
Bush, President George, 17, 75, 215
Butler's Pantry, 153
Buxton Court, 142, 146
Byers, John, 103
Byington, Steven, 105, 106
Bylaw of 1895, 209

C

Camp Andover, 56, 213
Camp, Dresser & McKee, 196
Camp Manning, 56, 213
Camp Maude Eaton, 56
Campbell, Eleanor, 20
Campbell Highlanders, 54
Campbell, Marie, 47
Campion, J. H., 135, 142
Canadians, 119
Candiano, Joseph P., 75
Canobie Lake Park, 178, 213
Cantone, David, 187
Capitol Diner, 138
Carriage Trade Shop, 147
Carmel Hill (Mount Carmel), 33
Carmel Woods, 32, 206
Caronel Court, 141
Carter, Sarah Wilson, 34
Carter's Corner, 49
Castle family, 237

Castle, Hanne and Frank, 42
Caswell, Helen, 51
Catholic Daughters, 107
Catholic Mothers, 107
Celus Fasteners, 96
Cemetery, Sons of Israel, 114
Center Street, 141
Central Andover Residents' Association, 50
Central Catholic High School, 140
Central Elementary School, 160, 161, 162
Central Industrial Labs, 96
Central Schools PTA, 56
Central Street, 11, 42, 55, 79, 100, 102, 103, 107, 126, 131, 148, 185, 186, 204, 210, 214, 244
Chabad Jewish Center of the Merrimack Valley, 111, 253
Chamber of Commerce, 152
Chandler, Beth, 169
Chandler Road, 41, 66, 77, 111, 115, 121, 123, 194
Chapel Avenue, 35
Chapel Cemetery, 18
Chapel Inn, 138
Chapell, Richard, 146
Chapman, Ovid, 147, 215
Chase, Barbara Landis, 170, 234
Chase, Herbert F., 134, 137
Chase, Omar, 137
Chase, Omar Paper Store, 133
Cheever, Alice Bancroft, 22
Cheever Circle, 22
Cheever, Frederick E., 21, 22
Cheever House, 36, 43
Cheever, William Abbot, 20
Chester building, 36
Chestnut Court, 183, 199, 56
Chestnut Street, 24, 34, 107, 147, 214, 236, 238
Cheyne, George, 142
Chiklis, Michael, 18
Children's Theater Workshop, 56-57
Chin Dang & Company, 136
Chinese, 129
Chinese laundry, 136
Chlebowski, Stanley, 191
Chocolate Shop, 152
Christ Church, 24, 32, 69, 96, 103, 114, 146, 167, 186, 250
Christian Science Church, 115, 116
Christie, Jim, 207
Christina's bridal shop, 153
Christopher, Dorothy and Jim, 43
Church Basketball League, 207
Church Street, 106
Civil War, 11, 69
Civil War cannons, 146
Civilian Conservation Corps, (CCC), 33, 176
Clark, Esq., Hon. Hobart, 225
Clark, Jared, 42, 191
Clark Motor Company, 147, 150
Clark Road, 106, 194
Clark, Thomas, 83
Clemens' Camp, Maynard, 203
Cleveland, Ruth, 18
Clist, Charlie, 44
Clothes Shop, 142
Clown Town, 52, 219
Cobblestones, 136, 146, 197
Coburn, Andrew, 20
Coburn, Rose, 210
Cochichawicke, 11, 189
Cochran Chapel, Phillips Academy, 101, 102, 170, 234, 249
Cochran, Thomas, 36, 140, 170, 172, 234

Coconuts, 141
Coffee Connection, 152
Coffee Mill (restaurant), 73, 147, 215, 216
Coffin, Rev. William Sloane, 18
Cohen, Jerry, 25, 29
Cohen, Marsha, 116
Cohen, Sheldon S., 191
Colby, A. M., 135
Cole, Albert Jr. and John, 194
Cole, Constance, 168
Cole Hardware, 140, 147
Cole, John N., 19, 31, 136, 137, 236, 238
Cole, Lt. Albert, 194
Cole, Milton, 147, 159
Cole, Minnie White, 19
Cole, Philip P., 136, 137, 236
Cole, Virginia, 49
Colleary, William B., 175
Collins Center, 24, 28, 233
Collins, Elizabeth Abbot, 28
Collins, Everett, 191
Collins, J. Everett, 28, 29, 189, 207
Collins, John, 168
Collins, Mary, 190
Colmore, Perry, 147
Colombo Yogurt, 69
Colombosian, Bob, 67
Colombosian family, 68, 123
Colombosian, Rose, and Sarkis, 67
Colonial Pre-Built Homes, Air Conditioning and Equipment Service Colonial Spinning Mills, 145
Colonial Theater, 138, 177
Combs, Allen, 50
Commons, Phillips Academy, 170
Community Chest, 25
Community Council for Recreation, 215
Compusource Incorporated, 94
Computer Associates International Incorporated, 94
Computers, 197
Congregation Tifereth Isreal, 253
Connolly, Sgt. Barbara, 192
Conservation Commission, 33, 37, 38, 39, 40, 42, 44, 134, 199
Convenant Housing, 99
Converse Rubber, 88
Coolidge, President Calvin, 215
Coon, Gary, 201
Coon, Howard, 20
Corcoran Company, 88
Cormier, Yvon, 149, 223
Cornell Fund, 34
Coulter Fibers, 80
Council on Aging, 199
Courtney's, 153
Coutts, Jessie Ann, 54
Coutts, William, 54
Crafts-in-the-Park, 218
Craighead and Kintz, 53, 80, 127
Crane, Mary H., 169, 235
Cronin family, John, 108
Cronin, Paul, 25, 29, 83, 84, 187
Cross Coal Company, 135, 137, 150, 210
Cross family, 135, 150, 166
Cross, Jerome W. ("Jerry"), Jr., 135, 150, 214, 236
Cross Street, 184
Crowley (drugstore), 140
Crowley, W. C., 136
Crowley, Woodrow, 210
Crusader Paperboard, 96
Crystal Ballroom, 91, 166, 205
Cub Scouts, 218
Cuba Street, 82, 83, 214
Cumberland Farms, 144

Cunningham, Agnes, 23
Cunningham, Christie, 59
Currier, Gerald F., 75
Curtis, Albert, Mrs., 51
Curtis, Irene, 69
Cushing Hall, Merrimack College, 175
Cushing, Richard, Cardinal, 108, 166, 174
Cutshamache, 11, 188, 189
CVS Pharmacy, 137, 152

D

Dagdigian, Hovenes and Vartar, 91
Daher's Shoes, 151, 153
Dahlgren, Joanne and Alfred, 116
Dale Street, 79, 80
Daley, Leo, 26
Daley, Rev. James, 108
Dalton, Carolyn, 151, 236
Dalton, Charles, 146, 207
Dalton family, 20, 24, 43, 158
Dalton, Kathleen M., 172
Dalton, Mary, 158
Dalton, William (Bill), 75, 146, 151, 199, 208, 209, 236
Dalton's Drug Store, 24, 140, 215
Daly & Co., P. J., 134
Daly, Francis, 83
Daly, Jeremiah, 135
Daly, Vera Downs, 83
Dana's Sport Shop, 151
Dancing classes, 51
Dane, George A., 192, 194
Dang, Chau, 118, 119
Dang family, 118, 119
Daniel, Rev. Jack, 104
Danton Realty Trust, 149
Dantos, George and Peter, 141
Dantos, Phidias, 69, 92, 141, 149
Dargoonhian family, 123
Darling Associates Incorporated, 24
Darling, Beverly, 24, 25, 180
DASA Corporation, 86, 183
Davidson, Agnes, 223
Davidson, Charles, 147
Davidson, John, 92, 149
Davidson, Leon "Doc," 147, 215, 223
Davies, Charles, 20
Davis, Margaret, 213
Day, Melville Cox, 169
De Rosa, Jean, 20
Deacon, William and Nancy, 58
Deane/Lyman Partnership, 80
Death, causes of, 178, 180
Dec-Tam Corporation, 96
Deer Jump Reservation, 41
Delaney, Dana, 18
Democratic Town Committee, 29
Demolition Delay Ordinance, 43
Demoulas, 58, 148
Dengler, Claus, 31, 32, 55
Dengler, Eartha, 55
Department of Community Development and Planning, 199
Department of Community Services, 215
Depot, 153
Depression, 66, 144, 160, 169, 206
Design Advisory Group, 199
Designing Kitchens, 151
Development and Industrial Commission, 29, 92, 93
Deyermond, Jack, 192
Deyermond, Robert V., 120
Deyermond, Warren C., 75
Diamond, Rev. James, 103
Digital Consulting Incorporated, 80

Digital Equipment Corporation, 95, 96
Disabled American Veterans, 48
District schoolhouses, 155, 156
Dobbie, Isabell, 155, 156, 157, 160
Dodd, Bruce and Lee, 178, 179, 180
Dodd, Douglas, 180
Dodge, Margaret, 35, 189
Doherty family, 23, 24, 144, 227
Doherty Insurance Agency, Incorporated, 144, 227
Doherty, James D., 24, 46, 74, 144, 199, 216, 227
Doherty, John, 23, 74
Doherty, Rachel, 73
Doherty School, 163
Doherty, William A., 23, 144, 227
Dole, Burton, 93
Dole, Percy and Retta, 140
Domingue, Robert, 20, 47
Domino's Pizza, 153
Donohue, Edward and Ruth, 223
Donovan, Anniek, 138
Donovan, Daniel, 138
Dorman-Bogdonoff Corporation, 86
Dove, John, 23, 81, 88, 104
Dove School, John, 56, 158, 162
Dow, George Francis, 35
Downs, William, 77, 194, 201
Doyle Lumber, 66, 115, 149
Dragon's Lair, 233
Draper (Block) 136, 236
Draper Hall, Abbot Academy, 45, 168, 169
Draper, Warren, 137, 168, 236
Driscoll, Jack, 144
Driscoll, Rev. Arthur, 108
Drosos, Maude, 184
Duff, Thomas, 191
Dufton, Charles H., Prof., 102
Dufton, George, 91
Dukakis, Michael S., Gov., 92, 180
Dundee Park, 79, 81, 84, 175
Dundee Properties of Andover, 80
Dunkin' Donuts, 153
Dunn, Donald, 216
Duxbury, Dana, 77

E
Eagle, 239
Eagle Investment, 151
Eagle-Tribune, 20, 38, 146, 183, 239
Earth Day, 77
East Junior High, 89
Easter Egg hunt, 216
Eastern Star, 53
Eastman, Edith, 140
Eastman, Edwin, 140
Eaton, Horace, 138
Eaton, Lucy, 167
Eaton, Thaxter, 190
Edgar, Gordon, 109
Edmonds, Thomas V., 42
Edwards, Rev. Justin, 99
Eisai Corporation, 95
Eisenhower, Dwight D., President, 223
Elander and Swanton, 243
Elander, Carl, 137
Electric Shop, 141
Eliot, T. S., 215
Elite Millinery, 135
Ellicott, Andrew, 59
Elm Farm, 147
Elm House, 134
Elm Square, 10, 134, 135, 138

Elm Street, 18, 25, 36, 38, 38, 46, 55, 104, 138, 167, 183, 204, 205, 227
Elm Street Service Station, 144
Elm Street Stables, 133
Elmer, Cathleen Burns, 168
Emerson, Charles F., 194
Emma Knox Millinery, 142
Enchanted Bridge, 8
English, 119, 129
Enzo's of Andover, 151
Equity Coalition Task Force, 130
Erickson, David, 92
Erickson, Edward I., 160, 191
Ermer, Arthur, 88
Essex Agricultural Institute, 64
Essex Company, 41, 62
Essex County Agricultural School, 66, 124
Essex Institute, 35
Essex Street, 62, 81, 107, 135, 146, 199, 214, 244, 245
Estabrook, Rolland, 210
Evening Study Program, 215
Evening Tribune, 24, 239
Everen, Louise Van, 41, 43

F
Fair Housing Committee, 199
Faith Lutheran Church, 109, 111, 252
Fardy, Thomas E., 244
Farmers, 65, 66, 67
Farrar, Esq. Samuel, 225
Farrington, Marcelle, 147
Faulkner, Edmond, 11
Feminist movement, 76
Field, Gloria (White), 168
Fieldstone's tearoom, 145
Finance Committee, 26, 36, 134, 190, 191, 243, 244
Finger, Louis, 134
Finlayson, Robert, 149
Finneran, Robert, 147
Fire station, 20, 56, 143, 194, 216
Fire Department, 36, 191, 192, 194, 218
First Baptist Church, 250
First Essex Savings Bank, 153, 224
First Federal Savings, 153
First National Stores, 139
First Universalist Church, 103
Fischer, Herbert, 142
Fish Brook, 185, 196
Fishing Derby, 216
Fitts, Dudley, 171
Fitts, Cornelia, 145
Fitzgerald, Rev. William, 109
Fitzgerald, Robert, 171
Flagg & Gould, 136
Flagg, Burton S., 46, 134, 142, 144, 168
Flagg, Timothy, 136, 236
Fleet Bank, 153
Fleming, William, 142
Flint family, 245
Flint farm, 245
Flint, George, 12
Flint, John, 46, 134
Flint, William and Millie, 109
Flood of 1936, 176, 184
Flood of 1979, 183
Florence Street, 141
Foley, Sister Veronica, 109
Follett, W. H., 223
Forbes, Wendy, 191
Ford Motor Credit Corporation, 94
Ford's Coffee Shop, 25, 140, 180, 215
Forest Fire of 1927, 184
Foster family, 56
Foster, Homer 213

Foster, Moses Estate, 38
Foster's Pond, 203, 238
Foxcroft Hall, Phillips Academy, 36, 172
Franklin Academy, 11
Franz Groceries, 138
Frechette, Maryann, 194
Free Christian Church, 28, 38, 83, 104, 107, 119, 120, 167, 250
Freitas, John, 144
French, 129
French, Alan, 45, 93
French, Edward V., 24
French, Mary Wentworth, 24
French, Phillip, 79
Friars Minor of the Immaculate Conception Province of the United States, 173
Friendly Fire Society, 194
Friendly Ice Cream, 150
Friends of Shawsheen, 49
Friends of the Library, 199
Froburg family, 193
Frontiero, Wendy, 37
Frye Circle, 183, 199
Frye, Samuel, 88
Frye Village, 14, 23, 35, 79, 81, 88, 89, 90, 157
Frye, William L., 194
FTP Software, 91
Fuess, Claude M., 19, 69, 170
Fuller, Samuel, 69
Furnari family, 127, 128

G
Gammon, Norma A., 42, 142, 199
Garabedian family, 123
Garbage collection, 77
Gardenia Boutique, 149
GCA Corporation, 95
Gendler, Everett, Rabbi, 102
Genetics Institute, 95, 209
George Washington Hall, Phillips Academy, 170
German, 127, 129
German Club, 53, 204
Germanium, 91
Gesell, Judge Gerhard, 18
Gilbert, Perley, 149, 188
Gilbreath, Richard, 75
Giles, Lincoln, 79, 149, 150
Gillette, 95, 209
Girl Scouts, 56, 218
Girls' Softball League, 208
Gleason, F. E., 135
Gleason, Louis, 164
Glendenning, Eve Cross, 210
Golden family, 76
Golden Gardens, 85
Golden Warriors Band, 218
Goldman, Paul, 114
Goldsmith, Bessie Punchard, 18, 19, 20, 51, 55, 189
Goldsmith Reservation, 18
Goldsmith, William G., 31, 33, 206
Goldwater, Barry, 215
Gordon, Donald, 169, 238
Gordon, Katherine M., 35
Gould, Abraham J., 136, 236
Government Study Committee, 190
Graber, Richard, 20, 21, 36, 72, 73
Graffam, Mary Louise, 99
Graham House, Phillips Academy, 102, 116
Grainger, Percy, 215
Grand Army of the Republic (GAR), 43, 48
Grandview Terrace, 199
Grange, 52, 216
Grant's, W. T., 148

Graves, Frederick H., 72
Great Depression, 22, 76, 142, 168, 245
Great Quadrangle, Phillips Academy, 172
Greater Lawrence Regional Vocational Technical High School, 31, 101, 164
Greater Lawrence Regional Vocational Technical High School, Superintendents of, 254
Greater Lawrence Sanitary District, 233
Grecoe Jewelers, 137, 143
Greeley, Anna, 190, 191
Greeley Company, James E., 190
Greeley, James, 142
Greeley, Roland, 63
Green & Woodlin, 135
Greenberg, Milton, 94
Greenwood Road, 62
Griswold, Jane, 38, 116
Grove, The, 203, 204
Grover, Elmer, 136
Grover, Ida, 161
Grullon, Juan D., Rev., 115
Guertin, Hervey, 207
Guild, 216
Gulf Station, 144
Gulf War, 74, 75, 218
Guthrie, George, 54

H
Habitat for Humanity, 107
Haggerty, Bernice, 42, 204, 205
Haggerty, John E., Brigadier General, 18
Haggett's Pond, 158, 195, 196, 233
Haggett's Pond Road, 108, 114, 245
Hagopian family, 123
Hahn, Kurt, 28
Hale, Emily, 215
Hall & Son, Edward, 149
Hall Avenue, 106
Halloween Parade, 216
Hamblin, Nathan C., 159
Hamilton, Jim, 149
Hammond, Edward, Sr., 39
Hammond Reservation, 39
Hammond, Ruth L. 147
Hammond, Virginia "Deena," 39, 45, 62, 63
Hancock, John, 91
Handy, Elizabeth, 50
Harding Street, 23
Harding, William H., 167
Hardy and Cole, 149
Hardy and Ross, 205
Hardy Brush Factory, 89
Hardy, Judith, 168
Hardy, Roy, 25, 46, 189
Harris Environmental Systems, 96
Harold Parker State Forest, 33, 44, 58
Hartigan's Drug Store, 142
Hartwell and Richardson, 103
Hartwell Abbot Bridge, 185, 204, 214
Harvard University, 173
Hastings, David, 117
Hatchery, 245
Haverhill, 132, 174
Haverhill Street, 14, 23, 59, 88, 89, 110, 176, 232
Havurat Shalom, 116
Hayes, Harold F., 194
Haynes, F. G., 135
Hayward, Henry, 135
Haven, The, 199
Hearsey, Marguerite, 169, 235
Henderson & Sons, George M., 149

Henderson, Robert, 39, 134
Heresy Trial, 172
Heritage Green, 110
Herman, Jack, 42
Herman, Karen, 41, 42, 43
Hersh, Kathy, 44
Heseltine, George, 151
Heseltine, Harold E., 25
Hewlett-Packard Company, 37, 93, 94, 208, 229
Hibernians, Ancient Order of, 54
Hickey, Raymond, 192
Higgins, Alice, 18
Higgins stables, 133, 135
Higginson, Joe, 18
High Plain, 41
High Plain Road, 37, 119, 184, 185, 245
High Street, 36, 46, 47, 77, 149, 199
Highvale Lane, 42
Hildreth, H. Frank, 147
Hill, Dot, 18
Hill Hardware, 147
Hill, Rod, 142
Hill, W. R., 142
Hiller, Bessie, 138
Hilton family, 96
Hilton, Georgianna, 155
Hilton, Henry L., 119, 191, 194
Hinton Ice Cream, 133
Hiscox Domestic Goods, 151
Hispanics, 129
Historical Commission, 35, 37, 42, 43, 45, 199
Hodgkins, William H., 79
Hoffman, Dustin, 215
Hoffman, Emil, 53
Hogan, Daniel E., 58
Holt and Company, T. A., 102
Holt, B. F., 135
Holt, Ballard, 2nd, 197
Holt District school, 158
Holt farmhouse, 33
Holt Hill (Ward Hill), 33, 185
Holt, John V., 34
Holt, T. A., 135, 135
Home & Abroad, 151
Homer, George, 133
Hood farm, 173, 183
Hood, William, 73
Horribles Parade, 217
Houghton, Leon, 145
House of Clean, 149
Housing Authority, 33, 199
Howard Johnson's, 146, 215
Howarth House, 83
Howarth Mill, 81
Howe, Charlie, 136
Howe, Clifford, 148, 243
Howe, Douglas Jr., 148, 243
Howe, Douglas N., Sr., 148, 243
Howe Insurance and Real Estate, 148, 243
Howe, Julia Ward, 51
Hsu, Ting-Shing, 55
Hughes (drugstore), 140
Hughes, Alan, 146
Hughes, Margaret M. (Peg), 42
Hugo, Robert, 151
Hulme, Albert E., 150, 151
Hurricane Bob, 187
Hurricane Carol, 186
Hurricane Edna, 187
Hurricane of 1938, 185
Hussein, Damergi, 144
Hussey's, Pond, 91, 210, 215
Hutchinson, John, 135

I
Iceland Road, 211
Inchcape Testing Services, 94
Indian Ridge, 21, 31, 33, 41, 188
Indian Ridge Association, 30
Indian Ridge Community Association, 49

Indian Ridge Country Club, 58
Indian Ridge Mothers' Club, 82
Indian Ridge School, 56, 155, 157, 211
Indianapolis Symphony, 215
Industrial Materials Technology, 95-96
Infant mortality, 178
Internal Revenue Service, 93
International Institute of Lawrence, 99
International Order of Odd Fellows, 53
Irish, 119, 129
ISI Systems Incorporated, 94
Italians, 127, 129, 196

J
Jackson School, Samuel, 56, 140, 161
Jacobson family, 123
Jacobson, Nancy, 197, 198
Jamison Farm, 242
Jay, Michael, 147
Jenkins, Dr. Roger, 18
Jenkins Road, 18
Jewish refugees, 128
Johnny's Supermarket, 147, 150
Johnson Acres, 22
Johnson, James F., 192, 194
Johnson, Preston, 168
Johnston, Clan, 53, 120
Josef's Men's Hair Styling, 151
Junior Football, 207
Junior League, 207

K
K&D Block, 141, 142, 145, 241
Kapelson, Richard, 148
KAPS Menswear, 10, 148
Karahalios, George, Rev., 115
Kasabian family, 123
Katz, Elaine, 77
Kearn Equipment, S. W., 245
Kearn family, 109, 245
Kearn, Stephen and Gwen, 245
Kearn, Warren, 109
Keck, Margaret (Peggy), 39, 92
Keller, Helen, 215
Kelly, Susan, 20
Kelsey, Katherine, 168
Kemper, John M., 170, 235, 237
Kemper Memorial Chapel, Sylvia (Phillips Academy), 102, 237
Kennedy, John F., Jr., 18, 25
Kennedy, Patrick, 18
Keough, 202
Kidder, Francis, 225
Killorin, Karl C. and Geneva H., 18, 149
Kim, Sung, Rev., 115
Kimball, Margaret and John, 34
Kirkshire House tearoom, 145
Kittredge, Esq. Joseph, 225
Klie, Robert, 58
Knights of Columbus, 48
Knights of Pythias, 53
Koch, Katherine, 52
Konjoian family, 66, 123
Koravos, Stella, 25
Koravos, Tom, 25, 180
Korean War, 69, 72, 87, 218
Korslund, LeNormand, and Quann, 164
Krikorian family, 123
Krinsky, Hyman and Rebecca, 17
Krinsky, Morris, 17
Kuo, Evelyn, 198
Kuo, Stephanie and Jeff, 55
Kurth, Bill and Barbara (Nichols), 186

L
Laaf, Marion, 191
Laarson, Larry, 201
Ladies Benevolent Society ("Benevie,") 47
LaDu, Rev. Joseph, 100
Lake, Janet, 190
Lally, Richard, 144
Langrock's Men Store, 147
Lantern Brunch, 151
Lardner, Ring, Jr., 18
Larsen, Nancy, 42
Lasser, Don, 114
Latham, Edith Saunders, 125, 126
Latin Commons, Phillips Academy, 37
Laurel Lane, 66
Lawrence, 13, 20, 23, 28, 38, 41, 47, 56, 61, 66, 73, 77, 80, 109, 112, 114, 115, 121, 122, 126, 127, 128, 144, 153, 158, 164, 177, 179, 187, 194, 200, 222, 232, 244, 245
Lawrence American, 239
Lawrence, Cornelia, 126
Lawrence Daily Eagle, 24, 239
Lawrence Gas and Electric, 136, 148
Lawrence General Hospital, 96
Lawrence, Margaret Woods, 137
Lawrence Pumps Incorporated, 191, 141, 152, 153, 193, 232
Lawrence Street, 25
Lawrence Telegram, 19
Le Boutillier, Addison, 22
Leaf, Monro, 20
League of Women Voters, 23, 24, 29, 39, 49, 77, 190, 191
Lebanese, 121
Lebow, Hildegarde, 128, 129
Lee, Donald, Jr., 72
Lee-Antoine Dress Shoppe, 147
Legendre, Al, 137
Leland, Francis, 79
LeLeche League, 57
Lemmon, Jack, 18
Leno, Jay, 17
Leon's Spa, 147
Lewis, Dorothy, 64
Lewis, Ellsworth and Hilda, 223
Lewis farm, 67, 93, 229
Lewis, Roger, 66
Lewis Street, 185
Lewis, Warren "Bud," 45, 179, 204
Liberty Group, 151
Liggett's Drug Store, 148
Lily, Josiah, 136
Lincoln, Emma, 31
Lincoln, Abraham, President, 18
Lindsay, Dr. Richard and Betty, 149
Lindsay, Stafford, 108, 213
Lions Club, 53
Liponis, Charles, 149
Little League, 207
Little Sanhedran, Phillips Academy, 36
Livingston Apple Farm, 155
Lloyd, Susan McIntosh, 20, 169, 171, 172
Locke, Abby, 237
Locke family, 237
Locke, James, 225
Locke Street, 31, 51, 112
Locke Tavern, 222, 225
Lodge, Henry Cabot, 51
Loizeaux, Marie Suzanne, 18
Long, William, 197
Longfellow, Gertrude Currier, and Loring Eugene, 242
Look, Donald, 20, 146, 192
Loomer, Amos, 138-139
Loomer, Barbara, 47, 189, 190

Loosigian, Alice, 122
Loosigian family, 67, 123, 124
Loosigian, Harry, 123
Loosigian, Peter, 119, 123, 124
Love Lane, 51
Lovejoy, William, Captain, 210
Lovejoy, Pompey, 210
Lovejoy Road, 64
Lovely, Eugene "Pop," 159, 207
Lowe, Mildred, 47
Lowe's Drug Store, 136, 140, 146
Lowell, 22, 25, 45, 55, 101, 109, 115
Lowell, Guy, 170
Lowell Junction, 64, 95, 146
Lowell Street, 67, 92, 112, 113, 114, 114, 145, 155, 204
Luedtke, Barbara E., 37
Lundgren, Everett, 138
Lupine Road, 41, 204, 209
Luscutoff, Jim, 18
Luscutoff, Lynn, 18
Lydia's Hair and Nails, 151
Lynch family, 193
Lynch, Lt. John K., 193
Lyons, John, 163
Lyster Chemical, 138

M
M. T. Stevens and Sons, The Marland Mills, 83, 84, 85, 86, 96, 183, 186
Macartney, Robert and Gardner, 148, 199
MacKenzie, Sgt. William, 193
MacPherson, Clan, 54, 219
Mahony, Gratia, 42, 233
Mahony, Kenneth A., 43, 191, 199, 233
Main Street, 23, 24, 34, 35, 36, 38, 47, 55, 58, 62, 73, 79, 103, 116, 126, 132-152, 148, 167, 194, 197, 206, 218, 222, 227, 234, 236, 238, 241
Main Street Terrace, 36
Majahad, Carol, 42
Mallory, John, Rev., 109
Malone, Joe, Massachusetts State Treasurer, 18
Mannarino, Dominic, 229
Mansco Construction Company, 43
Maple Avenue, 140
Maple Street, 185
Mararian family, 123
Markey, Francis P., 69, 199
Marland, Abraham, 84, 85, 96, 103
Marland, Edna and Charlotte, 167
Marland family, 96
Marland house, 79
Marland, John, 62, 78, 84
Marland Manufacturing Company, 84
Marland Mill Associates, 80
Marland School, 167
Marland Street, 84, 105
Marland Village, 79, 84, 176
Marland, William, 84
Marshall, Karl and Louise, 61
Marshall, Louise, 62
Marshall's, 91
Marson, Virgil, 147
Martin, Jon, Rev., 109
Mary Ann's Card Shop, 150
Masons, St. Matthew's Lodge of, 46, 47, 53, 132, 149
Massachusetts Historical Commission, 37, 42
Massachusetts School of Law, 175
Mast Industries, 95
Master Plan, 63

Master Plan Committee, 28
Matses, Charles, 115
Mazza, Joe, 144
McArdle, Miriam Sweeney, 50, 125
McBride, Frank, 210, 211
McCabe, Mary, 172
McCarthy, Eugene, Senator, 215
McCullom, Charlie, 207
McCurdy, M. S., Mrs., 56
McDonough, Marsha, 164
McGann, Joseph, 175
McGovern, James E., 135
McKeen Hall, Abbot Academy, 45
McKeen, George, Mrs., 51
McKeen, Philena, 168
McLellan Gift Shop, 144
McNemar, Donald, 170, 172, 235
McNulty, Mary, 205
McQuade, Robert E., 195, 196
McQuade, Vincent A., 174
McQuillian, Mark, Dr., 163
Means, Emily Adams, 168
Mears, George, 192, 194
Memorial Auditorium, 69, 93, 161, 205, 216, 219
Memorial Circle, 199
Memorial Day, 218
Memorial Gateway, Phillips Academy, 236
Memorial Hall, 51
Memorial Hall Auditorium, 89
Memorial Hall Library, 11, 26, 42, 56, 61, 72, 96, 175, 197, 198, 199, 233
Memorial Tower, Phillips Academy, 69, 234
Merchants' building, 142, 152, 241
Merrill Gate, 169
Merrill Lynch, 151
Merrimack Card Clothing Company, 146
Merrimack College, 20, 26, 29, 55, 174, 175, 200
Merrimack Mutual Fire Insurance Company, 132, 134, 141, 168
Merrimack River, 37, 41, 77, 176, 195, 229
Merrimack River Girl Scout Council, 56
Merrimack River Trail, 44
Merrimack River Valley Sewage Board, 26
Merrimack River Watershed Coucil, 44
Merrimack Valley, 96, 239, 240, 243, 244
Merrimack Valley National Bank, 133, 225
Merrimack Valley Transit Authority, 18
Messinesi, Despina Plakias, 18
Methodist Episcopal Church in Ballardvale, 103, 104, 105, 250
Methuen, 20, 38, 62, 68, 77, 91, 113, 114, 157, 164, 222, 232, 244
Metropolitan Bakery, 24, 158
Mexican War, 69
Meyers, Milton, Dr., 160
Meyers, Richard, 130
Meyerscough and Buchan, 138
Mid-Asian imports, 153
Middleton, 33
Mikula, Tom, 58
Mill, Victor J., Jr. 191
Miller, Fran, 51
Miller, Henry, 144
Miller, Janvier Lange, 77
Mills, Frank, 206
Miner, Joshua L., 28, 170
MKS Instruments, 95

Modicon, 91
Mofford, Juliet Haines, 20, 31, 41
Monastery of St. Clare, 109
Moncrieff Cochran Sanctuary, Phillips Academy, 36
Monette, Paul, 20, 171
Monette, Robert, 167
Monro, John, 209
Moody, Barbara, 160, 190
Moody, P. W., 80, 146
Morehardt, Nancy, 115, 116
Morris, Mary McGarry, 20
Morrissey stable, 135, 192
Morrison & O'Connell, 135
Morrison Block, 54
Morrison, Henry, 237
Morrison, John, 88, 138
Morse Hall, Phillips Academy, 170
Morse Hardware 142
Morton, Dean, 93
Morton Street, 103, 214
Mother Connection, 57
Mothers' Club, 56
Mulligan, Gerald, 134
Mulvey, Donald, 51, 214
Mulvey, Joseph, 129, 137
Mulvey, Nancy, 112
Munroe, Vaughn, 205
Murdock, Linda, 111
Murnane, Jack, 53
Murphy residence, 174
Murray, John, 144
Murray Tire & Supply, 145
Musgrove building, 21, 36, 50, 51, 134, 135, 136, 143, 146, 151, 227
My Brother's Pizza Place, 153
Mystic Warehouse, 96

N
National Register Historic District, 91
National Register of Historic Places, 42, 43, 51, 91, 152
Native Americans, 21, 37, 130, 131, 206
Nazarian's, 153
Neil, Tom, 184
Network, The, 91
New England Bible Church, 110, 111, 253
New England Classical Singers, 50
New England Solid Waste Commission, 233
Newcomers' Club, 56
Newman, Charles H., 20, 133
Newman, Mark H., 225, 236
Newton, Charles, 66
Newton Theological Institution, 173
Nicholas, Barbara Skeirik, 122
Nicholas, Elias, 122
Nicholas family, 122
Nichols, Arita, 18, 186
Nichols, Edward C., 134
Nichols, William E., 134
Nicoll, David L., 119, 191, 194
North Andover, 11, 20, 33, 38, 67, 77, 145, 151, 153, 164, 167, 174, 175, 189, 190, 194, 200, 203, 222
North Boston Korean United Methodist Church, 114, 253
North Main Street, 9, 23, 76, 85, 86, 87, 88, 116, 176, 183, 185, 194
North Parish, 189
North Parish Unitarian Church, 99
North Reading, 67
North Reading Choral Society, 50
North School, 49, 211, 214

North Street, 199
Northeast Document
    Conservation Center, 91, 92
Northern Rubber Company, 79
November Club, 20, 31, 50, 51,
    55, 112, 115
Noyes, Lee and Forrest, 149

O
O'Brien, Bridget, 138
O'Brien, Dick, 142
O'Brien, John, 201
O'Connell, William, Cardinal,
    177
O'Connor, Brian R., 75
O'Connor, Rose, 51
O'Donnell Sanatorium, 141
Old River Road, 134
Old Stone Chapel, Phillips
    Academy, 36
Old Town Hall, 200
Olde Andover Village, 57, 150,
    163, 236
Oleson, George, Jr., 163
Oliver Wendell Holmes Library,
    Phillips Academy, 170
Olivetti, Dino, 237
Olmsted Brothers, 170
Olmsted, Frederick Law, 234
Onasch, Ella, 138
One Elm Square, 149
Open classroom, 160
Open-air classroom, 158
Orchard Crossing, 37
Orchard Street, 22
Order of Scottish Clans, 82
Order of St. Augustine, 174
Ordman, M. Louise, 199
Orlando, Michael, 43
Ormsby, Charles, 203
Outward Bound, 28
Ozoonian family, 123

P
Paley, Bertram R., 86
Palmer, Rev. Frederick, 32
Pantelis, Paul, Rev., 115
Paradise, Scott H., 19
Parent to Parent, 57
Parents' League, 24, 56
Park, Agnes, 34
Park, The, 50, 126, 206, 219
Park commissioners, 206
Park Street, 17, 24, 25, 36, 54,
    146
Park Street Garage, 120
Park Street Stables, 133, 138
Park Street Village, 149
Parker, George A., 32
Parker, Nancy, 130
Parker's on the Shawsheen, 204
Patrakis, Joan, 99, 121, 122
Patriot missiles, 75
Patullo family, 193
Paul Revere Hall, Phillips
    Academy, 170
Peabody House at Phillips
    Academy, 109, 110
Peabody Museum of
    Archaeology, Robert S.,
    Phillips Academy, 234
Pearce, Clark, 41
Pearson, "Stretch," 207
Pearson, Dr. Eliphalet, 236
Pearson Hall, Phillips Academy,
    36, 172
Peatman, Arthur, 52, 53, 64, 65,
    66
Peatman, Glenn, 53
Pee Wee Hockey, 207, 215
Pellegrino, Joseph, 54
Penguin Park, 211
Penney, Everett, 177
Pentucket Medical Associates,
    84
People's Ice Company, 135, 210

Perfecto's, 153
Peters Street, 174
Pettingill, Merrill, 47
Petzold, Sharon, 18
Phelps, Elizabeth Stuart, 16, 18,
    137
Phelps, Marion and Marian,
    Revs., 106
Phillips Academy, 11, 17, 18, 18,
    19, 20, 23, 26, 28, 35, 40,
    41, 45, 53, 56, 69, 77, 93,
    101, 102, 138, 140, 142,
    144, 150, 167, 168, 169,
    170, 171, 172, 175, 178,
    183, 197, 200, 209, 214,
    215, 234, 235, 236, 238
Phillips Academy's Addison
    Gallery, 56
Phillips Academy, Cochran
    Sanctuary, 36
Phillips Academy Heads, 255
Phillips Hall, Andover
    Theological Seminary, 173
Phillips Inn, Phillips Academy,
    138, 170
Phillips, Samuel, 84, 99, 169
Phillips Street, 38, 214
Phinney, Mr & Mrs. Harold, 205
Phinney, Robert W., 199
Phinney's TV and Records, 151
Physical Sciences Incorporated,
    95
PictureTel, 92
Pierce, Franklin, President, 11
Piercy, Dorothy, 25, 209
Pike, Cynthia E., 167, 240, 245
Pike, Edson, Rev., 103
Pike School, 109, 167, 168, 240,
    245
Pike School Heads, 254
Pike School Parents Association,
    240
Pike, Walter, 245
Pine Grove, 245
Pinkham, Daniel, 18
Pitman Building Supplies, J. E.,
    149
Planning Board, 26, 39, 68, 152,
    199
Platt, Charles, 101, 170, 234
Playdon Florist, 133
Playground programs, 69, 211,
    213
Playground Committee, 211, 213
Playstead, 207, 211, 215
Pleasant Street, 245
Poland, Wiliam, 137
Pole Hill, 89
Police Department, 183, 191,
    192, 193, 194, 205
Polio, 177, 178, 179
Polish, 129
Polly Prim Beauty Shoe, 142
Pomeroy, Llewellyn P., 194
Pomp's Pond, 33, 56, 209, 210,
    211
Pony League, 208
Poor & Riley, 139
Poor, Albert, 206
Poor, William, 89
Poor's Pond, 89
Porter Road, 167
Porter, Walter, 229
Porter's dry goods, 138
post office, 62, 79, 84, 90, 244,
    134, 134, 141, 142, 232
Post Office Avenue, 134, 138,
    143, 146
Powel, Virginia, 57
Powers, Josephine, 23
Powers, Leslie Ford, 25
Pratt family, 237
Presidents of Merrimack
    College, 255
Proposition 2 1/2, 233
Public Safety Center, 87, 150

Public Welfare Committee, 28
Public Works, 195
Puerto Rican Labor, 66
Punchard/Andover High School,
    Principals of, 254
Punchard Avenue, 29, 47, 103,
    243
Punchard, Benjamin, 84, 96, 159
Punchard Free School, 133, 159
Punchard Girls' Band, 50
Punchard High School, 17, 20,
    22, 31, 42, 48, 96, 140, 155,
    159, 161, 161, 189, 207
Purdon, Susanne Smith, 35, 96
Purity Supreme, 150
Pustell, Margaret and Robert, 39,
    44
Putnam, Clara, 33
Putnam, Miriam, 197
Pythian Sisters, 53

Q
Quaker Meeting, 116
Quattlebaum, Ruth, 234, 235

R
Rabbit Pond, 195, 215
Rachmaninoff, Sergei, 215
Radio stations, 147
Rafton, Harold R., 31, 33, 39,
    40, 41, 94
Rafton, Helen, 40
Rafton Reservation, 41
Railroad Avenue, 87, 88, 104,
    107, 145
Raven Beauty Parlor, 140
Raytheon, 66, 91, 92, 93, 180,
    205
Reading, 132, 153, 185, 215
Rebekahs, 53
Recreation Department, 216
Recreation Lodge, 213
Recreation Park, 213, 216
Recycling, 77, 195
Red Cross, 25, 26, 47, 69, 152,
    243, 244
Red Spring Road, 81, 146
Redman Card Clothing
    Company, 146
Redman family, 81
Regan, Edward, 163
Reichhold Chemical Company,
    95
Reilly family, 144, 166
Reilly, Francis, 79
Reilly, Helen, 141, 166
Reinhold, William, 144
Rennie farm, 66
Reservation Road, 31, 204
Resnick, Sam, 138, 147
Retelle, Albert, 31
Revere Hall, Paul, Phillips
    Academy, 36
Revolution, 11, 69, 210
Reynolds, David, 86, 87, 144
Reynolds, Mary (May), 87
Richards, Laura Earley, 49
Richardson, Darius, 136
Richardson Field, 206
Richardson School, 56, 157
Rickey's Variety, 147
River Road, 37, 38, 41, 53, 64,
    66, 93, 94, 95, 109, 149,
    173, 175, 183, 229
River Road Industrial Park, 93
River Street, 79, 203
roads, 196, 197
Robbie's furs, 146
Robbins, Sarah Stuart, 137
Roberge family, 61
Roberge, Louise, 61
Roberts, Margaret, 42, 214
Robinson, Julia Underhill, 35,
    147
Rocky Hill, 49
Roddy, Edward, Ph.D., 20

Rogers, Alexander, 24
Rogers, Alexander, II, 239
Rogers, Barnett, 134, 146, 239
Roger's Brook, 126, 133, 152,
    187, 206
Roger's Dell, 41
Rogers family, 24, 134, 136,
    146, 147, 149, 238, 239
Rogers Family Foundation, 96
Rogers, Irving E., "Chip," III,
    147, 239
Rogers, Irving E., Sr., 96
Rogers, Irving, Jr., 147, 238, 239
Rogers, Samuel S., 84, 85, 96,
    186
Rogers, Walter E. 239
Rolling Acres Farm, 242
Romeo, Betty and Edward, 145
Rooney, Marsha, 41
Roosevelt, Theodore, 215
Rose Cottage Tea Room, 139
Rose Glen, 26
Ross, Donald, 223
Rotary Club, 129, 152
Roth, Rabbi Harry A., 114
Route 125 Bypass, 146, 197
Route 128, 60, 229
Route 28, 66, 146, 197
Route 495, 38, 41, 60, 61, 107,
    122
Route 93, 38, 41, 60, 67, 92, 93,
    94, 108
Royal-Barry Wills, 110, 116
Royal Jewelers, 137, 243
Russell, Officer Roy, 193
Russians, 129

S
Sacred Heart School, 91, 92,
    166, 205
Saints Constantine and Helen
    Greek Orthodox Church,
    115, 253
Saltonstall, Leverett, Governor,
    26, 27, 87
Samaritan House, Phillips
    Academy, 36
Samuel Phillips Hall, Phillips
    Academy, 172
Sanborn, Henry C., 159
Sanborn, Emma, M.D., 135
Sanborn School, 157
Sandard Duplicating Machines,
    96
Santa Claus Parade, 218
Sarkisian family, 123
Saunders family, 136
Sawyer, Annie, 185
Scanlon, William J., 147, 152
Scanlon's Hardware, 152
Scanlon's Inn, 145
Schiffer, Joseph J., 112
School Administration Building,
    199
School Building Needs
    Committee, 190
School Committee, 23, 61, 156,
    157, 160, 160, 163, 190, 227
School Street, 41, 210, 214
School Street, Phillips Academy,
    36
School transportation, 158
Schussel, George and Sandra, 80
Scot, William Donald, 88
Scotland District School, 156
Scots, 82, 119, 129, 193, 219
Scott, Cyrus, 150
Scott-Stowers house, 150, 151
Scottish, 104
Scrima, Claude, Rev., 174
Sealskin Gasket & Packing
    Company, 145
Seifert, Dr. Kenneth, 163, 164
Selectmen, 38, 46, 89, 93, 94,
    187, 189, 190, 191, 192,
    197, 199, 214, 218, 233, 255

Sellars, Peter, 18
Senior Center, 54, 56
Servicemen's Fund, 48, 217
Sessions, Barbara, 35
Sewer, 77, 93, 195, 196
Shannon, U.S. Rep. Jim, 18
Sharpe, Ruth, 42, 106, 127, 198,
    203
Shattuck, Catherine, 37
Shattuck, Edward, 190
Shattuck Farm, 37, 93, 229
Shattuck, Charles, M.D., 135
Shattuck, Mrs., 67
Shattuck's Drug Store, 203
Shawmut Bank, 142, 152, 153,
    241
Shawsheen, 203, 210, 215
Shawsheen Civic Association, 91
Shawsheen Co-operative Bank,
    141
Shawsheen Dairy, 141
Shawsheen Garage(s), 141
Shawsheen Hairdressing Parlor,
    141
Shawsheen Homestead
    Association, 91
Shawsheen Laundry, 141, 184
Shawsheen Manor, 14, 37, 43,
    90, 141
Shawsheen Market, 141
Shawsheen Motor Mart, 141,
    147
Shawsheen PTA, 56
Shawsheen Pharmacy, 141
Shawsheen Plaza, 85, 76, 92,
    147
Shawsheen River, 8, 52, 54, 79,
    82, 88, 100, 203, 215, 155,
    159
Shawsheen Rubber Co., 80, 146
Shawsheen School, 22, 130, 157
Shawsheen Spring Bottling
    Company, 91
Shawsheen Steam Fire Engine
    Company, 194
Shawsheen Tailor, 141
Shawsheen Village, 14, 23, 35,
    58, 61, 62, 79, 89, 90, 91,
    134, 141, 149, 167, 176, 232
Shawsheen Village Improvement
    Society, 28, 49
Shawsheen Village Woman's
    Club, 51
Sheehy, Augustine, 83, 84
Sheehys, Johnny, Mary, and Bob,
    68
Shepard, Howell F., 95
Sherman, Leonard, 188, 189
Shetland Properties, 91
Shoe Tree, 151
Shulze, Carlton, 146
Siddha Yoga Meditation Center
    of Andover, 253
Sidewalk Bazaar, 52, 218
Siemens, 94
Silverado, 153
Silverman, Gerald ("Jerry") H.,
    43, 200, 201
Simeone Block, 142
Simeone Drug Store, 143
Sisters of Notre Dame, 107, 166
Sizer, Theodore R., 170, 172,
    175, 183, 235
Sjostrom, Olga, 138
Skolnick, Janice, 116
Slavery, 103
Smart & Flagg Insurance, 142
Smith & Dove, 81, 82, 83, 89,
    96, 101, 119, 198, 209
Smith & Dove mills, 85
Smith & Manning, 135
Smith & Nephew Dyonics, 96
Smith, Charlotte, 41, 42
Smith, Frank M., 194
Smith, Henry ,Very Rev., 107,
    108

Smith, James, 57
Smith, John, 14, 81, 83, 88, 90, 104, 198
Smith, Mary Byers, 199
Smith, Nathaniel B., 40, 41
Smith, Peter, 81, 82, 88, 96, 101
Smith-Purdon Family Foundation, 96
Smyth, Joseph, Rev., 109
Snow Sanatorium, 141
Snyder, John 141
Soccer Program, 208
Sochrens, John, 133
Soldiers' Aid Society, 48
Sons of Italy, 54
Sons of the American Revolution, 54
Soong, Max, 43
Sousa, Wiliam, 94
South Center schoolhouse, 147
South Church, 25, 46, 51, 96, 98, 99, 103, 189, 214, 249
South Lawrence, 11
South Main Street, 37, 49, 110
South Parish, 189
South School, 130
Spade and Trowel Garden Club, 55
Spanish Influenza, 177
Spar and Spindle, 56
Spaulding, Amos, Esq., Hon., 225
Spiegel, Lawrence, 92
Spock, Dr. Benjamin, 18
Spring Grove Cemetery, 26
Square and Compass Club, 46, 47, 120, 149
Sridhar family, 130
St. Anthony Festival, 173
St. Augustine's Catholic School Guild, 56
St. Augustine's Church, 23, 26, 107, 114, 119, 147, 252
St. Augustine's School, 23, 107, 166, 186
St. Augustine's School, Principals of, 254
St. Francis Seraphic Seminary, 41, 109, 173, 174, 183, 216, 255
St. Joseph's Church, 108
St. Matthew's Lodge of Mason, 218
St. Robert Bellarmine Church, 108, 167, 245, 252
St. Vincent de Paul, 107
Stack family, 157
Standard International Corporation, 149
Standex Corporation, 58
Stapczynski, Reginald "Buzz" S., 191, 201
Stark, J. S., 135
State Police, 197
State Reservation and Game Sanctuary, 33
Stearns, Alfred E., 170, 234
Stearns Garden, Andover Historical Society, 55
Steinberg, Stephen, 151
Steinert, Arthur E., 149
Stephenson, Harry 145
Stern family, 128, 129
Stern, Herta, 128, 129
Stern, Peter, 51
Stevens, Abbot, 225
Stevens, Betty Bodwell, 135, 211
Stevens, Captain Nathaniel, 225
Stevens family, 96, 133
Stevens Foundations, 96
Stevens, John, 100
Stevens, Moses, T., 84
Stevens, Nathaniel, 42
Stevens, Nathaniel, Captain, 84

Stevens Street, 82, 84, 85
Stewart, Dora, 18
Stewart, William, 38, 191
Stillman, Howell, 190
Stott, Frederic A., 15, 43, 93, 199
Stowe, Calvin E., 18
Stowe Court, 199
Stowe, Harriet Beecher, 18, 19, 47, 137
Stowe School, 155, 157, 161
Stowe house, 35
Stowers, Nathaniel, 150
Strawberry Hill Farm, 123
Strong, William L., 79
Stuart, Moses, 136
Suburban Health Care Clinic, 86
Sullivan, Daniel J., 18
Sullivan, David, 20
Sullivan, Jane, 169
Sullivan, Jeremiah, 80
Sullivan, John, 42, 45, 160
Sullivan Hall, Merrimack College, 175
Summer people, 203
Summer Street, 50, 87, 157, 182, 185, 242
Summerstart, 112
Sun Micro Systems, 95
Sunset Rock Road, 140, 167
Supercuts, 151
Susie Sweets Bakery, 151
Sutherland's, 151
Sutton family, 96
Sutton, James, 199
Swain, Marilyn, 18
Swanton, Stanley, 137
Sweeney, Dennis, 135
Sweet Adelines, 50
Swift, Barbara, 42
Swift, Jonathan, 147
Sylvan Hollow Poultry Farm, 66

T
Tarbox, Fred, 164
Tateosian family, 123
Taylor Shop, Millie Vogel's, 152
Teen center, 53, 216
Telephones, 84, 147
Temple Emanuel, 28, 113, 113, 114, 167, 253
Temple Place, 140
Temple's Radio Shop, 142, 205
Ten Footer, The, 209
Tentarelli, Liz, 44, 45
Tewksbury, 44, 222
Tewksbury Street, 105
Thanksgiving parade, 216
Thibault, Barbara, 41, 42
Thomas, Marie, 141
Thompson, Kenneth P., 146
Thompson, M. E. "Chip," Rev., 111
Thompson's Stationers, 149
Thomson family, 237
Thoren, Sally, 110
Thorndale Stock Farm, 138
Thornton, Burke, 53
350th Anniversary celebration, 199
350th Anniversary Committee, 11
Tifereth Israel, 114
Topham, Fardy & Co., 244
Topham, Walter W., 244
Torrisi, Charles, 144
Tot lot playgrounds, 233
Town Charter, 190
Town Dump, 77, 147, 195
Town House, 13, 20, 22, 43, 55, 58, 69, 73, 133, 183, 187, 188, 194, 218, 233
Town Manager, 15, 49, 190, 191, 256

Town Meeting, 17, 28, 36, 38, 39, 40, 45, 49, 62, 77, 91, 92, 93, 149, 159, 180, 189, 191, 194, 195, 149, 43
Town Printing, 244
Town Seal, 188, 189
Townsman Press, 136
Train, 203
Trautmann family, 127, 203
Traver, Ted and Ann, 1208
Treble Chorus of New England, 50
Trickett, George, 42
Trolley, 132, 146, 158
Truman, Harry S., President, 72
Trustees of Reservations, The, 34
Tsongas, Paul, 29
Tucker, Susan, 25, 29
Tucker, William, 238
Tuesday Club, 52
Turner farm, 37
Turner, Samuel E., 72
Twilight Baseball League, 207
250th Anniversary, 188
Twomey family, 238
Twomey, Gerard N., Pfc., 238
Tyer family, 33, 47, 87, 134, 211
Tyer Rubber Company, 61, 75, 85, 86, 87, 134, 185
Tynan, William, 144
Tyning, Harold, Jr., 100, 101
Tyning, Priscilla Batchelder, 100

U
Ukranians, 129
Underhill, Caroline, 35, 189
Union Congregational Church, 251
Union Congregational Church of Ballard Vale, 105
Unitarian Church, 73
Unitarian Universalist Congregation in Andover, 51, 111, 112, 114, 167, 252
United States Post Office, 34
Urban renewal, 149

V
Valpey Brothers, 134, 135
Valz, Dino, 136
Vartabedian family, 123
Vasconcellos, Linda, 117
Vena Coco Collection, 151
Ventura, "Bennie," 144
Veterans Day, 218
Veterans of Foreign Wars, 48, 51
Victory Free Methodist Church, 115, 253
Vierne, Louis, 215
Vietnam War, 29, 72, 73, 74, 76, 218
Vietnamese, 119
Village Garden Club, 56
Vincenzo's Restaurant, 153
Visiting Nurse Association, 47, 152
Volunteers, 42, 191

W
Wakefield's meat market, 12, 135
Walbuck Crayon Company, 145
Waldenbooks, 153
Walker, Gwyneth, 18
Walker, William, 135
War of 1812, 69
Ward, Charles W., 33, 34, 203
Ward Hill (Holt), 203
Ward, Mabel Saunders 33, 34
Ward Reservation, Charles W., 34, 45
Warner, William, 162
Warshaw, Bernice and Thayer, 22, 28, 102, 114, 179
Washington, Booker T., 215

Washington, George, 215
Washington Park Apartments, 85, 148, 183
Water system, 77, 195, 196
Waters, John M., 240
Watson, Bill, 117
Watson, Laura Sophia, 168
Watson-Park Chemical, 95, 124, 146
Watters, Robert A., 113
WCCM, 147
Webb, Reuben, 184
Webster, Robert, 151
Webster Street, 245
Wennik, Hal, 207
Wertheimer, Walter, 114
Wesson, Charles, Jr., 201
West Andover, 64, 66, 89, 90, 93, 108, 195, 207, 245
West Andover fire station, 194
West Andover Neighborhood Association, 49
West Center School, 155, 156, 157, 211
West Elementary School, 117, 155, 156, 160
West Middle School, 28, 155
West Parish Cemetery, 52, 101, 245
West Parish Church, 12, 20, 52, 53, 96, 99, 100, 104, 111, 114, 167, 189, 216, 249
Western Electric, 180, 190
Western Union, 137
Wetterau, 95
What's Cooking? 151
Whipple File Company, 13, 80, 87
White, James, 151
White, Marian, 110
White, Sideny P., 25, 26, 46, 64, 69, 113, 189, 190, 191
White, Winthrop, 185
Whiting, John Edward, 133, 188, 189
Whittier Street, 38
Whyte, Chaplain James, 101
Whyte, John, 120
Wilbur Block, 140
Wild Rose Farm, 26, 113
Wilkins, Roy, 215
Wilkinson, Helen, 18
Willard, Lewis, 80
Williams Jewelry, 151
Wills, Royal-Barry, 110, 116
Wilmington, 190
Wilson, Alan, 146
Wilson, LeRoy, 146
Wilson, Penry "Pop," 146
Wilson's Corner, 174
Winslow, George, 190
Winters, Laurie, 42
Witch Trials, 11
WLAW, 147
Woburn Street, 77, 141, 183
Wolfson, Henry, 191
Women's Relief Corps, 48
Wonderland, 138
Wood, Cornelius, A., Jr., and Rosalyn, 23
Wood, Ellen Ayer, 51
Wood family, 23, 96, 202, 203
Wood Funds, 96
Wood Hill Road, 184
Wood Mill, 23
Wood, Muriel and Cornelius, 115, 116
Wood, William, Jr. and Rosalind, 202
Wood, William Madison, 20, 22, 23, 32, 33, 35, 58, 62, 87, 89, 90, 91, 101, 123, 141, 223, 242
Wood-Ayer Realty, 86
Woodbridge, John, Rev., 11
Woodburn, Grace, 178

Woodbury, Helen, 47
Woodworth Motors, 141
Wool Warehouse Corporation, 80
Woolworth building, 142, 143, 146, 148
World War I, 22, 69, 75, 90, 177
World War II, 22, 43, 48, 49, 55, 63, 69, 75, 86, 87, 91, 136, 146, 161, 217, 218, 235
Wormley, Sheryl, 169
Wragg, John, 163
Wright, Adeline, 62, 159, 160
Wright, Alvah, 158
Wright Farm, 64
Wrigley, Clifford, 188, 189
Wu family, 129
Wu, Jennifer, 55
Wyeth-Ayerst Labs, 96
Wynne, Rev. William J., O.S.A., 174, 175

Y
Yancy family, 125, 126
Yankee Lady, 151
YMAC (Young Men's Athletic Club), 58
YMCA, 48, 59, 134, 216
Yoga group, Siddha, 116
Yogurt, 68
Young, David, 147
Young, Ernest, 237
Young Fashions, 151
Young, John, 51
Young, Shirley, 18
Yunggebauer, Gustave, 138

Z
Zaeder, Philip, Rev., 102, 183
Zahka, Joseph, 112
Znamierowski, Carol Winkley, 155
Zock, Nick, 65
Zoning Board, 38
Zoning Board of Appeals, 199
Zoning Ordinance, 62

CENTRE ST

OAK ST

MARLAND ST

B B

RIVER ST

Gongregational Church
Methodist   "
Catholic   "
School.
Post Office and Depot.

Ballardv